Y0-CDC-985

A 364.1523   007886388   85

LANE, BRIAN
MURDER UPDATE

72164

MURDER
UPDATE

Brian Lane

LP830   21

Carroll & Graf Publishers Inc.
New York

First published in Great Britain 1991
First Carroll & Graf edition 1991

Carroll & Graf Publishers, Inc.
260 Fifth Avenue
New York
NY 10001

Copyright © 1991 by Brian Lane. The right of Brian Lane to be
identified as author of this work has been asserted by him in accordance
with the Copyright, Designs and Patents Act 1988

ISBN: 0–88184–740–2

All rights reserved
Printed in Great Britain

LC 24174

CONTENTS

ACKNOWLEDGEMENTS

Unlike books where an author is their single fount of inspiration, endeavours such as *Murder Update* are necessarily indebted to so many different sources, so many different people and organizations, that it would take a second volume to list them. In a way, the present author has acted merely as a catalyst, a final editor for the huge quantity of material gathered from around the world on the subject of contemporary crime.

Once again, the largest single group of contributors has been the international membership of *The Murder Club*, whose regular contributions to our archive have provided the basis for much of the material contained here – we have a 'Man' almost everywhere but in Havana.

I have spent more hours than I care to contemplate among dusty back copies in a score and more newspaper offices around the country, and even longer peering into a microfilm reader in the National Newspaper Library at Colindale; to all their patient staffs the contents of this book are my thanks. For although the words contained between these covers are my own, the book draws necessarily on the painstaking research and journalistic skills of reporters around the world.

For his imaginative response in developing the idea of *Murder Update*, thanks to publisher Nick Robinson; and for his uncanny ability to mix oil and water, my agent, Julian Alexander, deserves my continuing gratitude.

Brian Lane
1991

INTRODUCTION

Like many books of its kind, *Murder Update* has very mixed origins. The present concept began in Geneva with the creation of an installation sculpture titled 'When We Heard The News', one of a number of rambling pieces of quasi-polemic that later found themselves transmuted into the written word. This developed into the 'Crime Diary', which in its turn incorporated constructive suggestions from our present publisher, and crystallized into *Murder Update*.

The overall feature that characterized all three manifestations was that they offered a broad comment on things as they are and things as they might be. *Murder Update*, like its ancestors, charts the development not only of man's capacity for wickedness, but his resilience in combating the greater excesses, and the remoulding of his society to protect against the greater evils.

Although the period covered by this book is notionally the year 1990, this may only be the date of the most significant episode in the case. In most instances it will be the trial, for it is frequently only with the hindsight offered by legal process that a complex crime such as homicide can be fully comprehended, analyzed and set into a narrative.

We know that it is possible in the People's Republic of China for an accused person to be arrested, tried, convicted, sentenced, appealed and executed all within

*Information derived from *When the State Kills*, Amnesty International, London 1989.

the space of one week*, but the legal machinery in most of the civilized world moves more cautiously, more slowly – and in general is the fairer and safer for it. For this reason, to call *Murder Update* a 'yearbook' would present a slightly misleading impression, since the crimes selected for inclusion here do not on the whole fit comfortably into a single twelve-month span.

As an indication of how hit-and-miss the yearbook approach can be, it was planned to cover the extraordinary case of Simone Weber – 'The She-Devil of Nantes'. Madame Weber was arrested in November 1985 and charged with the dismemberment of a faithless lover with a chain-saw and the poisoning of her eighty-year-old husband after only weeks of marriage. Four years later her case had still not come to court, and in what was becoming a record even for the notoriously ponderous progress of French law, the trial did not open until February 1991. It was not only the longest remand in modern French judicial history, it was also just too late for inclusion in the 1990 *Update*.

On the other hand, the pace of Christian Brando's case was most 'convenient'. Between the fatal shooting of Dag Drollet on 16 May 1990, to the unfortunate Christian's sentencing in February 1991, was just nine months – thanks to a little plea bargaining.

However, most of the crimes covered by this volume span at least one year – in Britain it is almost one year to the month between the arrest of an accused person and their trial; it is about the same duration in the United States and Australia. So most of the important trials of 1990 will have had their origins in 1989. There are the inevitable glaring exceptions, such as the trial of David Lashley in London in 1990, for a brutal murder he committed *thirteen years* previously.

For those few crimes which were important enough to mention in the absence of a trial, an 'update' will be given in the next volume of this ongoing series.

The memory of some crimes lingers on long after due process of law has added the final dramatic act to the tragedy and dispensed punishment (and hopefully justice) to the satisfaction of at least the main participants. These are the cases which, for reasons not always clear to see, cannot be confined quietly behind prison walls; cases which are on the first stage of their elevation to the status of 'crime classics'. Sometimes they refuse to lie down because of some lingering doubt that justice may not have been done, and this applies to the appalling murder of Police Constable Keith Blakelock and the subsequent imprisonment of the 'Tottenham Three' for the crime. Then there are the unsolved cases – like the killing of Hilda Murrell, and of Ian Erskine – which continue to exert a fascination over the amateur sleuth that resides within us all. In other instances, perhaps, we are exhibiting an unhealthy eagerness to lionize the criminal – if this were not so, why do the brothers Kray occupy an almost heroic status in the popular mythology? Or the murderous Jack Abbott become a darling of the New York literati? Why do we return again and again to the monstrous crimes of Brady and Hindley, and find ourselves engrossed in the continued exploits of the Sutcliffe family?

In the section on capital punishment, it will be noticed that because of the often cumbersome system of appeals against the death penalty in the United States, many executions take place years, sometimes a decade or more, after sentencing. So we find that of the twenty-two executions carried out in 1990, the crimes which were being punished were committed at dates between 1976 and 1989.

Finally, the brief but essential chapter on crime statistics has been the last to be included in order to make use of the most recent available figures for 1990. As the years pass, and new volumes are added to the *Murder Update* series, these facts and figures will build into a uniquely useful body of comparative information.

Brian Lane
1991

THE STATISTICS OF CRIME

MURDER STATISTICS

Almost the only certain thing about crime statistics is that they rise, and the transition from the last decade to this was no exception.

Because of the requirement for figures to be fully integrated, analyzed and cross-referenced, it is only practical for crime statistics (at least in Great Britain and the United States) to be published in detailed form during the year following the twelve months covered. Thus for both countries, the tables relate to homicide statistics for the year 1989.

In addition, the British Home Office publishes advance statistics comprising basic figures on broad categories of indictable offences reported to the police in the previous year at the beginning of the current year; so there is a note appended on the statistics for 1990.

Murder of any kind is a comparatively rare statistical occurrence, but the chance of being killed by a stranger with no provocation is a negligible event. Homicide figures are among the most reliable crime statistics because few incidents go unreported (as distinct from other serious offences against the person such as rape), and based on figures for 1989 when there were 576[1] offences (comprising murder, manslaughter and infanticide), the overall chance of being unlawfully killed was 11.4 per one million of the population – a proportion which reduces significantly according to circumstances as shown in the charts below (*Who Kills?*).

Who Kills?

Still by far the largest proportion of murders are committed by people related to, or at least known by, the victim. However, one of the greatest causes for concern is that the proportion of victims killed by strangers has risen by approximately 5%.

The most dramatic difference in percentage statistics is seen between male and female victims – not least that 48% of female victims were killed by a spouse, cohabitant, lover or ex-spouse, - cohabitant or - lover. The comparative figure for male victims was 10%.

Why?

Of the three principal ingredients of homicide – motive, opportunity and method – the first is traditionally the most powerful, and as such affords an investigating officer his best chance of solving the crime.

Murders, according to one eminent writer on the subject, can always be conveniently filed in one of six classes of motive – gain, jealousy, revenge, elimination, lust and conviction – and allowing for those rare exceptions which prove the rule there is no reason to doubt the broad truth of this even today.

When dealing with statistics, however, it is necessary to take a broader and more prosaic view of motive, abandoning the 'code of six' in favour of a simpler classification.

Significant results are obtained by comparing figures for Stranger and Acquaintance related homicides, showing for example a hefty 62% of all homicides arising from quarrels committed by people acquainted with the victim, while only 26% of the same category were committed by strangers.

More predictably, the figures for homicide in the furtherance

---

[1]These consist of what are called 'currently recorded offences', as distinct from the 'initially recorded' figure of 627, of which 51 were not subsequently found to be homicide.

of theft were 15% for stranger-perpetrated offences and a low 4% for persons known to the victim.

Homicides 'attributed to an act of terrorism' were at an uncharacteristic high because of one single incident in which eleven young bandsmen were killed in the IRA bombing of the Royal Marines barracks at Deal, Kent (previous figures 1985:1, 1986:1, 1987:7, 1988:1).

Two categories in which no motive can be correctly given for a homicide are cases in which the killer takes his or her own life before a motive can be established, and those in which the suspect is so mentally disturbed that it is impossible to ascertain with certainty a reason for the crime.

. . . And What With?

For many reasons, not least their excellent accessibility: effectiveness ratio, sharp instruments (mostly knives) were the most commonly used weapons again in 1989 (contrast this with United States statistics below).

England and Wales 1990

The overall figures shown in the *Home Office Statistical Bulletin (4/91)* for the 'Notifiable Offences Recorded by the Police in England and Wales, 1990' do not permit detailed analysis, and do not go as far as separating 'Homicide' from 'More Serious Wounding,' and in the overall figures both these categories are amalgamated with 'Less Serious Wounding' under the heading 'Violence Against the Person'.

Offence	Number 1990	Percentage rise (over 1989)
Violence against the person	185,000	+4
Sexual offences	29,000	−2
Robbery	36,000	+9
Total Violent Crime	250,000	+4

Observations
1. Two thirds of violent crimes fall into the category 'Less Serious Wounding'.

2. 'Violence Against the Person' as a composite category increased by 7700 cases in 1990, representing a 4% rise over 1989. Although disappointing, the increase compares favourably with around 12% in each of the previous years.

Provisional Figures

Although they will be subject to greater or lesser reclassification between publication now and analysis later in 1991, provisional Homicide and Attempted Murder figures are available for comparison with previous years:

Offence Classification	1986	1987	1988	1989	1990*	Change 89–90 Number	%
1 Murder							
4.1 Manslaughter } Homicide	661	688	624	641	676	35	+5.5
4.2 Infanticide							
2 Attempted Murder	159	291	368	376	477	101	+26.9
3. Threat or Conspiracy to Murder	1340	1785	2730	3579	4160	581	+16.2
4.3 Child Destruction	–	2	8	2	0	−2	(−100)

*Provisional

United States 1989[2]

The sheer scale of crime in the United States seems to the British eye both bewildering and a little frightening – there were, for example, 21,500 homicides in the nation in 1989. This is a rate of 8.7 killings per 100,000 inhabitants, compared with a British equivalent of 1.1 per 100,000 of population. Even so, the American murder rate represents only 1% of all reported violent crimes.

As the Unites States has been conveniently divided into four distinct regions, each with its own characteristics of geography, population and economy, so the statistics vary between regions:

[2]Derived from Uniform Crime Reports *Crime in the United States 1989* (Publ. US Department of Justice, Washington DC, August 1990). Murder is defined as 'the willful (non-negligent) killing of one human being by another', and the classification is based 'solely on police investigation as opposed to the determination of a court, medical examiner, coroner, jury or other judicial body. Not included in the count for this offense classification are deaths caused by negligence, suicide or accident; justifiable homicides; and attempts to murder or assaults to murder, which are scored as aggravated assault.'

Region	% of Total	% Increase	Rate per 100,000	Rate* %
Southern States	43	+6	11	+5
Western States	20	+1	8	−2
Midwestern States	19	+4	8	+3
Northeastern States	18	+4	7	+4

* Over previous year (1988)

Like the British statistics above, those for the United States are calculated in the categories 'Who? Why? What With?', though the cross referencing tends to be slightly more detailed.

Friend or Foe?

More than half the victims of homicide in the US were related to (15%) or acquainted with (39%) their assailants, while strangers accounted for 13%.

The percentage where the relationship was unknown appears high in America at 33% (Britain: less than 10%) which may reflect the rather lower clear-up rate in the United States:

Southern States:	73%
Western States:	65%
Midwestern States:	73%
Northeastern States:	60%
Overall average:	68%
British average:	In excess of 90%

The Desire to Kill

'If the desire to kill and the opportunity to kill came always together, who would escape hanging?'

(Mark Twain)

Apparent motive, or 'circumstances' are categorized differently in the United States statistics, and it is interesting to observe that while British figures allow for a category headed 'Gang warfare, feud or faction fighting' (although such offences amount to only 2% of homicides), the American figures appear to split their alarmingly high gang murder rate among other categories such as narcotics felonies and 'arguments'.

Motives for murder are becoming increasingly prosaic on the

streets of America's cities and the subways beneath them. In the most alarming trend in murderous robberies – and one that is gradually being imported to other parts of the world, including Britain – young muggers are targeting teenagers' designer clothing and footwear. In New York in one month alone (December 1990) six young people were shot, three of them fatally, and their jackets stolen. Already teenagers are giving up wearing expensive clothing and accessories on the streets and transport systems, and in an escalation of violence have themselves taken to carrying weapons to protect themselves and their possessions against young thugs. One seventeen-year-old is reported as promising defiantly: 'If I buy something, I'm going to wear it. If anybody tries to steal something we [he and his friends] can get him.' Others were more fatalistic: 'There's a 50% chance I'll come home with it [his coat] and a 50% chance I won't.' This writer has been reliably informed by a correspondent that the most sought after item of the winter was the '8-Ball Jacket' – a hooded bomber jacket constructed from panels of brightly coloured leather, so called because of the motif on the back of a figure '8' on a circle, looking like a pool ball.

'Swift as pelet out of gonne'

It will come as no surprise that firearms head the list of murder weapons in the United States, though it is a shock to note that the use of guns is as much as four times more prevalent than the next most favoured weapon, the 'cutting or stabbing instrument'. Comparative figures for Britain shows almost exactly the reverse, with guns rather low on the chart.

After twenty years of decline, the figure for people shot by New York City police rose over a three-year period to a record of 108 people shot and 41 killed in 1990; this despite the fact that the force had one of the most restrictive codes of firearms practice in the country. In fact, aside from the disappointing fatality rate, police officers fired their weapons only 304 times in 1990, against 329 the previous year, and there has been a steady increase in the number of occasions when police would have been justified in using their weapons but did not – even though they were being shot *at* increasingly frequently (in 1989, 760 officers received gunshot wounds and three were killed).

An independent panel of inquiry set up in November 1990 under former police commissioner Patrick V. Murphy concluded that one of the main reasons for this increase was 'more violence, more young people with guns involved in drug traffic. The cops read about these things. They might not hesitate that extra second if they come on a kid with a gun.'

Captain John Cerar, commanding officer of the police firearms training course, praises the products of his college: 'Based on the circumstances today, their restraint is unbelievable. What has affected the police officer is that thirty years ago when an officer said put your hands up in the air, they did. Now they don't. And more people have guns than ever before.'

However, despite the obvious effort made by the city police to use restraint with firearms, their record is not beyond criticism. The New York Civil Liberties Union, for example, have suggested that: 'The cops feel they have carte blanche to do whatever they want to do . . . There is no punishment for an officer who uses his weapon improperly.' The civil liberties lobby insist that more training is required to enable young officers to come to terms with the increasing levels of street violence without automatic recourse to firearms, claiming that at present the police themselves are being seen as openly aggressive. Recruits to the New York City police force receive a single week's intensive firearms training, supplemented every year after they have been sworn in by two sessions of practice and tactical training, amounting altogether to one and a half days.

Although there have been accusations by lawyers acting for families bereaved in police shooting incidents that 'the cops don't worry, they know the system will protect them', some officers do find themselves answerable in open court in cases of suspected misuse of firearms. In the first days of 1991, a 25-year-old New York State policeman was indicted by a Bronx jury in an incident where a Bronx woman was shot dead. Police said she had grabbed the officer's night stick and threatened him after he had arrived to sort out a domestic dispute between the woman and her daughter. The victim's family denies she ever had the night stick in her hands, and that if she had, it could not be seen as life threatening.

New York, New York . . .

There is not the space in this section to examine in detail the differences in scale and type of crime in individual states of the US, let alone its cities, so one example will have to stand representative of that country's trend in homicide. More than a dozen major American cities broke the records in 1990, and statistics for eight of the twenty largest were up 3% over the previous year with a total of 7647 deaths. In 1989, Federal Bureau of Investigation statistics listed New York City as the ninth most criminous city (the top three were, respectively, Washington – retaining its long-held distinction as Murder Capital of America – Detroit and Miami).

On the morning of 21 December, the last day of 1990, police authorities in New York announced that, assuming the next 24 hours went according to familiar pattern, the city's homicide rate would top 2200 for the twelve months – a new record; as were both the previous two years: 1896 deaths in 1988 and 1905 in 1989. In percentage of population this translates as 14.6 people per 100,000 of population (Washington averaged 36.1 per 100,000).

The biggest fear to emerge from the overall New York pattern was the trend towards casual, unpredictable killings in which 'You could be innocently minding your own business and you could get shot!' Five years previously, in 1985, four people were killed by stray bullets. In 1990 the figure was forty, mostly innocent bystanders finding themselves sandwiched between belligerent parties in the drug war.

Other increases were 26 subway homicides (20 in 1989) and 32 cab drivers murdered (28 in 1989).

Other alarming figures revealed that 75 children under the age of sixteen were killed, 39 with guns and ten by stray bullets. 21 police officers had been wounded, while police themselves had shot 106 people, 41 fatally (30 in 1989).

Firearms were used in around two-thirds of the killings in New York (see national figures above), and police expected by 1 January 1991 to have confiscated more than 17,000 illegal guns in the previous twelve months (800 more than in 1989).

It is a sobering experience to examine in detail a single twelve-hour period in this record-breaking year's statistics. On 21 November, the *New York Times* carried out just such an exercise over the night of Monday, 19 November and the following morning, based on police records:

4.30 pm: A gunman in a passing car opened fire on a man in a 1985 Chevrolet at Suydam Street and Wyckoff Avenue in the Bushwick section of Brooklyn, chasing the victim until he lost control and slammed into a parked car. The driver, still unidentified last night, was found dead in the back seat of the wrecked sedan with several bullet wounds in his head. A .38 calibre revolver was found in the car next to him. A bystander was also wounded in the incident.

6.10 pm: A 34-year-old man was shot in the chest and killed at East 138th Street and Brook Avenue in the Motthaven section of the Bronx. The police last night had found no witnesses to the killing and were still trying to determine the man's identity.

8.00 pm: Victor Lacroix, aged 27, of Lucas Street in Queens, was stabbed once in the chest and killed when he tried to defend his nephew, Gordon Rodriguez, from two youths who were beating him because he jostled them on the street. The stabbing took place in front of a house in 214th Street and St Albans, Queens, where Lacroix and Rodriguez were visiting relatives. Shortly afterwards police arrested Michael Holly, aged nineteen, of Francis Lewis Boulevard, Queens, and charged him with murder.

9.00 pm: A 53-year-old Staten Island man and his girlfriend were stabbed repeatedly with a kitchen knife in their apartment at 11 Pine Street, reportedly by a close friend after a petty argument. Lieutenant William Quinn of the Staten Island detectives said the man, Robert Vasser, bled to death in his living-room with six stab wounds; his companion Barbara Forrest, 43, was stabbed twice and taken to St Vincent's Hospital where she was in a stable condition. Kenneth Little, aged 28, of Lafayette Avenue, a friend of the victims, was arrested at his home and charged with murder and assault.

10.00 pm: In the Kensington Park section of Brooklyn, a twenty-year-old man, identified as Achelleus Henry of Nostrand Avenue in the Crown Heights, was shot once in the back outside a house in Ocean Avenue. He was found lying face down with $40 in his hand. Detectives said they thought he was killed by drug dealers.

11.15 pm: A seventeen-year-old youth watching a street fight between two other teenagers in front of 1702 Davidson Avenue, in the Tremont section of the Bronx, was accidentally shot in the chest and killed when one of the youths pulled out a small calibre revolver and tried to shoot his adversary. The victim, Earl Bruce Hunter, died at Lincoln Hospital at 11.43 pm.

12.15 am: Two men were shot and killed on the top floor of an apartment building at Sands Street in the Farragut Houses in downtown Brooklyn. The victims, Horace Simmons, a 48-year-old sanitation worker of Manhattan, and Gary Buford, a 39-year-old maintenance worker who lived in the building, were moving furniture to a friend's apartment when they apparently stumbled on a drug transaction.

4.20 am: A person walking a dog found the body of George Van Name, aged 23, who worked for a landscape architect, on a secluded stretch of Freedom Avenue, near Travis Avenue in Staten Island. Mr Van Name had been brought to the spot in a car and shot three times in the right side of the head and once in the face with a .25 calibre pistol. The motive was unknown.

An Endangered Species

A report issued in December 1990 by the Federal Center for Disease Control, in Atlanta, Georgia, stated that the homicide rate among black males aged between fifteen and twenty-four had risen by two-thirds in the past five years: 'In some areas of the country it is now more likely for a black male between his fifteenth and twenty-fifth birthday to die from homicide than it was for a United States soldier to be killed on a tour of duty in Vietnam.' The latest statistics show that one in 1000 black males died as a result of homicide (almost always with firearms as the weapon) a rate which is about six times that of the rest of the population in the same age group – in fact, it is the major cause of death in this group. One counsellor is reported as commenting: 'Young blacks are an endangered species; they are dying out like the condor, out there in the streets . . . Violence has become a way of life, homicide has gotten to the point where it is almost a recreation.'

KEEPING IT IN THE FAMILY

BLACK AND WHITE
The Case of Charles 'Chuck' Stuart

'State Police, Boston.'

'. . . My wife's been shot . . . I've been shot.'

'Where is this, sir?'

'I've no idea.'

'Try to give me an indication of where you might be; a crossroads, anything . . .'

Silence.

'Hello.'

'Yes, sir, go ahead.'

'He got into the car at Huntington Avenue; I drove through Huntington Avenue.'

'Where are you now, sir? Can you indicate to me?'

'No. I don't know. He drove us, he made us go to an abandoned area.'

'OK, can you see out of the windows, can you tell me where you are?'

'No, I don't know. I can't see any signs. Oh God.'

'What kind of car do you have, sir?'

'A Toyota Cressida.'

'You're in the city of Boston?'

'Yes.'

'Can you give me any indication where you might be; any buildings?'

'No.'

'OK, your wife has been shot as well?'

'Yes . . . In the head.'

'OK. Bear with me now, stay on the phone with me.'

'Should I try to drive?'

'No. The people who shot you, are they in the area right there?'

'No, they took off.'

'OK, can you look out? Can you get out of the vehicle and look around to see where you are? I'm trying to get assistance to you.'

'Should I drive up to the corner of the street?'

'If you can drive without hurting yourself, yes. Just try to give me a crossroads. If you can drive, give me any street indicator and stay there, I'll get someone right to you.'

'I'll start the car . . . He took the keys, but I have a spare set. Oooh, man . . . I'm starting the car.'

'OK. What's your name, sir?'

'Stuart, Chuck Stuart . . . Ah, man . . .'

'Bear with me Chuck. I'm going to get someone to you. Hang in with me now.'

'I'm at a place, but I can't read it.'

'Just try to read it, Chuck; just stay calm, I'm going to get help to you. Help is on the way.'

'I'm coming up to an intersection, but there's no . . .'

'What colour's your car, buddy?'

'Blue.'

'A blue Toyota Cressida?'

'Yes.'

'OK Chuck, help is on the way. Bear with me. Is your wife breathing?'

'. . . She's still gurgling . . . There's a busy street up ahead, but I can't see where I am.'

'Hang in there Chuck, just try to give me any indication of where you might be. Can you see a building?'

'I'm driving with my lights off . . . I can't reach forward . . . too painful . . .'

'Just tell me what street it is, Chuck.'

'Aaah, man . . . I'm pulling over . . . Tremont Street . . .'

'You're at Tremont?'

'Ohhh, man . . . I'm going to pass out . . . my wife has stopped gurgling, she's stopped breathing. I'm going to try to drive straight to the hospital.'

'Can you drive?'

'I'm trying.'

'Chuck, pull over to the side of the street and talk to any passer-by, so I have an indication where you are.'

'I can't move . . . Oh God!'

'Chuck, can you see anyone on the street?'

'My car just died . . . Oh, man.'

'Chuck, can you see anything . . . Chuck . . . Chuck . . . Can you hear a siren?'

'Yes, I can hear a siren.'

'Chuck, can you hear me? Pick up the car phone; I can hear you breathing, come on, buddy.'

'I hear the police. They're right here. The Boston Police . . .'

It was 8.30 on the night of 23 October 1989, and this desperate conversation had been passing between despatcher Gary McLaughlin of the Massachusetts State Police Communications Center and Charles Stuart in his car on the streets of Boston's Mission Hill district. It was the overture to one of the most bizarre, most cynical homicides in modern American criminal history.

Stuart and his wife, Carol, had earlier left the Brigham and Women's Hospital on Francis Street, where they both attended the regular Lamaze class for couples expecting babies. Their route home to the northern suburb of Reading took the Stuarts through the predominantly black, ghettoized area of Mission Hill. Despite being home to such distinguished institutions as the Museum of Fine Arts, Northeastern University and the Symphony Hall, it was a district that enjoyed an unenviable reputation for violence, particularly with the white middle-classes in whose midst it nestled. Were it not that Brigham and Women's was a nationally respected maternity hospital – and only the best was good enough for Chuck and Carol Stuart – they would never have been in the district by choice.

When officers of the Boston Police Department arrived to rescue the Stuarts, they found Carol slumped in the passenger seat of the car, a bullet wound in her head; Chuck was behind the wheel, bleeding massively from the abdomen. Rushed respectively to Brigham and Women's and Boston City Hospital, Carol and Chuck were wheeled straight into surgery for emergency treatment.

Carol Stuart was barely alive when she reached the operating table, suffering extensive brain damage, and died a few hours later without regaining consciousness. Meanwhile, her baby had been removed by caesarean; two months premature, the infant would, like his mother, enjoy a pitifully short life.

Charles Stuart had also suffered a single bullet wound, and it was nearly as fatal, causing greater or lesser damage to the stomach, intestine, liver and urological tract, as well as severing several major blood vessels. In all, Chuck spent more than a month in intensive care.

As soon as he regained consciousness, however, Stuart was eager to help the police investigation, and kicked off with a detailed description of his nightmare drive and of his attacker. Shortly after leaving the hospital, so Chuck's story went, while their car was stationary at a traffic light, a black man carrying a silver-coloured pistol forced his way into the back seat, and in a 'raspy, sing-song voice' announced that he was going to rob them, warning: 'Don't look in the rear view mirror.'

The man then gave Chuck directions until they reached the broken-down housing project at Bromley and Heath. When Stuart stopped the car, the gunman snatched the keys from the ignition and robbed them of money and jewellery. Then, according to Chuck's narrative, the robber noticed the car phone, immediately assumed they were police and started shooting. First he put a bullet into Carol's head, then he took aim at Chuck's but missed when he ducked. The man leaned over the seat and shot Stuart in the side and was about to fire again but found the chamber empty. Pocketing his loot, the assassin fled into the night. Fortunately, Chuck had a spare set of keys to the car in his pocket, and despite considerable pain he tried to drive back to safety after dialling 911 on the cellphone and contacting despatcher McLaughlin.

A point that seemed to puzzle nobody at the time was how, despite the darkness, the panic, the armed threat not to look in the rear view mirror, Chuck Stuart was able to give a precise – some might say meticulous – description of his assailant: brown skinned, brown eyed, with high cheek bones and a bony, stubbly jaw, a medium 'Nubian' nose and a short Afro haircut; he was five feet ten inches tall, aged between 28 and 34, and slim – weighing 150–160 pounds. The man was wearing a black sweatsuit over a dark shirt, and the sweatsuit had two or three red stripes on the sleeve. He was wearing a baseball cap on his head and black driving gloves with the knuckles cut out; he was right-handed, and of course there was the unmistakable raspy voice.

It was one of those bizarre tricks of fate that the paramedic group arriving with the police team that found the injured couple was being covered by a camera crew from television's *Rescue 911* programme; this meant that news of the appalling crime was accompanied by live on-the-spot media coverage. When the newspapers broke the story on the following morning, the text was accompanied by grisly photographs, taken through the Toyota's windscreen, of the carnage within.

As a story it shocked the nation. But in Boston itself the effect was not dissimilar to that generated by the riots that ripped through the Roxbury and Mission Hill districts in the wake of the assassination in Memphis of Dr Martin Luther King Jnr in early 1968. The Black Nemesis, it seemed, was back to haunt the white middle-classes of New England, and the political consequences of the Stuart case will reverberate through the city of Boston for many years to come.

America could not have asked for two more perfect martyrs; the ideal suburban couple who fell prey to the savage beasts of the urban jungle. Chuck, 29 at the time of the shooting, met Carol (a year older) in 1979 while they were both working at a restaurant called the Driftwood in Revere – he as a cook, she as a waitress.

Carol DiMaiti, born into a solid Catholic Italian-American family, was a popular girl with many friends and a quick brain that earned her high grades at school, and ultimately the chance to study law at Boston College. It was just after she graduated that Carol took the job at the Driftwood. Charles Stuart was an almost perfect match; like Carol he came from hard-working Catholic stock, with origins in Ireland. Like her he was outgoing with friends, though it was later recalled that he could be quiet, almost sullen in strange company. He enjoyed sports and was well liked among his peers. If he could not quite equal Carol in academic achievement (he later felt the need to fabricate the story of a college scholarship), then at least Chuck was industrious and ambitious for his future security. In December 1983 Chuck and Carol became engaged, and on 13 October 1985, they were married. Both were now enthusiastically climbing the ladder to emerge into what became known as the 'yuppie' lifestyle. Carol had secured a job as tax attorney with Cahners Publishing Company, and her future looked endlessly optimistic; Chuck, by dint of personality and hard work, was now the valued general manager of Kakas and Sons, an old-established and highly respected Boston furrier, situated in fashionable

Newbury Street. With increased responsibility came increased pay cheques, and Chuck and Carol Stuart were able to sell their first home in Medford and buy a large split-level home in the suburb of Reading. Among his fondest plans for the future, Chuck included owning a restaurant – it was an expensive ambition, which would be clearly remembered in the light of revelations to come. In spring 1989 Carol became proudly pregnant, and both she and Chuck enrolled at the Brigham and Women's. Outwardly, the Stuarts were the perfect couple, close and loving in their own relationship, warm and generous with friends, unstinting in the time and affection they gave to their families. It was this, the American dream, that was shattered on the night of 23 October 1989.

Brothers-in-arms

The police responded to the crisis created by the shooting of Carol and Chuck Stuart by putting a veritable army of officers on to the streets of the Mission Hill district in a blanket stop-and-search exercise. It did not go unremarked, though, that Mayor Flynn had been less enthusiastic in his use of law enforcement time and manpower when the victims of homicide had been poor blacks.

On Saturday, 28 October, Carol Stuart was buried, and a funeral service was held at St James's church, Medford, where she and Chuck had been married. Chuck himself was still too weak to attend, but his closest friend, Brian Parsons, read aloud to the mourners the farewell eulogy penned by Chuck while on his sick-bed. It read in part: 'Good night sweet wife, my love. God has called you to his hands not to take you away from me, but to bring you away from the cruelty and violence that fill this world.'

Then, dramatically, the city authorities announced with undisguised glee that they had apprehended a likely suspect in the person of 39-year-old habitual criminal Willie Bennett. Bennett had a record far longer than his arm, starting with petty theft in his early teens and progressing to robbery and assault. In 1973 he had shot at and wounded a police officer.

Just weeks before the Stuart shooting, a man identified as Bennett was said to have held up a video store in Boston using a 'silver' revolver and speaking, according to the shop's manager and clerk, with a 'raspy' voice.

Now Willie Bennett had made himself a lot of very bad luck in his life, but what happened next took the prize. Willie had a nephew named Joey, who also lived around Mission Hill. Joey hero-worshipped his uncle; he loved having a gangster in the family – even one as inept as Uncle Willie – and if Willie was taking a breather between 'exploits', Joey would just make them up. Which is how he came to spread the rumour that Uncle Willie had shot the Stuarts. Travelling fast, as it usually does, this piece of neighbourhood gossip was not long in reaching the ears of the police. Willie Bennett was well and truly 'in the frame'.

But now something happened that pushed the drama to ever more poignant heights. After struggling valiantly for life during the past seventeen days, the Stuarts' baby – which had been hurriedly baptized Christopher – died at Brigham and Women's Hospital on 9 November.

The fury and anguish continued unabated, and consequently the pressure on police to present a culprit to the public was relentless. On the night of 11 November, Willie Bennett was arrested at his girlfriend's home in Burlington. In the absence of any concrete evidence to link him to the Stuart case, Bennett was held on charges arising from the hold-up of the video store. Willie had already protested that he was there with his girlfriend in her apartment on the night of 23 October, and she had confirmed it. Unluckily for Willie Bennett, his two sisters proved as much a hindrance to his freedom as his nephew. According to their story, Willie was in no such place as Burlington – he had been with *them* on the night of the shooting, in a Mission Hill bar! It was one piece of family loyalty that Willie could have well done without. He could also have done without the identity parade.

It was now December, and Chuck Stuart was beginning to respond to the medical treatment and care lavished on their distinguished patient by the staff of the Boston City Hospital. He was receiving a constant stream of visitors, and spent a lot of time telephoning a young woman named Debbie Allen. It was never established quite what level this friendship was on, apart from the fact that she and Chuck had met when Ms Allen took a summer vacation job at Kakas and Sons. Chuck was released from hospital on 5 December and went to stay at the family home in Revere. In hindsight it must have been a strange homecoming, for something very dramatic indeed had happened among the Stuart siblings. Just three days after the shooting of Chuck and Carol, 23-year-old Matthew Stuart made a startling confession to elder brother Michael. There is no knowing *exactly* what passed between the brothers – neither has said – but it could have left Michael in no doubt that both Chuck and Matthew were deeply implicated in the shooting incident. Nevertheless, the secret was safely kept, and one of Chuck's first errands was to set in motion the machinery whereby he could claim on Carol's life insurance policies. After what must have been a very low-key Christmas in the Stuart household, Chuck was asked to attend an identity parade in which Willie Bennett would have a starring part. As each of the participants passed in front of him, Chuck scrutinized the man carefully before declaring at the end that Bennett 'most resembles the person who shot my wife and I'. Amazingly, none of the men on the line-up was asked to speak, and as far as we know Chuck Stuart was incurious as to whether the man he had fingered had a 'raspy, sing-song voice'. The spectre of a very long prison sentence must have loomed large to Willie Bennett, though he was not yet charged with murder.

Meanwhile Matthew Stuart had been talking again; this time to his girlfriend Janet Monteforte. Janet had talked to her parents, and Mr and Mrs Monteforte had talked to a lawyer. As the number of persons privy to the darker secrets of the Stuarts widened, so Michael realized that their only salvation lay in a concerted family effort. On the first day of 1990, it is rumoured that the clan met at an undisclosed location; it is considered unlikely that Chuck was in attendance. The result was that Matthew began to feel decidedly uncomfortable, and he announced that on 3 January, as soon as the New Year holiday was over, he intended to spill the beans to the state prosecutor's office.

As it was to turn out, Chuck would steal his thunder.

Nevertheless, on 3 January Matthew kept his appointment with the district attorney. There is no convenient transcript of that vital meeting, but in his painstaking and convincing reconstruction of the Stuart case,[1] Ken Englade suggests that Chuck had recruited his younger, wilder brother ostensibly to defraud the insurance companies by staging a phoney break-in. The details are hazy, though it is thought that while Matthew took care of the bogus burglary, Chuck intended to slip off and kill Carol. In any event, the whole thing was bungled and Carol lived to see another day. On 22 October – the day before the

[1] *Murder in Boston*, Ken Englade. St Martin's Press, New York, 1990.

fatal shooting – Chuck took Matthew on a tour of Mission Hill and pointed out a spot where he was to wait in his car on the following night for brother Chuck to drive past and hand him a package, which Matthew was under instruction to dispose of – permanently.

And that is perhaps what happened. The only difference may have been that when Chuck met his brother he was in considerably more pain than he had anticipated. What was meant to be a self-inflicted flesh wound in the thigh, through an ironic error of judgement, nearly cost Chuck his own life. Charles Stuart then drove from the rendezvous, telephoned 911, and the rest is history.

As for Matthew, he and his passenger, a close friend, drove out to the north of Revere and threw the bundle of jewellery and then the 'silver' gun far out into the Pines River. Almost as though he knew he might need proof, Matthew held back Carol's engagement ring from the package and presented it to the prosecutor. That was his story, and soon there would be nobody around to contradict it.

It was obvious that Chuck, perhaps through a family contact, was well aware of Matthew's imminent confession, and the predicament in which it would inevitably put him. The story was now outside the Stuart clan, beyond his control, and at about the same time that his brother was relaying his drama, effectively to the world, the main actor was preparing his stage exit.

In the late afternoon of 3 January, Chuck Stuart drove the new car he had purchased only the previous day (and partly paid for with the money from his late wife's life insurance) to his own home in Reading. He then visited the family lawyer who declined to act on his behalf. It is interesting to speculate on how the rest of Chuck's day – the rest of Chuck's life! – would have changed if John Dawly had taken the case. As it was, Charles Stuart drove across Boston to the Braintree district south of the city, and booked in at the Sheraton-Tara Hotel; it was around ten at night, Matthew had told his tale, and the police would be on the lookout for Chuck. At 4.30 on the morning of the 4th he was awakened by the alarm call booked the previous evening, and shortly afterwards left the hotel. It was the last time anybody remembers seeing Chuck Stuart alive.

At 6.50 am, a state trooper spotted Chuck's newly acquired Nissan Stanza abandoned on the huge Tobin Bridge over the Mystic River and Boston's Inner Harbour. The car's engine was running and the emergency lights were flashing. Of the occupant there was no sign save the driving licence issued to Charles Stuart and a note written on Sheraton-Tata headed paper expressing regret at having caused 'so much trouble'.

Within a few hours, state police divers had raised the body of Chuck Stuart from the muddy bottom of the Mystic. Not long afterwards, a different team of divers recovered the bundle of jewellery that Matthew had hurled into the Pines River; followed later by the gun which would be confirmed as the weapon used in the 23 October shootings. It would also be revealed that a similar gun had gone missing from the safe of Kakas and Sons, furriers.

Needless to say, Willie Bennett was freed from suspicion by an embarrassed Boston police authority. But it was not to be as easy as that, for the crime of Charles Stuart had gone far beyond killing his wife, and indirectly his child, out of sheer greed. He had divided a whole city in a way that made it difficult for the holes to be repaired. In choosing a black ghetto as his location, and a black gunman as his villain, Chuck Stuart had found his way to the very root of the fears of white America, a population just waiting to have its worst fears, its worst prejudices, confirmed.

Newspapers and black community workers were not slow to remark how spontaneous the reactions of Boston's white-run authorities were in saturating the area around the scene of the shooting with law enforcement officers, their willingness to believe any excess Chuck cared to describe, so long as the culprit was black. They pointed out, too, how at variance this was with the experience of black victims of violence in their dealings with the police. And we should not ignore the role of the television crew at the murder scene, showing with unprecedented immediacy the horror of the incident as it unfolded. The crime was *inescapable*, and it is a crime of which we are unlikely to have heard the last.

On 12 January 1990, a grand jury was convened to hear evidence in the Stuart case. The jury adjourned and reconvened over the best part of the year, its purpose to determine on the testimony whether there is sufficient evidence for the case to go to trial. At present the official blanket of silence thrown over the case has all but stifled that ambition. A report published in November 1990 stated that on the 5th of the month the Massachusetts Supreme Court ruled that the lawyer visited by Charles Stuart for advice, John T. Dawley, could not be forced to testify before the grand jury. The court ruled by a majority that the confidentiality of a lawyer-client relationship must stand even though the 'client' – Stuart – was dead: 'The mouth of the attorney shall be forever sealed.'

Legal observers have stated that this ruling indicates strongly that prosecutors might never now be able to assemble sufficient facts with which to bring the Stuart case to trial.

Update

It was exactly one year after the incident at Mission Hill that the city of Boston was forced once again to remind itself of the weakness in the fabric of its society, as exposed by the arrest and confinement of Willie Bennett.

At the end of October 1990, the body of a young black woman was found in Franklin Field, a Boston park. She had been raped and murdered. It was the 128th killing in the city so far that year, and it was not – unlike the shooting of Carol Stuart – a case which seemed to attract much official attention.

Indeed, the police made every effort to play the case down; the victim was a prostitute, and she was dead. That was about it.

It was not until three weeks later that the victim was identified as 26-year-old Kimberley Rae Harbour, and she had fallen foul of a local gang who called themselves the Pistons out on a Halloween 'wilding' spree. They also revealed that she had been stripped, raped, bludgeoned with a tree branch and stabbed more than 130 times with a knife and a broken beer bottle.

A spokeswoman for the Boston chapter of the National Association for the Advancement of Coloured People claimed: 'If it had happened in any other community they would have let people know that there was harm out there. We have some major issues of public policy that need to be resolved.'

The director of the Black Community Information Center added: 'This community should have been informed. The alleged perpetrators have been walking the streets for three weeks and there could have been other victims.'

A morally wounded spokesman for the District Attorney's office made a statement that the police had *not* provided the media with information *because* of the Stuart case, where the authorities had been heavily criticized for revealing too much of the *mis*information that originated from Chuck Stuart: 'We have no obligation to tell the media anything other than the scant details when things are under investigation. In the Stuart case the community was upset with the police and the prosecution for publicizing the case. Now they are criticizing us. You're really just damned if you do and damned if you don't.'

Both of Boston's leading newspapers – the *Globe* and the *Herald* – reported having difficulties prising information out of the police: 'We were chased away from the scene of the crime,' complained one reporter, while L. Kim Tan of the *Boston Herald* confirmed that since the Stuart affair he was having great problems, especially in the current case, where 'all the affidavits for the search warrants used in the arrests have been impounded . . . There is very little detail available, and very little about the circumstances.'

Meanwhile, as the city tries to live itself down, three of the attackers of Kimberley Harbour who are to be tried as adults and five juveniles are facing charges of murder, aggravated rape and armed robbery.

THE MESSENGER OF MISERY
The Case of Christian Brando

It was announced as America's scandal of the year, though whether the scandal was in the crime itself or in the media circus that it became is arguable. What is certain is that an otherwise commonplace shooting would have been no 'scandal' at all had it not involved the son of America's greatest living actor.

It was a simple, if sordid, story of violent death US-style, a fatal cocktail of alcohol, domestic dispute and guns. Without its capacity to flush out the Great Man and ensure that after more than thirty years avoiding it, Marlon Brando would be obliged for the sake of family loyalty to cooperate with the media, the saga would have been a non-runner.

It all began on the night of 16 May 1990, although by the time the police had arrived at the two-acre Brando family residence it was all over. The scene that faced detectives, and would make headlines around the world, was an almost pitiful anti-climax. In the television room of the rambling mansion on Mulholland Drive, high in the exclusive residential area of the Hollywood Hills, sat the victim, 26-year-old Tahitian Dag Drollet. At first glance, he might just have dozed off in front of the big game, a cigarette lighter clutched in one hand, a tobacco pouch lying beside him on the white sofa. But then you noticed the small round wound on Drollet's face where a .45 bullet had ripped through flesh and bone from almost point blank range, peppering the skin with a tattoo of burnt powder, before exiting at the base of the neck.

The one thing that struck investigating officers was how neat it all was, no sign of a struggle. And that did not seem to add up, because the other leading player in this drama, Christian Brando, Marlon's 32-year-old son, had already told his father and the police that there had been a fight: 'I didn't mean to shoot him, he fought for the gun . . . we were rolling around on the couch . . .' Then he was handcuffed and taken into custody; and along with Christian they took his arsenal of firearms – the .45 semi-automatic SIG-Sauer handgun which had robbed Dag Drollet of his life, an Uzi submachine gun, an M14 rifle and another pistol.

The house would normally have been home only to the reclusive actor, but Brando had invited to stay his common-law wife, Polynesian actress Tarita Teriipia, their daughter Cheyenne, and Cheyenne's lover and father of her unborn child, Dag Drollet. The three of them had just arrived from Tahiti where Cheyenne had been recovering from a serious motor accident sustained the previous year, and where Drollet's father was a leading politician.

Christian was at the family home only because his father had insisted he lodge his guns there for safe keeping – although he and Cheyenne had earlier in the evening gone out to a restaurant for supper. What conversation passed between the younger Brandos we will never know for sure, but in the light of subsequent events this may have been the occasion that Cheyenne chose to tell her half-brother that Dag Drollet had been knocking her around – a claim, incidentally, which has been denied by everybody except Cheyenne herself. In fact Marlon Brando was reported as describing Dag as 'a polite, low-key, fine young man'. Be that as it may, when the siblings returned from their meal at around 10 o'clock, Cheyenne followed Christian, apparently angry and, according to his own admission, the worse for drink and bent on seeking out Drollet, whom he found watching television in the den.

Within minutes, during which it is anybody's guess what was really said, what really happened, Dag Drollet was dead. By the time his father, attracted from another part of the house by the return of the children, reached the television room, Christian Brando was standing with a large pistol gripped in his hand. Cautiously, the actor took the weapon from his son while the boy, in an obvious state of distress and confusion, claimed that he had just shot Drollet. Brando tried mouth-to-mouth resuscitation, but Christian's victim was beyond help. There were now only two things to do – at around 10.45 pm a 911 telephone call summoned the police, and later a long-distance to New York brought top lawyer William Kunstler to the phone.

It was around midnight that Christian Brando got his opportunity to tell officers of the Los Angeles Police Department his version of what had happened earlier that night. Those who have heard the tape-recorded interview have remarked on Christian's agitated, almost neurotic delivery. The content of his statement alternates between contrition and braggadocio. Brando starts by repeating that 'We got in a struggle and the gun went off in his face. I didn't want to hurt him; I didn't want to kill him', followed by a more aggressive claim that 'You know, we got in a struggle . . . I'd been drinking . . . I didn't go up to him and go *Boom*! in my dad's house. If I was going to do that I'd take him down the road and knock him off.' Later in the interview, Christian seems to get into his stride: 'If I was going to do something devious like this [murder], I would have said [to Drollet] "Hey, let's go out, you know, check out the mine shafts on the Mojave." You know, or something like that. Whoops! He fell down a hole. Couldn't help it. "See you later sucker!" You know, I mean, all delicately laid – take him out to Death Valley, no clothes on, and give him three gallons of water "Get a suntan!"'

Of great importance during this interview, Brando admits that it was on the way home from the restaurant with Cheyenne that he stopped off at a girlfriend's apartment and picked up the weapon that killed Dag Drollet. Until then he had maintained that it was already in the room where the shooting took place.

'A Tragic Accident'

On the following morning, represented by the Brando lawyer, William Kunstler, a woebegone Christian who gave his occupation as 'self-employed welder' stood handcuffed and unshaven, wearing grey prison issue, in the dock of the Los Angeles court. Kunstler entered a formal plea of 'not guilty' on his client's behalf, claiming, 'The weapon was fired accidentally during a struggle. There was no intent to harm anyone. This was not a murder by any means.' It was clear at this early stage that William Kunstler intended to press for a manslaughter charge. He pointed out that Christian's confession made to police officers on the night of the shooting was the result of alcohol – in other words, he was so drunk he didn't know what he was saying.

Christian's half-sister Cheyenne and his former wife Mary McKenna were in court; his father, notoriously reclusive, was not. Nevertheless lawyer Kunstler volunteered: 'He will be available for his son.'

Despite his having threatened to kill her and her mother during their acrimonious divorce proceedings, Mary McKenna added her unqualified support of Christian's innocence: 'He is not a killer . . . there must have been a reason for it.'

Five days later, on 22 May, Marlon Brando, true to his word, was there in Division 91 of Los Angeles Municipal Court for his son's bail hearing. Next to Marlon sat Tarita Teriipia, their son Teihotu, and his son and daughter by a previous marriage. In support of their charge of first-degree murder, the District Attorney's representative, Steven Barshop, emphasized to the court that not only had the fatal bullet entered the victim's head from an angle that indicated he was shot by a person standing above him, but the fact that he was still gripping a cigarette lighter in one hand and a television remote control unit in the other (Marlon Brando had removed this during his attempt to breathe life back into Drollet) seemed to disprove Christian's insistence that a struggle had taken place on the couch and the gun went off accidentally.

Despite his father's undertaking to ensure that Christian would not abscond, the judge refused bail and the defendant was returned to prison. After the hearing, Marlon Brando stoically faced a media that he had turned his back on so long ago to broadcast his belief in his son's innocence and to add, poetically, that 'the Messenger of Death has come to my house. He also came to the house of Jacques Drollet [Dag's father] in Tahiti.'

In the middle of June, after lawyer William Kunstler had failed to win bail for him, Christian Brando's defence passed into the care of Robert Shapiro. Shapiro announced that in collaboration with 'the country's most respected criminologist', he would stage a reconstruction of the shooting incident in order to demonstrate how Dag Drollet's death had been a simple, if tragic accident.

However, although the words 'plea-bargain' were not used, it was understood that Mr Shapiro might offer a no-contest plea in exchange for lesser charges. The court was promised that a date for Christian's preliminary hearing would be set on 25 June.

Cheyenne, for her part, had made only the briefest of statements to the police, but it was to the effect that Christian had 'just walked in and killed Dag'. She was prevented from making any further damaging observations by being flown back to Tahiti. She remained on the island, far from the clutches of the district attorney's office, and gave birth to Dag Drollet's child.

In the meantime, Tinseltown's hangers-on, anyone who could claim an acquaintance with him or, as Christian put it, 'I fucked once or twice', were telling their stories to the highest media bidder. Some made more out of it than others; Ms Shirley Cumpanas, wife of Christian's closest pal, and billed by one English tabloid who carried her 'Exclusive Confessions' as a half-Apache Indian, claimed a seven-year affair with 'Marlon Brando's son'. She was also, according to other reports, hawking photographs of herself to *Penthouse* and *Playboy*.

At Christian's preliminary hearing, a blow was struck to the prosecution case by the court's refusal to admit as evidence the tape-recorded interview which he had made at police headquarters. The reason was purely a technicality – officer Steve Osti had failed to advise Brando of his right to a lawyer before the interview began. Another officer on duty after the killing told the court: 'Christian stated he didn't care for the guy [Drollet] a whole lot, but he didn't want him killed; if something happened to him to that effect it would be OK, but he didn't want him to be killed.'

On 24 July a further setback occurred when Municipal Court judge Larry Fidler also ruled inadmissible the statement by Cheyenne Brando that Christian was angry at Drollet before allegedly killing him. Prosecutors were seeking to prove murder, and investigating officers' evidence that Cheyenne had told them her half-brother became enraged when she told him that the victim had physically abused her were fundamental to the case. Nevertheless, the judge's ruling was again on a technicality – that the statement alone, without Cheyenne's personal testimony, would deprive the defence attorney of the right to cross-examine. It was also made clear that Ms Brando would be remaining in Tahiti on medical grounds.

The court finally ruled that Brando *would* face trial for murder: 'There is no doubt there has been a killing; there is no doubt that the defendant pulled the trigger.'

Christian was also facing two other firearm offences – not for firing them, but for not having them licensed. Bail was set at the extraordinary level of $10 million (£5.5 million) which was to prove less of a problem than the requirement to surrender his passport, which could not be found. The likelihood of Christian becoming a fugitive was remote, but given that the only other witness to the killing – Cheyenne Brando – had fled to Tahiti and dug her heels in was guaranteed to make the district attorney's office cautious. Thus Christian remained a prisoner without bail.

A week into August (during which time the passport remained elusive) lawyer Robert L. Shapiro made application to the court that Christian's bail be reduced to that which might be asked from 'an ordinary person in his situation'. There was not a bond company in the country, he suggested, with the equivalent of almost £6m available in cash.

By the following week an agreement seemed to have been reached whereby Marlon Brando was allowed to put up, as collateral for a reduced bail security, his own Hollywood home. Christian's obviously contrite offer to wear an electronic security tagging device was rejected by the judge as being 'unnecessary'. Having secured his client's temporary freedom, Robert Shapiro indicated that he was willing to enter into a plea-bargain whereby Christian would exchange his not guilty plea for guilty to a lesser charge of voluntary manslaughter.

Christian Brando was formally released from prison on bail on 15 August 1990.

In the middle of September, moves were being made by the Los Angeles deputy district attorney to flush Cheyenne Brando out of her Tahitian retreat to give evidence in court. It was a move resisted not only by the witness herself, but also by the French authorities on the island who refused to comply with the American request. Within a week the matter became academic – Cheyenne Brando tried unsuccessfully to take her own life with an overdose of drugs, and when she emerged from the coma was declared by a French judge in Tahiti to be incapable of looking after herself and placed under the care of her mother on the island.

Meanwhile, with the unlikelihood of their star witness ever appearing before a court, the prosecuting authorities at the end of the year decided to cut their losses and agree to a reduced charge of voluntary manslaughter in exchange for a plea of guilty.

As expected, Christian Brando formally pleaded guilty to the voluntary manslaughter of Dag Drollet after a plea-bargaining agreement between his lawyer and the prosecutor's office. However, despite the reduced charge, the district attorney announced that he would press for a maximum sentence when Brando appeared before the sentencing hearing on 26 February 1991.

One man clearly dissatisfied with the way the case was ending was the victim's father, Tahitian politician Jacques Drollet, who according to one newspaper asked: 'What kind of justice is this?' The truth will be hidden for ever in the drawers of Marlon Brando and his slick lawyers.'

In a memorandum to the sentencing court, the deputy district attorneys Steven Barshop and William Clark recommended that Christian Brando, whom they described as 'vicious, callous and a serious danger to society', should be sentenced to no less than sixteen years.

At the sentencing itself, Christian and his father seemed closer than anyone remembered for years, adversity seeming to have welded at least a temporary bond. For his part, Christian Brando made public his remorse in an interview with a Los Angeles newspaper: 'It is a tragedy and I do feel bad. If I could give my life to have Dag come back, I'd do it, but there's nothing I can do. I have to live with this for the rest of my life; wake up with it and go to sleep with it.'

Marlon Brando, pulled at last into the public limelight, loyally took the witness stand on his son's behalf and gave testimony that Christian's early problems with the family's relationships were greatly responsible for what one psychiatrist described as a 'low-profile, low self-esteemed personality', which had driven him into a spiral of alcohol and drug abuse.

In the end, after all the ballyhoo and tub-thumping had died down, Christian Brando was sentenced to ten years' imprisonment. It was, as everybody had predicted, an affair from which only the lawyers gained. For Marlon Brando there was the unwelcome intrusion by the world into his treasured privacy; for Cheyenne a further jolt to an already unsettled mind. For the Drollet family, the loss of a son and perhaps disillusion with the American way of justice. For Dag, the ultimate loss, his life – which for all Christian's 'feeling bad' can never be given back to him.

But perhaps the most haunting figure in this almost fictional Hollywood script is Christian Brando himself . . .

Drugs and Drink

Born in May 1958, Christian Devi was the son of Marlon Brando and Anna Kashfi, an actress who had gone to Hollywood in 1955. Her Indian appearance – which she did everything to accentuate with saris and exotic jewellery – belied the fact that Anna was in reality the daughter of a Welshman named O'Callaghan and whose only genuine claim to the subcontinent was to have been born there while her father was working for the State Railway. By the time this shattering news was revealed, it was too late; she had become pregnant by Brando, and although Marlon felt a strong sense of betrayal, the couple married in secret in October 1957.

After Christian was born, there was almost permanent open hostility between his parents, with the unfortunate child being pushed around like a pawn in Marlon and Anna's games of one-upmanship. Accusations of violence and insanity and alcohol and drug abuse flew thick and fast in those formative years, and a succession of custody orders ensured that Christian was lobbed around fairly equally between his parents' ambitions – or more realistically between a series of nannies and nursemaids.

By the end of 1964, Anna Kashfi was so badly affected by drink and drugs that she attempted suicide; subsequently she was allowed access to her son only in the presence of an attorney. In 1965, the child was removed from Marlon Brando's custody by a court order and placed temporarily in the care of Marlon's sister Frances. During this period neither parent gave any particular demonstration of affection, but by October 1965 Christian was back with his mother.

Meanwhile, Marlon had met Tarita Teriipia while making *Mutiny on the Bounty*; they had a son – Teihotu – in 1963, and would have Cheyenne in 1970. In 1971, Christian was in joint custody and once again pushed and pulled from every direction. He went missing from boarding school and was eventually tracked down by Marlon's private detectives living the life of a hippie in Southern California. Kashfi was accused of masterminding a 'kidnap' which resulted in Brando once again being given sole custody of his son, whom he whisked away to the Tahitian island paradise of Tetiaroa. When he returned, predictably wild and undisciplined, Christian was put into private school from which he dropped out at the age of eighteen – to the disappointment of all and the surprise of very few. Marlon is said to have temporarily banned him from the house.

The relationship between father and son continued to deteriorate until Christian married Mary McKenna in 1981; from this point until his trial, Marlon was always on call for some favour or other – usually money. Shortly after the marriage, Christian met a minor actor named Bill Cable, who was also skilled as a tree surgeon and got Christian interested in the job. Christian was also taking an above average interest in drugs, alcohol and guns, which he began to collect; he collected a succession of women too, few lasting longer than a week. In 1988, Christian Brando came into an annuity of $100,000 a year, which simply allowed him access to more excess; by the time he shot Dag Drollet in May 1990, it would have been difficult to have described Christian as anything but a broken-down wreck. A weak boy, a foolish boy, it would nevertheless, in view of his upbringing, have been surprising if Christian had *not* become a drug-dependent alcoholic with a short temper and an unnatural love of firearms.

As Mike Bygraves so perceptively wrote in the English *Independent* newspaper during the trial: 'He is popular with women who see him as a little boy lost – which is hardly surprising since Christian has been lost since he was a little boy.'

REVENGE OF A PLAYTHING
The Case of Kiranjit Ahluwalia

On the night of 9 May 1989, neighbours in Coombe Close, Crawley, West Sussex, heard an agonized scream pierce the dark from the direction of the house that Deepak Ahluwalia shared with his wife Kiranjit and their children. Looking out to see what the commotion might be, they saw an Asian woman, barefoot and apparently in distress, climbing from a downstairs window, a child in her arms, and fleeing from a house that was rapidly becoming engulfed in flames.

At just before 3.00 a.m, the police and fire brigade reached the house, and within a very short time the investigators became convinced that this was no fire with a 'natural' origin. Somebody had clearly set fire to the house. Nor did it take long to establish who that somebody was. When Mrs Ahluwalia was picked up and taken to Crawley police station for questioning, she gave every cooperation and during her recorded interview admitted setting fire to her own home and, along with it, her husband.

'You poured petrol on him?'[1]

'Yes; on him and on the floor and on the [bed]sheets.'

'Was he in bed, then?'

'Yes.'

'How much petrol did you pour on him?'

[1]Derived from Mrs Ahluwalia's recorded statement to the police.

'More than in that glass [tumbler]. I couldn't put any more on; I was frightened because he's always aggressive. I just put the bucket over on the floor . . . I got fire but it went out.'

'Was there petrol in the bucket.'

'Yes.'

Like many of the dozen or so women every year who kill their partners, Mrs Ahluwalia had endured years of the most intense physical and mental abuse – ten of them in all. Trapped by her religion and her culture into a life of suffering in silence, she could finally take no more.

Kiranjit Ahluwalia never denied killing her husband, and in court she pleaded guilty to manslaughter. The plea, however, was rejected on legal grounds, and the defendant was charged with, and eventually convicted of, murder. When she appeared before the Lewes Crown Court in December 1989, Mrs Ahluwalia did not feel confident enough to give evidence on her own behalf (and in Britain at least, it is the unassailable right of the accused *not* to be put in the box – and for there to be no inference of guilt as a result). Had she done so, the jury would have heard from her own lips the catalogue of appalling domestic violence from which Deepak's death represented the only available means of escape.

'Tell us what happened.'

'I was thinking, if I kill him . . . if I kill myself . . . who's going to look after my babies, because he's having an affair with another lady. Then I just made up my mind.'

'Made up your mind to do what?'

'To burn him, because it hurts. He hit me every day, I just wanted to give him pain. So much pain I get when he hits me.'

'What sort of pain do you think you were going to give him pouring this much petrol over him?'

'Because he was giving me pain; breaking every part of my body. Last week he gave me a blue eye. I was unconscious, he kept hitting me – he broke my tooth . . . he gave me a punch there, my lips were so swollen I couldn't go to work for five days.'

Victim of Custom

There are, of course, an alarming number of women the world over who could tell much the same story – an increasing number of women's refuges and divorce courts are filled with these victims of male violence. But for Asian women there is a far greater cultural pressure to remain with a husband no matter how intolerable the marriage may be. The wife is simply told, as Kiranjit was, to 'try harder'. The custom is called *izzat*.

Kiranjit was the subject of the quite common Asian practice of arranged marriages, and in 1979 she embarked on her future with great optimism and enthusiasm as the wife of Deepak Ahluwalia, a Sikh from the same caste as herself. It was not long before Kiranjit Ahluwalia learned to regret and fear her new life; most of all she feared her husband's violent abuse and threats of death. He would, for example, lock her in a room for days on end with neither food and drink nor any normal facilities for hygiene. He once burned her face with an electric iron . . .

Despite telling her own family, and her husband's violence being well known to his own, nothing was done to help or protect Kiranjit Ahluwalia. Eventually she made an unsuccessful attempt to take her own life.

Fortunately for her (and potentially for other women in the same invidious position) Kiranjit has had her case enthusiastically championed by Crawley Women's Aid, in her home county of Sussex, and the Southall Black Sisters group in north London. On 29 June 1990, they launched a nationwide campaign to have Mrs Ahluwalia's case reopened in an attempt to secure her freedom.

It was to be a difficult task, involving a fundamental rethinking of the law of provocation, for Kiranjit's attorney had already tried unsuccessfully to advance such a defence at her trial. At present, in the instance of murder (unlike any other crime), provocation is a legal defence that will result in a verdict of 'voluntary manslaughter' – where the defendant had intended to kill or 'otherwise had the mental element for murder'. A life sentence is never given for a provoked killing. There is, moreover, an implicit requirement to distinguish between homicide committed in 'hot blood', where there is no calculation before the act, and a killing in 'cold blood', where a deliberate decision is involved (also called in legal terms 'malice aforethought').

The problem faced by Mrs Ahluwalia's defence counsel was that although his client had been 'provoked' in the moral sense of having suffered years of beatings, in the legal sense she had calculatedly waited for her husband to fall asleep, collected various paraphernalia from around the house – petrol, candles, matches – and then set fire to him. For the same technical reason, a plea of self-defence would fail against the fact that Deepak Ahluwalia was asleep at the time he was set alight.

At a public meeting in Crawley, packed with representatives from both the Asian and white communities (and including Mrs Ahluwalia's own family and in-laws), the victim herself, for the first time in public, spoke of her deep suffering. Through the medium of a tape recording made by her while in prison, Kiranjit Ahluwalia told her audience *exactly* what it was like to be the victim of an abuse of *izzat*:

'My heart is full of things to say, but it's difficult to know where to start my story. My culture is like my blood, it is in every vein of my body. The culture into which I was born and grew up sees the woman as the "honour" of the house. In order to uphold this false "honour" and "glory" she is taught to endure in silence many kinds of oppression and pain. Also, religion teaches her that her husband is god, and fulfilling his every desire is her religious duty. A woman who does not follow this path in our society has no respect or place in it; she suffers abuse and slander, and she has to face attacks and much hurt – entirely alone. She is responsible not only for her husband's happiness but also for his entire family's. For ten years I tried to fulfil the duties endorsed by religion – I don't mean to praise myself, but I was a good daughter-in-law, wife and mother. I tried to make my husband and my in-laws happy in every possible way, I put up with everything . . . A couple of times I tried to escape from the trap of my anguished life, but I gave in to the pressure of upholding the family honour and my desire to keep up appearances. So now at my age [she was 33] I am a prisoner – jailed; far from my children [her two sons were put into the care of her mother-in-law]. What have they done to be robbed of their mother's love having already lost their father's? . . . Today I have come out of my husband's prison and entered the jail of the law. But I have found a new life in this legal jail; it's in this cage I've found a kind of freedom . . .'

An Act of Clemency

For those who have loyally supported Kiranjit Ahluwalia there is a ray of hope. It comes not from the hallowed bastions of the English law-courts by whom she was tried, but from the United States, and a state governor who, with his wife, once opened their own home as a refuge for battered women.

On 22 December 1990, 25 inmates of Ohio's state prison received an early Christmas present beyond their most extravagant expectations. Governor Richard F. Celeste granted clemency to the 25 women convicted of murdering the men who had physically abused them. This extraordinary move – the first such mass release of prisoners in the United States – was guaranteed to provoke extreme reactions. Women's rights activists were obviously optimistic, while judges and prosecutors were predictably less enchanted.

In the first review since a historic decision was taken by the state's Supreme Court earlier in the year (that a defence of 'battered woman syndrome' was legally valid), Governor Celeste examined the records of more than 100 cases of women who had killed their spouses or male companions, and decided to commute the sentences of 21 immediately and a further four after two years. Mr Celeste explained: 'These women were entrapped emotionally and physically. They were the victims of violence, repeated violence. They loved these men even though they beat them and frightened them. They were so emotionally entangled they were incapable of walking away. If I thought they would be a threat [to society], I wouldn't have commuted their sentences.'

Prosecutors gave voice to their fear that the previous Supreme Court ruling and Governor Celeste's present action would encourage women to take murder as the escape route from domestic abuse, in effect offering the defence that being battered validated doing the battering. As the President of the Ohio Prosecuting Attorneys' Association expressed it: 'Now instead of going to the courts or getting a divorce, these women will think, "Maybe I'll kill him" . . . Taking human life is not something we want to promote.'

Other detractors feared that although some women would be able to substantiate a defence of 'battered woman syndrome', there would always be 'some of these women making it up'.

Governor Celeste saw no such problems: 'I don't believe anyone in their right mind should take this as any kind of licence to kill. Being battered is no guarantee of acquittal.' A sentiment no doubt endorsed by women's rights workers everywhere: 'This is a signal to the rest of the country that women will no longer permit themselves to be battered and abused by men . . . Women don't kill men unless they've been pushed to a point of desperation.'

It was indeed taken as a signal by other parts of the country. Within days of the Ohio decision, the King County Coalition Against Domestic Violence, based in Seattle, approached the governor of Washington to take similar action. Governor Gardner has already used his power of clemency in the past to commute the sentence of a woman who had been physically abused, and he has undertaken to look into the current cases of 65 women serving sentences in the state prison.

But how long will it take for Britain to catch up with this radical approach to sentencing? It is fitting perhaps to hear, once again, the plea of one woman caught in this trap: 'Nobody asked *why* all this had happened, and though I had two little children and worked without rest for 50 or 60 hours a week in order to build up my home I should set fire to that house . . . why did everyone use me as they chose? This is the essence of my culture, society and religion, where a woman is a toy, a plaything. She can be stuck together at will, broken at will. For ten years I lived a life of beatings and degradation and no one noticed. Now the law has decreed that I should serve a sentence for life. Why?'

It is a question that deserves urgent and careful study. Not because there is any doubt that Mrs Ahluwalia was correctly convicted – it is clear that she was convicted and sentenced correctly *according to the law*. What is in question is whether that law should be qualified to take account of such exceptional cases of suffering.

LIFE IMITATES HOLLYWOOD
The Murder of Jose and Kitty Menendez

According to their own story, Erik and Lyle Menendez went to
see the popular *Batman* film for a second time on the night of 20
August 1989. Then, again according to evidence that they gave
to the police, they kept up the happy atmosphere by taking in
a wine and food festival in Santa Monica before arriving for a
supper appointment with a friend back in Beverly Hills.

It was approaching midnight when the brothers reached home
and found their parents in the den. Jose Menendez had been shot
eight times at point-blank range before the shotgun had been
forced into his mouth and a final cartridge blew the back of his
head away. His wife Kitty had been shot five times. At 11.47
pm Beverly Hills police logged an hysterical telephone call from
Lyle Menendez: 'They killed my Mom and my Dad.' According
to neighbours, Erik was out on the porch sobbing as though his
heart would break.

The case made headlines – not just in Los Angeles, not just in
California; the Menendez killings are world-wide news. And
from a country with more than 20,000 other homicides in the
same year, it must have been something special.

But then, the Menendez family were not exactly ordinary. For
a start they were rich, very rich. And they lived in Hollywood;
in fact they lived in the reputedly $5 million mansion once the

home of a succession of rock superstars such as Elton John and Michael Jackson. Jose Menendez himself had been big in the entertainment business. A refugee from Fidel Castro's revolution in Cuba, 45-year-old Menendez had risen to executive positions in a number of companies, and at the time of his death was on the board of directors of Carolco, the company which made the blockbusting series of 'Rocky' films; Sylvester Stallone was a fellow board member. Jose was also chief executive of Live Entertainment, a major music and video company.

Now he was dead in what at first was thought to be a Mafia execution – the hit carried out quickly (there was no sign of forced entry or a struggle at the scene of the shootings), and cleanly (whoever pulled the trigger had also been meticulous at picking up the spent cartridge cases).

Yet when, in March 1990, the Menendez brothers Erik and Lyle were arrested and charged with parricide it was a media dream come true; real life was imitating Hollywood. And now at least four television 'docudramas' were in the making, a film or two, and the usual clutch of books about these, the latest 'celebrity' murders.

Wait a minute, though! All these storylines assume that Erik and Lyle are guilty; there would not be much of a plot otherwise. *But* the Menendez brothers have not even been put on trial yet. True, they have been held for some time without bail; true, police and prosecution have released enough tasty morsels of evidence to keep the public's interest in the boys' guilt going. *But* whatever happened to the concept of innocent until proven guilty?

There are many, not least of the immediate family, who have been vociferous in their belief that twenty-two-year-old Lyle and nineteen-year-old Erik Menendez could never have killed their own parents. One uncle is reported as believing that 'the whole situation with the kids is something the police have fallen into for lack of a better lead'.

Could it possibly be as he says?

It is true that the police did take a long time – more than six months – to press charges against the brothers for murder. It is also true that out of sympathy neither boy was checked for forensic evidence. Detectives had disposed fairly early of the 'Mafia hit-man' theory, partly because there was no evidence to suggest that Jose Menendez was in the grip of the mob, or had ever had any dealings, either wittingly or not, with gangsters; and partly because it is not characteristic of 'execution-type' assassins to create a bloodbath – the professional does not need to loose off a shotgun fourteen times to make his point.

Of course the Menendez brothers had been routinely questioned, and may even have been considered suspects in the early weeks of the investigation. But it was not until the heartbroken youths had begun to spend, spend, spend, that they once again came under official scrutiny. By this time the brothers – sole beneficiaries under their father's will – had taken delivery of the first instalment of the $400,000 insurance policy on his life. Erik's first step was to shelve plans to enter university and instead hire an expensive tennis coach in the hope that his already promising talent could be brought up to professional standard. Meanwhile, Lyle was at the Porsche showrooms selecting a new car, and was soon to move into the apartment he had bought in Princeton where he attended university. For good measure he also bought a restaurant in town. But what really attracted attention was the way Lyle Menendez had taken to being chauffeured around in a hired limousine flanked by bodyguards – protection, he claimed, against those disgruntled business associates who had robbed him of his parents.

Further revelations kept the media ball rolling during the latter part of 1989, when it was learned that two years previously, in collaboration with his pal Craig Cignarelli, Erik Menendez had written a screenplay. The script was called *Friends*, and told the story of an eighteen-year-old named Hamilton Cromwell who murders his parents for the $157 million inheritance. It contains this chilling passage: 'The door opens, exposing the luxurious suite of Mr and Mrs Hamilton Cromwell Sr lying in bed. Their faces are of questioning horror as Hamilton closes the door gently.' Kitty Menendez typed the manuscript for her son; we will never know what she made of such a plot.

The most significant, and the most controversial, piece of evidence gathered by the police investigators was a tape recording allegedly of the boys confessing murder to their psychologist Jerome Oziel. The existence of the recording had come to official attention in a most bizarre way. Another of Oziel's patients claimed she had been sitting in the waiting-room when she heard the conversation through the wall. It was subsequently established that such a feat would be virtually impossible, but that did not prevent officers seizing a number of tapes from Mr Oziel's consulting rooms and making application for them to be accepted as evidence in court. It is normally considered that secrets which pass between a doctor and his patient are sacrosanct, but according to Californian state procedure, such information *may* be revealed if the psychiatrist considers the patient to be a serious threat to himself or others. The content of the tapes has not yet been made public, but at the preliminary hearing a judge ruled that the tapes could be used by the prosecution as evidence: 'Dr Oziel had reasonable cause to believe that the brothers constituted a threat, and that it was necessary to disclose those communications to prevent the threatened danger.' It was a decision strongly opposed by the Menendez defence counsel, who has referred the ruling to a higher court.

On Thursday, 8 March 1990, Lyle Menendez was arrested on suspicion of murdering his father and mother; three days later Erik returned from a tennis tournament in Israel and was taken into custody at Los Angeles airport. Both young men have pleaded not guilty to charges that could carry the death penalty. Their trial is likely to begin in the summer of 1991, though judging by many media accounts it seems that due process of law is at best a formality, at worst an obstacle in the frantic race to get the story neatly parcelled and on the big screen.

The love of money . . .

If the brothers Lyle and Erik Menendez *are* convicted of parricide, then they will be only the latest in a long line of privileged children of wealthy Californian parents who have turned violently on their own families.

Ricky Kyle was one of them. The 23-year-old son of multi-millionaire business tycoon Henry Kyle was indulged in every possible way and lavished with every possible gift, except, if his own account of things is true, respect. And when what he saw as his father's drunken abuse became too much of a burden to Ricky's cocaine-addled brain, he shot Henry Kyle dead with a single bullet through the heart in July 1983. Unfortunately, Ricky Kyle had already boasted to friends that he had an eye on his father's fortune, so the provocation plea sounded a mite hollow. Even so, Kyle won a void at his first trial when the jury failed to reach a unanimous verdict. A second jury found him guilty, though he was sentenced to a comparatively light five years' imprisonment.

In the same year, Marguerite Miller was killed. The Millers, whose lavish home on the exclusive Palos Verdes estate outside Los Angeles had panoramic views of the Pacific Ocean, were often described as the 'perfect family'. Regular churchgoers with no known vices, Roy Miller was President Ronald Reagan's personal attorney and close White House confidante. The rest of the family had consisted of Marguerite Miller and their two adored sons. Jeff had attended the prestigious Dartmouth College in New Hampshire, but committed suicide in 1981 while undergoing psychiatric treatment. Michael was described as intelligent, sensitive and gentle, though he had dropped out of college after his brother's tragic death, and at the time of the murder was described as a 'beach bum'. On 24 March 1983, Roy Miller came home from work and called his wife's name; there was no reply. Then Miller saw the broken glass and the bloody towel, and immediately summoned the police. When they arrived, detectives found Mrs Miller's naked body sprawled on her bed – she had been bludgeoned to death with a wooden club and raped. On the following day Michael was taken into custody where he confessed to killing his mother, but blamed the 'demons' that took control of him. He, and they, are now confined in a secure mental hospital.

Only days after the Miller killing, Eric Washington bludgeoned and strangled his mother to death in their home at Long Beach. Thomas Tober added his own black mark in the same year, being charged with shooting his mother and sister dead in the middle-class Los Angeles suburb of Grenada Hills.

As elderly Gerald and Vera Woodman drove into the garage of their Brentwood, California, home, two gunmen stepped out of the shadows and shot them to death. It looked to the police as though robbery had been the motive – and in a way it was; in the most horrible way. The Woodmans' sons, Stewart and Neil, were well known to be thoroughly irritated at not yet being able to lay their hands on the family fortune, and in the end became so impatient that they hired a couple of professional hit-men to do what nature was taking so long about. In early 1990, 40-year-old Stewart Woodman was found guilty of murder and conspiracy and joined the two assassins in jail; brother Neil is likely to join them.

Wealth did not save Oscar Salvatierra from the murderous intentions of his son Arnel who, in the summer of 1986, blasted him at point-blank range with a Magnum as the older man slept.

Salvatiera had been the editor of a successful Filipino newspaper in Los Angeles but, if his son was to be believed, was a bully who frequently abused him in public. In fact the court did believe him, and despite contrary evidence that Arnel was really after his father's money, he was tried on the lesser charge of manslaughter.

So much for the American 'West-Coast Syndrome'. But although the murder of parents by their offspring is a statistically rare event, it is by no means confined to the sun-drenched acres of the Golden State.

In January 1991, Dr Elliott Leyton, Professor of Anthropology at Memorial University, Newfoundland, Canada, published his *Sole Survivor: Children Who Murder Their Families* (Penguin Books, London), a remarkable study covering a broad range of variations on familicide, from the English countryside of Essex to the Chesapeake Bay, as well as examining in detail four classic cases: 'The "aspiring millionaire" Steven Benson, who killed his mother, sister and brother with a car bomb; the military school cadet Harry de La Roche who didn't want to go back to school, so he shot his parents and two brothers in their beds; Butch Defeo, the eldest son of violent parents who destroyed the entire family – mother, father, two younger brothers and two sisters; and the middle-class poetess and dabbler in drugs and occultism, Marlene Olive, who planned and commanded the murder of her adopted parents by her subservient lover.'

MASSACRE OF THE INNOCENTS

DEATH OF A CHILD
The Case of John Heeley

Child murders are perhaps the worst of crimes, and the callous disregard for life that characterizes the killing of a defenceless infant is the most difficult with which to express sympathy or compassion for the murderer. Many would argue – not entirely without justification – that on a sliding scale of crime, the sexual abuse of children falls not far behind. Statistically, the two brutal acts are commonly part of the same crime, for it is rare to encounter the murder of a child which is not at root motivated by sexual perversion. Certainly it is one of the most unacceptable manifestations of man's tireless search for self-gratification.

The 1980s appeared to many observers as a decade in which these types of crime flourished as never before. And during the first year of the new decade it sometimes seemed that child abuse had become a national epidemic. In retrospect this appearance is misleading, and can in large part be explained by the greater willingness of parents and educational and social authorities to take children seriously when they relate their experiences of sexual abuse (whether in the home or outside), and by the efforts made by police and social service workers to follow up these complaints with the vigour they deserve.

For the fact that children are increasingly outspoken, we can thank the many support organizations that have emerged to deal with this insidious and previously 'secret' crime. *Childline*[1] was established in 1986, amid much trumpet blowing, by television personality Esther Rantzen, and by providing a national telephone line over which children unable to confide in anybody else had access to an instant 24-hour-a-day advice and counselling service, gave comfort and hope to thousands of once-silent victims. Organizations like *Kidscape*,[2] founded by Michele Elliott in 1984, dealt with the problem of personal safety for children who, with the collaboration of parents, teachers and police, are taught how to deal with bullies, getting lost, and approaches from strangers or even known adults who may try to abuse them.

Clearly the most fundamental advice to instil into children is a caution of strangers. The fact that this warning is so often ignored is rarely to be attributed to disobedience or naughtiness, or even plain silliness; rather it is the case that as adults we are expecting far greater psychological powers of analysis than a child may possess. A child's view of life is much more simplistic than our own; when we warn that if they talk to strangers or go off with them something bad might happen, a child is likely to think that the 'stranger' is a *bad* person, a 'monster' – not at all like the person who smiles and is nice to them and offers sweets or a ride in a car. These people are no longer even 'strangers'. And this, in part at least, is why despite repeated warnings at home and at school of 'Stranger Danger', a child could still, with unwitting compliance, fall victim to a molester, or worse.

The Stranger You Know

Her parents could not count the number of times nine-year-old Annette Wade had been told not to talk to strangers, not to take sweets from them, to run away if a stranger pestered her.

Tuesday 18 July had been another hot summer's day, and since the Wade family had moved from their flat in Blackpool the previous year to a new semi in the pleasant countryside around Carlton, just outside the Lancashire coastal resort, Annette had been allowed to play outside on her bicycle. At 3.30 pm Brian

[1]*Childline* has a free 24-hour helpline on 0800 1111.
[2]*Kidscape*: Information on child protection programmes, resources and the free booklet 'Keep them Safe' can be obtained from Kidscape, World Trade Centre, Europe House, London E1 9AA.

and Mary Wade had picked up their daughter and a couple of friends from Beck School and driven home to Blackpool Old Road, dropping off the other two youngsters on the way. Annette changed out of her school uniform and got ready to go out; that she seemed a bit more excited than usual was attributed to her looking forward to playing with her friends.

Just after 4 o'clock, Brian Wade watched his daughter wheel her bicycle across the road and walk it through the late afternoon sun in the direction of her friend's home opposite. When she arrived, Annette informed her two playmates that she could not stay as 'I've got to meet someone special'. The only other person she would talk to in her brief life was her killer, John Heeley.

Annette left her friends almost immediately to cycle out into the countryside, keeping her appointment with death. Thirty-year-old John Geoffrey Heeley (alias Higham) was exactly the sort of 'stranger' Annette had always been warned about. He had already been caught interfering with other children, and had recently been thrown out of his lodgings in Caunce Street, Blackpool, because of his appalling behaviour in inviting young girls back to watch pornographic videos. Heeley was due to reappear before the Blackpool magistrates on the following morning to answer charges of possessing an offensive weapon, behaviour likely to cause a breach of the peace, and using behaviour likely to cause alarm and distress – all over the period of the previous couple of weeks.

After losing his accommodation, John Heeley started living rough in a makeshift hideaway fashioned from branches and bracken in a thicket alongside a little-used path through Wood House Farm, off the Blackpool Road at Carlton. It was here that young Annette had her special meeting. We are unlikely ever to know precisely how the swarthy ex-fairground worker and general nuisance and bully came to meet Annette. Perhaps it was while she was enjoying some of her happiest moments in life, just walking and riding in the open countryside. Understandably, Annette might have been fascinated by this man who dressed like – and indeed claimed to be – a Red Indian, living in a 'wigwam' in the hedgerow; fascinated, too, perhaps by the dozens of tattoos that thickly patterned his hands and arms like living picture books (only later do we begin to mistrust such lifestyles as these). Perhaps Heeley, who not only claimed direct descent from Sitting Bull but also the British Royal family, told Annette his story about being related to the Queen Mother.

For all we know, it may have been a little joke about the badge Annette wore that introduced the conversation; it read 'Don't Talk To Strangers'. Anyway, that was where Annette was now bound for – the hideaway on Wood House Farm.

But John Heeley and his young guest had not been the only ones to be enjoying the warm evening around Carlton. Two anglers were engaged in a spot of leisurely fishing close by. Tragedy was about to strike.

It was around 5 o'clock that the fishermen spotted dense smoke billowing from a gully in a nearby field; as the men approached the fire, they noticed a scruffy figure dart through the hedgerow. They thought he looked a bit like a Red Indian. The two men alerted farmer Robert Aspden that there was a blaze on his land, and thinking some mischievous local children had started a fire, Aspden carried a couple of buckets of water down to try to prevent it spreading to the dry grass. The farmer then telephoned the police to report the fire, and at about 6 o'clock a constable arrived, inspected the damp, smouldering heap and made the awful discovery that it was not just a pile of rubbish that had been burning, but a small human body on a pyre of twigs and branches. On top of the blackened mound was a child's red bicycle.

At about the time farmer Aspden was trying to douse the fire in his field, two elderly women, Mrs Knowles and Mrs Bennett, were confronting a scruffily dressed man getting into a green Austin Metro car. They took this rather courageous step because they knew that the car had been stolen; by coincidence, the real owner was an acquaintance of theirs. Not surprisingly, the man drove off at speed without waiting to explain himself. Actually the car had been stolen from outside a house after a burglary in the nearby village of Carleton – not far from the Wades' home. The police had, in fact, already found the vehicle at 5.15 pm and had driven away to summon a scene-of-crimes officer to examine it. However, between then and 5.40 the thief had returned, had his showdown with the two ladies, and made good his escape. The car was eventually abandoned in the Finchley Road in north London, where officers of the Metropolitan Police found it at 8 o'clock the following morning. Of the driver there was no sign save a piece of saliva-stained cloth found in the car which would later prove, by means of genetic profiling, to be John Heeley's (by odds of some ten and a half million to one).

At a press conference called on 20 July – only two days after Annette Wade's murder – the police took the unusual step of issuing a photograph with a description of the man they wanted to question in connection with her death – John Geoffrey Heeley from Clowne, Derbyshire, five feet seven inches in height, dark brown cropped hair, and of course the unmistakable tattoos, described by one witness as 'so close together it looked almost as if he was just dirty'. What the police did keep to themselves was their reason for suspecting Heeley.

Never could a case be more complete. The pathologist had by now examined the sad remains of the victim and pronounced that she had died as the result of four stab wounds – three in the neck and one to the left of her chest. She had been subjected to a brutal rape, and her body placed on the fire, causing it to suffer considerable burning.

Police were convinced that Heeley was the killer and had now associated him with the figure seen by the anglers running from the scene of the crime, the same man encountered by the elderly ladies in Poulton, and the driver of the green Austin Metro abandoned on the streets of the capital. The difficulty was finding John Heeley himself.

The announcement of the suspect's name had given investigating officers a predictably strong public response. It transpired that just before the murder of Annette Wade, Heeley had bought a British temporary visitor's passport in a local post office. He had casually told the postmaster he intended to go to France; and it was later discovered that Heeley had a woman-friend in Versailles. It was clear the investigation would have to cast its net wider, and 10,000 bilingual 'Wanted' notices were distributed on both sides of the Channel. Soon every gendarme at the French ports and every policeman on the English side were on the lookout for Annette's killer.

At 3 o'clock on the afternoon of Wednesday, 26 July 1989, Britain's most wanted man was placed under police arrest. After a tip-off, Special Branch detectives had singled Heeley out of a boatload of day trippers from Boulogne disembarking the P&O ferry *Pride of Hythe* at Dover's Eastern Docks. The search for Annette Wade's dangerous killer had lasted less than ten days. It would be another ten months before he faced a jury.

The trial opened before Mr Justice Kennedy at Liverpool Crown Court at the end of April 1990. In a novel and dramatic variation to the trial's procedure, the prisoner, judge, jury and court officials were taken on a coach trip to the location of the crime. Mr Justice Kennedy officially convened the court in the car park of the *Castle Gardens* public house, Carleton. When they arrived at the meadow on Wood House Farm, the judge and jury were given a guided tour of the spot where the anglers had seen the fire, and viewed the now bulldozed thicket in which Heeley had built his lair.

Despite his defence that he had been lounging on Blackpool Pleasure Beach at the time Annette was killed, the weight of evidence presented against Heeley left the jury in no doubt about his guilt.

One more 'stranger', one more menace to civilized society had been removed. But 1990 had not seen an end to the abuse of its children.

THE BABES IN THE WOOD
The Case of Russell Bishop

On Thursday evening, 9 October 1986, ten-year-old Nicola Fellows and nine-year-old Karen Hadaway set off from their homes in Newick Road on the sprawling Brighton municipal estate of Moulescoomb; neighbours and close friends, Nicola and Karen were on their way to the local fish and chip shop. Although the girls reached the Seafare fish shop, they never returned home. Twenty-two hours later, after an intensive search of the area by more than 150 police officers, dog handlers, a helicopter and a group of neighbours led by the girls' distressed parents, the tragic pair were found, like the babes in the wood, lying together in dense undergrowth in Brighton's Wild Park close to their homes. There was no sign of a struggle, and no attempt had been made to conceal the bodies. The children were fully clothed, but despite initial statements to the contrary, Nicola and Karen had been sexually assaulted. Death, it was to be established later, was caused by manual strangulation.

In the biggest manhunt ever mounted in the south-coast town, Sussex police began the time-consuming but always vital procedure of interviewing anybody and everybody who might have – however unwittingly – the merest shred of information revealing the identity of the man described to the media as an 'animal' by distraught father Barrie Fellows. Within hours of finding the children's bodies, a squad of 160 police officers had interviewed more than 1000 people – by the end of the week they had spoken to upwards of 7000 residents in more than 2000 homes on the Moulescoomb estate. Senior detectives led by Superintendent Bernie Wells had already made public their suspicion that 'this vicious murderer' was a local man, possibly a neighbour of the victims – a theory that was supported by the girls' parents who were convinced that neither child would have gone off with a stranger.

Ironically, over the past seventeen days there had already been an alarming series of reports involving young children around the Brighton area. In Lewes, Rottingdean and Newick, in separate incidents, a man described as being plump, about 25 years old, with ginger hair and spectacles, tried to lure young girls into his car. His technique had been to park outside schools and tell his proposed victim that her mother had sent him to collect her. The incidents had led to a widespread campaign around the local schools under the operational name 'Stranger Danger', and advice had been given by teachers and police emphasizing the dangers of accepting lifts or gifts from strangers. During this line of inquiry a possible link was established when one witness reported seeing a similar 'dirty blue' car outside the Seafare fish shop at about the time Nicola and Karen disappeared.

While the police manhunt escalated, a congregation smitten by tragedy said farewell to two of its flock at a Sunday service in the Church of the Holy Nativity. Tearful friends and neighbours of the two heartbroken families filled the pews, while outside the church an overspill of mourners stood silent as five children carried fresh flowers along the aisle and laid them on the altar. After leading prayers for the young victims, Father Michael Porteous asked God's forgiveness for their brutal killer.

There comes a point in most police inquiries when witness statements, interviews and information received begin to lead the investigation in one or more positive directions. Often these leads, no matter how firm they may seem at the time, prove to be red herrings, leading to nowhere but a dead end. Still, every clue must be relentlessly followed up.

So it was with the sighting of the 'two youths'. Investigating officers (now in the overall charge of the head of Sussex CID, Detective Chief Superintendent John McConnell) had always been puzzled that one of the girls had not managed to break free and run for help while their attacker was preoccupied with her friend; also that the scene of the murders had shown no sign of their putting up a resistance. After a week details began to emerge that might solve the riddle by implicating *two* attackers. A woman out walking her dog saw the men, in their late teens or early twenties, run down a flight of steps called Jacob's Steps only one hundred yards from where the bodies of Nicola and Karen were found in the Wild Park; they then ran across the busy A27 Brighton-Lewes road which borders the park, and into the Moulescoomb estate. The pair, wearing sweatshirts and jeans, separated and ran off in opposite directions. Within 24 hours, five more witnesses recalled spotting the fleeing youths. Despite urgent appeals for more information and for the men to come forward, no more was ever learned about who the youths were or why they appeared to be running from the scene of a murder. That they existed is in little doubt – too many people reported seeing them for it to be a figment of one person's imagination – though whether they remained anonymous for reasons of a guilty conscience over some other misdemeanour, or whether they simply feared involvement in a crime in which they played no part, that particular avenue of investigation was closed.

Another possible lead that fizzled out was a mystery dog walker – a 30-year-old man, using a golf club as a walking stick, exercising a dog in the Wild Park between 6.00 and 6.30 on the evening of the girls' deaths. The man never offered his help to the police and they never identified him during their house-to-house inquiries.

Finger of Suspicion

Meanwhile, in a further attempt to jog the memories of the people around Moulescoomb estate, the police staged a full reconstruction of Nicola's and Karen's last known movements. Two of the girls' schoolfriends, Katrina Taylor, who was in the same class as Nicola at Moulescoomb Junior School, and Lianne Martin, who attended Coldean Junior with Karen, set off from the victims' homes wearing similar clothes and closely followed by their mothers and two policewomen. Katrina and Lianne walked from Newick Road to the fish and chip shop and then, as dusk began to turn to dark, they crossed the A27 to Wild Park.

As the reconstruction was taking place, a huge squad of 300 police officers were on duty, stopping some 5000 cars and interviewing more than 18,000 people whose memories might have been sparked by the two young actors. BBC Television's

Crimewatch team devoted a programme to a dramatized version of Nicola's and Karen's movements on the day of the crime, and one of the most comprehensive exercises ever staged by the police resulted in a public response described as 'overwhelming'.

Even so, it was not until Wednesday, 3 December, after interviewing him for 51 hours, then releasing him on bail, that police finally arrested twenty-year-old unemployed building labourer Russell Bishop for the 'Babes in the Wood' murders. As detectives had suspected throughout, he was a local man. Bizarrely, Bishop had once baby-sat for Nicola Fellows' parents, and had been one of the first to join the search party when the girls were reported missing. Clothing was taken for forensic examination from Bishop's house in Stephens Road which he shared with his partner Jenny and their twenty-month-old son Victor.

On the following day, Hove magistrates remanded Russell Bishop in custody, the first stage of the customary preparation for a major homicide trial, a procedure which was to occupy eleven months. Although most of the work would go on behind the scenes, occasional moments of drama punctuated the year-long wait. At the beginning of 1987, the redoubtable Mr Ralph Haeems, who was acting as Bishop's solicitor, made a public appeal to the child who had telephoned his London office three times claiming to have 'highly relevant' information. Mr Haeems said the caller, from the Brighton area, had seemed frightened and would only give a first name.

Later, on 14 January, the coroner finally released the bodies of Nicola Fellows and Karen Hadaway for burial. The two tragic youngsters were buried side-by-side in the same grave close to their homes. Today the memorial is still a place of pilgrimage for the girls' grieving families, and it is constantly tended and decorated with bright flowers and toys.

At the end of February, Russell Bishop appeared again before the magistrates at Hove for a committal hearing – where the Crown prosecution is obliged to present evidence before the examining magistrates to show that a *prima facie* case has been established so that the defendant can be committed for trial. There is a more modern form of committal based on written statements in which the magistrate does not need to consider evidence if the defendant does not wish it. In the case of Russell Bishop, an old-style committal was heard which was, in effect, his trial in microcosm.

The court heard Mr Robert Owen, prosecutor, open by saying that during his interviews with the police Bishop had made a number of misleading statements before unwittingly revealing details of the crime which could only have been known by a person who had seen the bodies – which he had not been allowed to do. Bishop had been one of the first people to join the search party when Karen and Nicola had been reported missing, and from the witness box a pregnant Michelle Hadaway, Karen's mother, gave evidence of the moments before and after the finding of the girls' bodies: 'Suddenly there were police swarming across the park and a helicopter came overhead and I saw the tape and I knew. I saw Russell [Bishop] and shouted at him because I wanted to know what was happening. He just put his hands over his face.' Earlier in the search, Bishop, a friend of both the murdered girls' families, had asked for an item of Karen's clothing to give his dog 'Misty' her scent.

Dealing with forensic evidence, Mr Owen revealed for the first time that only Nicola Fellows had been interfered with sexually, both before and after death. He also told the magistrate that 'cogent and compelling' forensic evidence would be presented in the form of a sweatshirt found in the park which carried fibre traces linking it with the girls' clothing, and stains linking it with Bishop. The defendant denied that the sweatshirt was his, or that he had killed Nicola and Karen.

On Friday, 6 March 1987, Hove magistrates decided that there was a case to answer, and in committing Russell Bishop to trial at Lewes Crown Court refused an application on his behalf for bail. Bishop left the dock in tears, shouting: 'I am innocent, I hope you realize that.'

Legacy of Hate

Wednesday, 12 November 1987; Russell Bishop faced Mr Justice Schiemann across the well of Lewes Crown Court, accused of the murders of Nicola Fellows and Karen Hadaway – a charge which Bishop denied. Much of Mr Brian Leary QC's opening speech for the Crown was a repetition of prosecution evidence presented at the committal proceedings nine months previously, and pivoted on the forensic evidence of the sweatshirt found along the route between the location of the murders and Bishop's home in Stephens Road, Brighton. Then Mr Leary hypothesized to the court about how the two young victims could only, according to the physical evidence at the scene of the crime, have been killed by somebody they knew well and trusted; somebody with whom they would be willing to go into the tangled underbrush of Brighton's Wild Park: 'The man with these girls was overcome with sexual desire and attempted to molest Nicola. He could not leave anyone alive who would identify him, so he strangled both little girls with his bare hands. There is only one person who could have done this, and that is the accused.'

The trial had lasted almost a month when, on 9 December, His Lordship Mr Justice Schiemann summed up the evidence for the benefit of the jury. The eight women and four men who had endured the painful details of the violent deaths of two innocent children needed no reminder of the judge's first remark: 'A murder of this kind,' he told them, 'is clearly a great worry to the community in which it takes place. There is immense pressure on the police to find the murderer because everyone is very keen the man should be inside and not carry on murdering.'

As the judge had correctly observed, there *was* a great deal of pressure on the police to find a callous child-killer. There will always be public disquiet when a murderer is at large in the community. But did this statement from the Bench go further? Were the jury to take it as an indication that the judge himself was not entirely happy with Bishop's arrest? His Lordship proceeded to advise the jury that it was no part of their duty to decide whether or not it was wise for the police to have arrested the defendant, but merely to decide whether he had committed the murders: 'We are not detectives. The structure of this court is not set up to be a sort of latter-day police inquiry, with everyone forming their own theories as to what might or could have happened. You are here to decide whether you are sure Mr Bishop committed these murders. You are not to convict unless you are sure.'

It seemed, on the face of it, to be a classic of what old-timers, wise in the unwritten codes of the court, might have called 'a summing-up for the defence'.

In the end, it took the jury two hours' deliberation to reach their verdict of 'Not Guilty'.

Amid shouts of approbation from the Bishop faction in the public gallery, and the evident distress of the victims' relatives, Mr Justice Schiemann, after appealing for silence, formally acquitted Russell Bishop.

What now? Two girls are dead, murdered in the most barbaric

circumstances. By whom? Not, it would seem, Russell Bishop – the jury said that; so what do the police do now, reopen the inquiry? An official spokesman is reported as saying after the trial: 'The inquiry into these murders is closed.' In other words, they are not looking for another suspect; there is no more *evidence*.

As for Russell Bishop, things will never be the same again. A man freed by the court need be innocent only in the judgement of 'twelve good men and true' – quite clearly Bishop had not been exonerated by his neighbours. In what he described as 'an orchestrated wave of hate', the Bishop household in Stephens Road was subjected to a firebomb attack, and posters bearing his photograph began to appear around Brighton with messages openly accusing him of being a child-killer. On top of this, Bishop claimed, he was being picked on by the police. After being arrested for non-payment of fines, Bishop was ordered to surrender himself at the local police station where he was held temporarily before being released on bail: 'I am being victimized. It could have been sorted out without me having to go down to the station. They're just harassing me because my lawyers destroyed their case.'

Nevertheless, no one was more vociferous in demands that police reopen their inquiry into the murders of Nicola Fellows and Karen Hadaway than Bishop, who joined both sets of parents and friends in street protests and marches aimed at forcing the authorities to take further action.

Not only did the Sussex police force not reopen the case, but it was no great secret that Russell Bishop was viewed as a 'long-term suspect', who would sooner or later attack again. Eventually the sullen atmosphere of hatred and suspicion that hovered around the drab streets of Moulescoomb became unbearable: 'I can't stand being around kids now, I don't even like taking mine out the door, because I'm looked at, even though there's no nasty comments there's that feeling I've always got, and it isn't a very nice one.' Bishop moved his family off the Hollingdean estate to a house at Preston Barracks on the Lewes Road. It was March 1988, and those whose lives were not directly touched by the tragedy of two children's deaths might have been forgiven for forgetting the name of Russell Bishop.

The Demon of Devil's Dyke

At around 3.30 on the Sunday afternoon of 4 February 1990, a seven-year-old girl was abducted close to her home on the Whitehawk Estate near the Marina at Brighton. Less than two hours later, at around 5.00, she was found by a middle-aged couple out for a stroll. She was still alive, but naked and in evident distress as she wandered close to the beauty spot known as Devil's Dyke on the Sussex Downs. The girl, whose name would not be revealed, had been half-strangled, sexually assaulted and left for dead. To a town that just two years previously had to face the possibility that an uncaught child-killer was in their midst, the pattern was horribly familiar. Like Nicola Fellows and Karen Hadaway, this sad seven-year-old had been on a trip to the local shop and was returning home when she was abducted – in her case it was thought by a man in a red car; she was assaulted and manually strangled only a few miles from the Wild Park where Nicola and Karen had been assaulted and strangled in October 1986. A further grim connection was a warning given to school children only two weeks previously after a man in a red car had been reported prowling near the Whitehawk Junior School. It was the driver of a red Ford Sierra spotted on Devil's Dyke that the police now wanted to interview.

Remarkable as it seems, the Devil's Dyke victim, despite her horrendous experience, was reunited with her family after needing only overnight observation at Brighton's Royal Alexandra Children's Hospital. In a description of her ordeal, praised by the police as 'very lucid', the child told how she had been roller skating towards her home when a man with a moustache leapt from behind a red car, grabbed her round the waist from the back and warned, 'Scream and I'll kill you.' She was then bundled into the boot of the car and driven away, all the time screaming and banging on the inside of the boot cover with a hammer she found inside. When they reached Devil's Dyke, the fair-haired youngster was dragged from the car boot, thrown on to the back seat and throttled until she lost consciousness.

As 100 police officers combed the scrub and thick gorse on the Devil's Dyke area in the search for clues, and a further unit made concentrated house-to-house enquiries around the district where the girl was last seen before her disappearance, three men previously associated with offences against children were being questioned. Not surprisingly, one of them was Russell Bishop. Bishop was taken into custody at midnight on the day of the assault and subjected to lengthy questioning.

On 8 February, Bishop appeared before the Brighton magistrates and was remanded in custody accused of attempted murder, kidnap and indecent assault. By this time, at the request of his solicitor, Russell Bishop had been put into an identity parade and identified by the young victim as her attacker. On 5 July, the same court committed him for trial.

Perhaps on the principle that it had already brought him a favourable result once, Russell Bishop asked to be tried at the Lewes Crown Court. Presenting the Crown case, Ms Ann Curnow described the shock of the middle-aged couple as the peace of their Sunday stroll was shattered by 'this apparition coming towards them, unsteadily, bleeding from the mouth and genital areas and covered in scratches'.

The first and most damning witness against Bishop was the victim herself – protected from the defendant's eye by the law's mercy, she spoke of her terrifying ordeal from behind a screen. In a calm, firm voice, the girl told the jury of her kidnap, and how she felt as if she was in a dream as her attacker pulled her from her car: 'He took me out of the boot and strangled me. He thought I was dead but I wasn't – I was in a deep sleep. He never strangled me long enough . . . When I woke up I was in the middle of bushes. I wasn't wearing any clothes.'

The child had declined the offer of giving evidence from the even greater security of a closed-circuit television, and throughout her hour-long appearance the public were excluded from the court. After putting her at her ease, talking of school and home, the judge, Mr Justice Nolan, asked her: 'Have you been brought up to tell the truth?' The girl said she had.

Questioned by Mr Ronald Thwaites QC, on behalf of Bishop, whether she had heard her attacker talk to anybody else before she passed out, the young witness replied: 'I dreamt he was talking to someone and he gave me a toy to play with and said "If you lose it, I'll kill you", and I dreamt I lost it.'

'Do you think that part of it was all a dream?'

'Yes.'

It was Russell Bishop's defence that he was nowhere near Devil's Dyke at the time of the assault, though witnesses testified to seeing a red Ford Cortina identical to the one owned by the defendant at the beauty spot. Raymond Symons and his wife were walking their dog when they came upon the car but attached no sinister importance to it: 'I noticed it was well misted up. I assumed at that stage there was probably a courting couple. There was a movement in the back of the car as if somebody had raised up and looked through the back window and then lowered down again.' Significantly, Mr Symons remembered the sign in the car's rear window: 'For Sale £750 ono' – the same sign that was found in the back of Russell Bishop's car. Furthermore, tyre tracks found close to the scene of the crime were also shown to be consistent with having been made by the tyres on Bishop's car.

On the fourteenth day of his trial, Russell Bishop stepped into the witness box to give evidence in his own defence. Strongly denying the charges against him, Bishop claimed that a concerted campaign of hate had been launched against him by police officers who thought he had been wrongly cleared of the murders of Nicola Fellows and Karen Hadaway. Asked by his counsel, Mr Ronald Thwaites, why people – the general public as well as police and scientists – should still think him guilty of the two killings, Bishop began crying as he pointed to one of the posters that had been displayed around Brighton at the time of the 'Babes in the Wood' murders reading: 'Russell Bishop Warning Notice. This Man is a Child Killer'.

'With leaflets like these,' he sobbed, 'what do you expect?'

Quickly pulling himself together, Bishop proceeded to accuse forensic scientists of faking the evidence that linked him with the present case. It was the police, he claimed, who drove *his* car to Devil's Dyke and deposited the tyre impressions.

The acquittal in 1987 could clearly not be erased from anybody's mind, and Bishop's own continual references to it during his accusations of police harassment ensured that the jury were constantly confronted with the previous case. It is doubtful whether Mr Justice Nolan's words of caution in summing up made any redress: 'So far as this case is concerned he was found not guilty of these crimes and that is the end of the matter. Normally it would not be mentioned in a trial. But we have heard the defence suggest throughout in cross-examination of many, if not most, of the prosecution witnesses that their evidence against the defendant has been coloured, motivated, or wickedly inspired and fabricated because of their suspicions that he was guilty of earlier crimes. These suggestions have been firmly denied by all the witnesses concerned, and it is for you to decide.'

That decision came the following day, Thursday, 13 December

1990. It was almost three years to the day since Russell Bishop, standing in the same dock accused now of attempted murder, had been acquitted of double murder. After a retirement of four hours and twenty minutes, the six men and six women returned a unanimous verdict of guilty – of kidnap, of sexual assault and of attempted murder.

Speaking of the assault and attempted murder of the seven-year-old victim, Mr Justice Nolan described the act as 'almost as dreadful as can be imagined . . . in the highest category of wickedness'. Sentencing Bishop to life imprisonment, His Lordship told him: 'I believe you are a very dangerous man, perhaps more dangerous than you yourself realize.'

As a tearful Russell Bishop was led from the dock to begin his sentence, the public gallery erupted into spontaneous cries of jubilation, not least from the parents of Nicola Fellows and Karen Hadaway. Despite the judge's caution, and statements made by Detective Chief Superintendent Tim O'Connor that 'The Babes in the Wood murders are still unsolved', for Michelle and Lee Hadaway, and for Susan and Barrie Fellows, the killer of their children was now facing a life behind bars. Mr Hadaway expressed their feelings: 'There is no doubt in my mind that Bishop was the man who killed my child. He is scum. Perhaps we can now start living our lives again. Justice has been done.'

Even so, not everybody was as ecstatic about the verdict. Apart from Russell Bishop himself, who was obviously dismayed at the outcome of the trial, there were almost fanatical expressions of loyalty from the rest of the Bishop camp. His mother, Mrs Sylvia Bishop, a well-known dog-breeder and writer on the subject, declared: 'I loved him to death, he was always my favourite . . . he was my baby. He was a gentle boy. I could never believe he did it. Never.'

Three days later Mrs Bishop and another of her sons, Alec, were the innocent victims of malicious firebomb attacks and were placed under police protection.

Russell Bishop's partner and mother of his three children, Jenny Johnson, had stood by him throughout his first trial and through the wave of violent threats and abuse that followed. When he was arrested on the Devil's Dyke charge, Ms Johnson is said to have become hysterical and threatened police officers with a metal poker, accusing them of 'fitting him up'.

It is only right that the final word should be given to the

remarkable little girl who had survived a murderous assault by the 'Demon of Devil's Dyke', and had miraculously sprung back to point an accusing finger at him. Described by the police as 'a diamond, the brightest, sharpest, bravest kid you could imagine', she wrote this thank-you letter to all the well-wishers who had sent her cards and toys as she recovered from the nightmare of her ordeal:

To all my friends: I would like to thank you for all the lovely presents you have given me. I am feeling well now and all my scratches have gone. I am having a lovely Christmas and I would like to wish you a merry Christmas.

KILLED ON DUTY

A TALE OF SIX CONFESSIONS
The Murder of PC Keith Blakelock

The Background

As horrific murders go it was one of the worst of its decade. A police officer, on duty in uniform, literally hacked to death by a screaming mob – not in some South African township where such violence has become tragically commonplace, but on the streets of England's capital.

The incident really began during Saturday, 5 October 1985.

While police officers were searching her home on the Broadwater Farm Estate in Tottenham, north London, Mrs Cynthia Jarrett collapsed with a heart attack and died before reaching hospital. The police had been looking for stolen property in the wake of having arrested Mrs Jarrett's son.

On the following day, 6 October, a demonstration of around 100 people congregated around Tottenham police station to protest at what they considered a fatal, though to them typical, example of heavy-handed policing in an area notorious for its racial sensitivity. No one could have predicted the outcome of this mainly peaceful protest.

By nightfall, the small demonstration had grown into a large and angry mob; any attempt to defuse or contain the riot failed. The whole area around the Broadwater Farm council development began to blaze with petrol bombs, and the air was filled with whatever missiles demonstrators could lay hands on. Hijacked cars were set alight and used as barricades against the police and emergency services. Officers of all services came under violent attack as did media reporters and film crews. Sporadic shooting claimed three wounded policemen. As one senior police officer later claimed: 'This was not London, but madness.'

Against this backdrop of uncontrolled hatred and violence, one police officer died, victim of the mob.

The Trial

By the time what had become known as 'The Blakelock Case' got to court, press and public seemed already to have tried the defendants, convicted them and handed down sentences.

On the morning of the second day of the trial, *The Sun* newspaper carried a front page headline that shouted: 'FACE OF MAN ON RIOT PC MURDER CHARGE' alongside a large portrait photograph of Winston Silcott. In its report of the opening speech for the prosecution, the newspaper wrote that 'Silcott was among a mob of 50-strong who tried to cut off the PC's head . . .' Referring to this article in court on the day of its publication, 22 January 1987, the trial judge Mr Justice Hodgson made it clear that he intended to refer the matter to the Attorney-General as a possible contempt of court. He told the jury: 'I can only say that in my view it is an entirely deplorable way of reporting the case . . . apparently there is at least one part of the press which cannot be trusted.' His Lordship directed that no other photographs or even 'artists' impressions' should be published during the remainder of the trial.

But although *The Sun* was clearly wanting in etiquette, it was just one example of the prejudice that had long since set in against Silcott and his co-defendants.

The trial began as all trials begin, with the legal formalities; the setting of the stage and the identification of the players. From an unprecedented 400-person panel, a jury was selected after the customary safeguards against interested parties bringing undue prejudice to the verdict: in this case, persons who lived on or very close to the Broadwater Farm estate or had relatives or close friends who did so were eliminated, as were those with relatives or close friends who were either serving with, or had served with, the police. Surprisingly, perhaps, it took only 40 minutes to select the eight men and two women, including two blacks, who would comprise the jury in this lengthy, complex and often harrowing trial.

After selection, the jury was released until the following day while Mr Justice Hodgson spent the afternoon hearing legal arguments. His Lordship cautioned: 'While you are trying the case, I have no doubt your relatives and friends will want to talk to you about it. You must resist any temptation to do so. It is vitally important each one of you should keep your own counsel throughout the time you are trying this case. Speak to no one about the case, and if anyone tries to speak to you about it, refuse to do so at once, and firmly and immediately tell a court official that you have been approached.'

The legal arguments that were to be heard in the jury's absence occupied much of the following day as well, so it was not until the morning of 21 January 1987, that The Blakelock Case began to be heard in the crowded Central Criminal Court in one of London's most famous streets – Old Bailey.

Six men stood before the court accused that, on 6 October 1985, they murdered PC Keith Blakelock, and on the same date engaged in riotous assembly and affray.

The six were Winston Silcott, aged twenty-seven, a greengrocer of Martlesham, Broadwater Farm; Mark Braithwaite, twenty, unemployed, of Islington; twenty-year-old Engin Raghip, unemployed, from Wood Green. In addition there were three juveniles (one aged fifteen, the others aged sixteen) who were not identified by order of the court. The defendants denied all charges against them.

Opening the case for the prosecution, Mr Roy Amlot outlined the events leading up to the affray at Tottenham in October 1985, following the tragic death of Mrs Cynthia Jarrett during a police raid at the Broadwater Farm estate. People on the estate had become inflamed by what they interpreted as characteristic brutality by the police against the ethnic minorities.

By the early evening of 6 October, all attempts to restore calm to the area failed and rioting broke out; in all, 250 police officers were injured that night.

PC Blakelock had been one of a party of twelve officers despatched to protect firemen trying to put out a blaze in a looted supermarket on the estate. When the fire-fighters began to turn their hoses on the building, they came under attack from gangs of youths. As the police and fire brigade retreated, they were assailed by a mob, many of whom were masked and armed with javelins, swords and spears made by taping knives to poles. One of the gang was reported to be trying to light a 'flame-thrower'. Police reported afterwards that the mob was chanting, 'This is the Farm', and threatened, 'You'll never get out alive'. By the time the police officers and firemen reached open ground they were being pursued by 100–200 people. As they continued to retreat to the safety of their vehicles, PC Blakelock was one of the last to run, and as he did so the constable slipped and fell. Almost at once, about 50 people pounced on him. One police observer said that he noticed seven or eight people with their arms lunging up and down.

Mr Amlot observed: 'The attack on that lone officer was brutal and without pity. He had no chance. It is clear they were intent on murdering him.'

The court would hear later just how intent the mob had been on murdering PC Blakelock when pathologist David Bowen presented the medical evidence of the wounds sustained by the officer. He had died as the result of multiple injuries, which included a savage six-inch slash wound across the right cheek starting at the lip and travelling to the back of the neck, which had fractured and splintered the lower jaw. Professor Bowen elaborated on his opinion as to the origin of this gash: 'An ordinary knife would not have been sufficient to cause this wound. It would have been a sharp, heavy weapon such as an axe, a machete or a sword.' There had also been a six-inch-long serrated blade knife embedded in PC Blakelock's neck up to the hilt. The pathologist also described two stab wounds beneath the left armpit and one beneath the right, all of which had entered the lungs. In addition, the catalogue of injuries contained multiple wounds to the head caused by a heavy blade and fourteen to the back; the officer's body was covered with various wounds and abrasions caused through kicking and stamping.

In fact, so horrific were the injuries that Mr Amlot disclosed that he intended to excuse the jury from the ordeal of looking at the photographs of PC Blakelock's body: 'We take the view that the photographs of the body are so horrifying that it would not be appropriate to place them in front of the jury.'[1]

[1] Mr Amlot reserved the right, however, to reintroduce the photographs in the event of an issue becoming dependent on the nature of the wounds.

Of the background to these horrendous injuries, the court would hear much more as a succession of police officers who had been with Keith Blakelock on the night of 6 October gave their evidence to the court.

PC Maxwell Roberts: 'I got there [to where Blakelock lay] and realized it was a policeman. I tried to help him up. I grabbed hold of his clothing but it came apart in my hands. I told him "Get up and run, bloody run." I helped him to his knees. He was still alive at that point, he tried to take two or three strides and just collapsed. I tried to help him to his feet again but he was a dead weight. We dragged him across the grass as fast as we could. I still did not know who it was because his face was covered with blood. He did not have a helmet on, his face was just a mass of red . . . I realized then it was Keith because I saw his moustache. I saw a bread knife sticking in his neck.'

PC Miles Barton: Described seeing PCs Blakelock and Coombs (who was later rescued) lying on the ground: 'The youth who had chased me with a machete was attacking the body on the ground. PC Blakelock seemed to be lifeless, his body was moving like a rag doll on the floor. [Coombs] was lying on the ground with another officer on top of him protecting him from blows with a long shield . . . he was not moving and I thought he was dead.'

PC Michael Shepherd: Running to help Blakelock, he was felled with an iron spike: 'I was struck twice while I was on the ground, the spike pierced my helmet.' Shepherd saw PC Coombs lying next to him: 'He was not moving. I could see he was cut badly on his face. I put my shield over his body to protect him. We were surrounded by youths – they were kicking and striking me. I saw a large coloured man; he had a large machete in his hand . . . I thought there was no way other officers would know we were down. I thought we were both going to be killed. My right arm was numb and there was no way I could drag PC Coombs out.'

Commander Colin Couch (Chief Superintendent at the time of the riot): Described being among the group of officers who rescued PC Blakelock: 'We ran with him backwards with his face upwards and his head down. At that stage I hoped he was merely unconscious. As I ran back we were being showered with missiles. I looked back to try to see what was going on. I saw one of the youths holding a protective helmet [which had been cut from Blakelock's head] in his right hand and he was laughing at me.'

About the frightening circumstances there could be no doubt – besides, tens of thousands of feet of film was being taken by camera crews covering the riot for news broadcasts, and photographers, amateur, media and official, were recording the events in all their horror.

Despite this, the police, whose unenviable job it was to investigate the case in its aftermath, had singularly little success in identifying any of the large number of people seen to be instrumental in Keith Blakelock's death. Murder it most certainly was – of the worst kind, of an innocent law enforcement officer carrying out his normal duties. A brave man butchered on a London street. Who, then, were the butchers?

The Metropolitan Police, after one of the largest single investigations ever carried out, were still no nearer their colleague's killer. Inquiries at the Broadwater Farm estate directed at finding eye witnesses had been met with a sullen silence. A combination of an acquired mistrust of the police, a fear of self-implication or of possible retribution from the killers conspired to keep lips tightly sealed. There was little usable forensic evidence, and those fingerprints which could be developed on weapons left at the scene of the riot were not helpful in identifying a culprit.

As none of the almost 1000 photographs taken by the police during the Tottenham affray matched any suspect, the only avenue of investigation left to the police was to round up and interview known trouble-makers seen on the night of the riot in the hope that they might incriminate PC Blakelock's murderers. It was this systematic questioning of 'suspects', many only teenagers, many without the benefit of a solicitor, that was to cast a dark shadow over the admissibility of much police evidence.

The method, however, certainly produced results. A statement made by one of the juvenile defendants on trial made headlines nationwide when it was repeated in court – a chilling accusation which did little to endear the prisoners' case to the public:

1.[2] 'I saw the policeman curled up on the grass screaming for help. He was lying on his side. A machete hit him on the side of

---

[2]Many of these statements made in police custody were subsequently withdrawn by suspects who claimed that they had been coerced into incriminating themselves. Indeed, some of the confession evidence was later ruled inadmissible by the judge. Where these statements were later questioned, they have been indented and numbered and will be discussed later in this report.

the head . . . they were trying to chop his head off. They said they were going to put it on a pole and plant it in the grass.'

The boy said that he had been pulled into the mêlée by one of the mob who forced a sword into his hand and made him put a token cut on PC Blakelock's leg and chest. In a subsequent statement the youth withdrew this statement, claiming that police had put pressure on him; he now said he had not been at the scene of the constable's murder.

During the Crown's presentation of its case, other defendants' interviews were read to the court. Engin Raghip had been named by one of the youths brought in for questioning and was subsequently interviewed ten times in the course of five days. All the conversations were recorded and signed. It was not until his third interview, when he had been in custody for 36 hours, that Raghip began materially to depart from his former claim that he had not been on the estate at the time of the riot. During the course of the fourth interview, he said that he had witnessed the attack on officer Blakelock:

2. 'It was like when you see a man in a film with dogs on him, it was quick. There were 10–30 people attacking him; the crowd were knocking each other over to get at him.' Later: 'You should have heard the noises coming from him as he was attacked. It was like a continuous "aaah" sound, as if he was really being hurt.' In one of the later interviews, Engin Raghip admitted having a broom handle as a weapon, but could not use it properly because of the crowd. Asked if he intended to kill PC Blakelock, Raghip replied: 'I might have kicked him or hit him with the broom handle, but I didn't touch him, that is the truth – I couldn't get in there.'

It was not until four months after the murder that Mark Braithwaite was arrested, and he immediately denied that he was present during the disturbances at Broadwater Farm estate: 'Murder, murder? What is this murder?'

3. The only reason that Braithwaite had been picked up at all was on the uncorroborated evidence of a single youth questioned after the riot. Like Engin Raghip, Braithwaite was interviewed without the benefit of a solicitor. It was during his fifth interview that he told police he was at the scene of PC Blakelock's murder, but could not identify any of the faces in the crowd. By the sixth interview: 'All I want to say is that I hit

him with a bar twice while he was on the ground. Others were stabbing and kicking. There were about ten around him, I was not the first or the last to kick him. The constable was covering his face and rolling on the ground.' When Mark Braithwaite was interviewed for a seventh time he appeared to have become unsure of the identity of 'his' victim, and thought that after all it was another policeman, not PC Blakelock, that he hit. In court, Mark Braithwaite retracted his confession, and in answer to counsel's questions claimed he had invented a story in the hope that the police would stop pressuring him and let him go. His so-called 'confession', Braithwaite now maintained, was cobbled together from snippets of information heard around the estate about the events of 6 October.

It was the third of the adult defendants, Winston Silcott, who police became convinced was the ringleader of the mob that attacked and killed Keith Blakelock. As in the case of the other two, there was no forensic evidence to link Silcott with the murder, no photographic evidence, and no direct eye-witness evidence – only Silcott's alleged statements made while in police custody.

4. Like Raghip and Braithwaite, Winston Silcott's name had been given to police by youngsters questioned in connection with the night of the rioting. Significantly, the descriptions given of his appearance and clothing and of the locations where he was supposed to have been seen were inconsistent to a quite remarkable degree. Two of these juvenile 'witnesses' were themselves to become defendants alongside Silcott, Braithwaite and Raghip. Their statements to the police would be discredited, and in throwing the evidence out of court, were described by Mr Justice Hodgson as 'fantastical make-believe'.

This left only the contested statement made by Silcott while under interrogation by police for the fifth time since being taken into custody:

Detective Chief Supt Graham Melvin: 'I believe that you were with others standing over PC Blakelock when he was on the ground. You had either a machete or something like a sword with which you struck the officer.'

Winston Silcott: 'Who told you that?'

Melvin: 'I am not prepared to tell you who has described your part in the murder of the officer. Suffice it to say that I have been told that you played an active part in murdering him.'

Silcott: 'They're only kids. No one's going to believe them. You say they say that, how do I know? I don't go with kids.'

Melvin: 'What makes you think that the people that I am referring to who have witnessed your part in the murder are young people?

Silcott: 'You've only had kids in so far, haven't you?'

Melvin: 'If only one person had told me of your part in this crime I would not be so confident in my belief that you were the ringleader that night. When there is more than one person saying the same thing the facts become clear.'

Silcott: [Stands up, moves to the window, looks out and returns to chair] 'You cunts. You cunts.' [Leans back in chair, tears in eyes, arms above head] 'Jesus. Jesus.'

Melvin: 'Did you murder Police Constable Blakelock?'

Silcott: 'You ain't got no evidence. Those kids will never go to court, you wait and see. Nobody else will talk to you. You can't keep me away from them.'

Melvin: 'What do you mean by that?'

Silcott: 'I can't say no more, and you've got a big surprise coming. You will be out of a job.'

Melvin: 'Are you telling me that any witness is in danger from you?'

Silcott: 'Just take me down and charge me, I'm not saying any more.'

This, then, was the bulk of the evidence offered by the Crown against the three adult defendants, Winston Silcott, Engin Raghip and Mark Braithwaite. All three accused were emphatic of their innocence of the murder of PC Blakelock, and from the witness box both Raghip and Braithwaite maintained that their 'confessions' were the result of unfair coercion on the part of investigating officers which made their use in evidence unreliable. Winston Silcott elected not to give evidence on his own behalf. This can be understood in view of the fact that had he done so it would have been perfectly permissible for him to be cross-examined on his previous record – which, given that he had recently been convicted of another murder committed before the October riot, would not have been in his own best interests. As it was, all that could be offered in evidence against him was his alleged statement that had been made without the presence of an independent third party (Silcott in common with the other defendants had not had access to solicitors), had not been tape-recorded, and the transcript of which had not been signed by Silcott because he disputed its content.

The vexed question of interviewees being refused the services of solicitors was partly explained by Detective Chief Superintendent Melvin in answer to a question from counsel: 'There were incidents which cropped up which led me to believe that the integrity of some firms of solicitors left a lot to be desired.' Mr Melvin added that he was afraid, either wittingly or not, that a message might be passed via a solicitor to some third party who might then tamper with or destroy some potentially valuable piece of evidence.

5. On 24 February the court witnessed the first signs that the prosecution case might be weaker than it appeared. Two of the three unnamed juveniles jointly accused with Silcott, Raghip and Braithwaite were cleared of the charge of murder. After legal discussions from which the jury was excluded, Mr Justice Hodgson instructed them in one case: 'As a matter of law, for reasons that do not concern you, I have decided that the interviews, the evidence of interviews in respect of this youth, and the evidence given regarding him is inadmissible.' He directed the jury to return a verdict of not guilty. In the matter of the other boy, the Crown decided not to proceed with the charge of murder against him.

The third teenager would be formally acquitted on 10 March after the judge ruled that his alleged confession was inadmissible as evidence.

On 16 March 1987, Mr Justice Hodgson began his summing up by warning the jury that they must not allow their decisions to be influenced by their revulsion over the means of the victim's death: 'You must approach the onerous task placed upon you coolly and dispassionately. The fate of these defendants is in your hands and you will not, I know, allow your decisions to be swayed by emotion or by the revulsion everyone who has anything to do with the conduct of this case feels and has expressed at the crime committed . . . *If not one of [Blakelock's] murderers is brought to book for that terrible crime it will be a great injustice. But I know you will agree it would be a far greater injustice if somebody not implicated was wrongly found guilty.*' [Author's emphasis.]

Amid growing fears of a new outbreak of violence and rioting on the Broadwater Farm estate, a jury that found it difficult enough to reach a common verdict on its first day of retirement was housed overnight at a London hotel. After a further day in court, without a verdict being reached, the jury spent a second night away from their friends and family – cloistered, according to the English law, against outside interference and influence. There were few people who would have exchanged places with a member of that jury.

After a retirement of three days, verdicts of guilty were announced on all three defendants, and as the trial judge began his sentencing it was to the clamour of disapprobation from the public gallery. When the shouting and swearing had been silenced, Mr Justice Hodgson sentenced Winston Silcott to life imprisonment for murder, with a recommendation that he serve at least 30 years. Engin Raghip and Mark Braithwaite were given life sentences with no recommendation. In addition, Silcott was given ten years for rioting and the others were each given eight years.

The Aftermath

It was no time at all before the predictable backlash hit the police following the sentences handed down to the 'Tottenham Three' – already heroic martyrs to many of their contemporaries around the Broadwater Farm Estate. By now a number of Haringey's Labour councillors (who had already been accused of deliberately obstructing the initial police inquiries), along with local community activists and relatives of the convicted men, were making such statements as 'The police acted like German Nazis', and one community leader likened the Tottenham police to the South African security forces.

As if the police had not suffered enough brickbats from their obvious 'opposition', senior Scotland Yard officials were reported as announcing that they would be studying criticisms made by the trial judge of police interview procedures which led to his ruling evidence inadmissible, and the Police Complaints Authority was already investigating complaints of police action during the Broadwater Farm riot and its aftermath.

On 7 April 1987, lawyers acting on behalf of Winston Silcott, jailed for 30 years, began appeal proceedings directed at overturning the verdict on grounds of insufficient evidence to convict. Mr Andrew Hall, Silcott's solicitor, said there was no scientific evidence linking his client to the killing of PC Blakelock, and the judge was incorrect in leaving the jury to interpret for themselves Silcott's evidence to the police.

During the next several years a number of events would help to keep the 'Tottenham Three' convictions in the public eye, culminating, in 1990, in a serious new assessment of the safety of the convictions.

October 1987: A factory worker named Danny Smith was passing a builder's skip on his way to work in north London when he saw a pack of legal documents among the rubbish. They turned out to be the files on one of the young Broadwater Farm defendants who had been acquitted by order of the judge at trial. Although every effort was made during the investigation and court proceedings to suppress the boy's identity, here was his name, address, date and place of birth, along with a lot of other official material documenting his time in police custody. Also with the papers was a copy of the youth's own account of his ordeal, which, thanks to the documents falling into press hands, are now in the public domain: 'At about 7.00 in the morning three or four policemen stormed into my bedroom. One told me to get up and then slammed me against the wall . . . I was put in the back of a van with my two brothers and my dad. [At the station] I think they asked me about the murder of PC Blakelock and told me that a witness told them I was there at his murder. I denied it. They told me I would be released after being interviewed if I co-operated . . . I remember telling the officers that I wasn't at the murder, that their witness was lying . . . Anyway, eventually I said I'd seen some black guys chopping PC Blakelock. I gave some information about the murder which ordinary members of the public wouldn't know; this is because my whole family heard first hand of the murder. I can't remember exactly how much I told the police, I do know they made me say it all. I was feeling all hot and flustered, and they kept putting words in my mouth. They even tried to make me say I shot the copper. I just kept telling them things so they'd let me out.'

These accusations of oppressive questioning without benefit of legal advice was set to haunt the Blakelock murder inquiry for a long time to come.

January 1988: Police Constable Keith Blakelock was among twelve officers awarded the Metropolitan Police force's highest bravery medal, the Commissioner's High Commendation. Mrs Elizabeth Blakelock accepted her late husband's award.

November 1988: PC Blakelock was posthumously awarded the Queen's Gallantry Medal, likewise collected by his widow. Eleven other Metropolitan Police officers on duty during the Broadwater Farm riots were also honoured.

December 1988: By the eve of their application to the Court of Appeal for leave to challenge their convictions, the 'Tottenham Three' already had a great weight of informed opinion on their side, and grave doubts had allegedly been expressed over the safety of those convictions. On the 12th of the month the Lord Chief Justice Lord Lane, Mr Justice Steyn, and Mr Justice McCowan heard appeals on behalf of Winston Silcott, Engin Raghip and Mark Braithwaite. None of the appellants was in court for the hearing.

On Silcott's behalf, his counsel, Ms Barbara Mills QC, pointed out to the court that there was no scientific evidence against her client, and he had not been identified on any of the thousands of photographs taken during the riot. The only evidence against him was a single interview with Detective Chief Superintendent Graham Melvin and Inspector Dingle in which Winston Silcott denied being involved in the killing of PC Blakelock. Ms Mills agreed, 'This was a horrific case. It was a terrible case. Fourteen people were involved in the slaughter of PC Blakelock, but at the end of the day only three people were left in the dock to stand convicted of it. One of them [Silcott] was constantly referred to as the ringleader; perhaps it is not surprising that the jury convicted him. We say that this is one of those rare cases where despite the fact that the trial was fairly conducted, you should review the situation and hold that it is not safe and satisfactory to convict a man on this sort of material.'

For Engin Raghip, Mr Michael Mansfield told their Lorships that a recent psychological report on his client showed that, with an IQ of 74, he was mentally in the bottom 4% of the population; he had a reading age of six. All the indications, said Mr Mansfield, were that Raghip, because of his mental deficiency, would either agree with or repeat anything which was suggested to him; this information should have been made available to the original trial jury.

As to the case against Mark Braithwaite, although he did not deny being involved in the general affray, and confessed to striking a police officer with an iron bar, there were no injuries on PC Blakelock's body consistent with such an attack. The appellant was represented by Mr Michael Kalisher.

On the following day, 13 December, the Court dismissed the applications to appeal in all three cases. Lord Lane described the convictions as 'safe and satisfactory', and praised the trial judge, Mr Justice Hodgson, for his impeccable handling of the case. The Lord Chief Justice emphasized that evidence as to Engin Raghip's mental condition did not affect the decision: 'It seems to us that the fact that this young man is more susceptible to suggestion than others does not make him mentally abnormal, nor does it put him outside the ordinary experience of a jury in assessing a fellow human being.' This will not by any means be the last word on the mental capacity of Mr Raghip.

April 1989: In a clearly provocative gesture, the Students Union of the London School of Economics elected, by a large majority, Winston Silcott as their honorary president. Silcott was nominated by a member of the College's Labour Club as 'a vote in favour of justice and a fair trial'. However ill-considered it might have been, the action was a further demonstration of disquiet over the Broadwater Farm murder convictions, which had also been voiced by Amnesty International. Mr Silcott's elevation was loudly condemned by PC Blakelock's colleagues, and was reported to have, quite understandably, 'disgusted' the policeman's widow. Members of Parliament described the election as 'an outrageous insult', and over the following few days calls were made to review the Governors' annual £260,000 funding of the LSE Student Union. The incident sparked controversy in the House of Commons when Mr Kenneth Baker, the then Conservative Secretary of State for Education and Science, said during question time: 'I very much hope that the decision will be changed, because the reputation of the London School of Economics should not depend on a small minority of the Loony Left.'

May 1989: Winston Silcott, through his solicitor, Mr Andrew Hall, resigned his honorary presidency of the London School of Economics Student Union, allegedly after students supporting him had received death threats. The statement read: 'A press campaign of hatred against me has ensured the public has never had an opportunity of looking at my case calmly and fairly. The same campaign has now been waged against students who had the courage to draw attention to the injustice of my conviction. I have never asked for honours, only for truth and justice. I thank from the bottom of my heart the students of the LSE for their courage. However, I have no wish for them to be made scapegoats, as I have been. I therefore resign as president. I hope that by this action the threats which have been made against them for speaking the truth, and for seeking justice, will be lifted.'

September 1989: Detective Chief Superintendent Graham Melvin, whose interview with Winston Silcott was the only evidence brought against him at his trial, was reported in the press to be facing disciplinary charges over the treatment of another suspect, Jason Hill, arrested during the Broadwater Farm night of unrest. The Police Complaints Authority decided that Mr Melvin does have a case to answer, and he will face a tribunal.

May 1990: After eight months, DCS Melvin considered that he had waited so long for a hearing that the tribunal should be abandoned. The Police Complaints Authority insisted that it *would* go ahead, and by June they made a decision. The tribunal, according to reports, found Detective Chief Superintendent Melvin guilty on three charges arising from the arrest of Jason Hill during the Broadwater Farm investigation. Hill, only thirteen years old at the time of his arrest, was originally picked up on burglary charges but held for three days without access to his parents or a solicitor, and interviewed while dressed only in his underwear. Jason Hill was eventually charged with murder along with five other defendants. When it became clear that Hill's alleged confession was, as the trial judge described it 'fantasy', he was formally acquitted, and Mr Justice Hodgson commented at the time that police action had been 'burdensome, harsh and wrong'. Afterwards spokespersons for the 'Tottenham Three' expressed the hope that the result of the tribunal would open the way for the release of the three men finally convicted of the murder of PC Keith Blakelock. According to one newspaper, the Chairman of the Metropolitan Police Federation said: 'I have always maintained that the Broadwater Three will be released, not because of their innocence, but because of political expediency. I believe Mr Melvin has been sacrificed to that expediency.'

September 1990: The Home Office launched an internal inquiry into the convictions and sentences of Winston Silcott, Engin Raghip and Mark Braithwaite, the so-called 'Tottenham Three'. At the root of the disquiet was the method of collecting and presenting the police evidence by the original team investigating the murder of PC Blakelock in 1985. It was reported that the special Home Office division C3, which investigates alleged miscarriages of justice, would soon begin examining documents relating to the trial. One of the determining factors in this new development must have been the decision to refer back to the Court of Appeal the case of the 'Birmingham Six' – six Irishmen who were currently serving life sentences for the bombing of two public houses in Birmingham in 1974. The hearing of new evidence in the case of the six began with the results of a new forensic technique called ESDA (Electro-Static Document Analysis) which demonstrated that a number of pages of police interview documents claimed to be verbatim records were in fact written at a different time and inserted into the report. In the event, the 'Birmingham Six' were released in early 1991. However, 1990 ended without further action in the case of the 'Tottenham Three'.

The Doubts

Meanwhile anxiety grew in many quarters over the convictions, and during 1990 a number of influential newspaper analyses of the evidence indicated a grave doubt as to the guilt of the three prisoners. In addition, the BBC TV *Inside Story* investigation 'Beyond Reasonable Doubt' presented even more challenging evidence in favour of the innocence of Winston Silcott, Engin Raghip and Mark Braithwaite.

Remember that throughout the trial there was never any more evidence offered by the prosecution than the statements made by the defendants themselves, and in Silcott's case not even signed. There was no scientific evidence to link the three with the murder of PC Blakelock, and no evidence of identification.

In this final analysis of the case, reference will be made to the numbered statements above.

Engin Raghip

Nineteen years old at the time of his arrest, Raghip was questioned repeatedly over a period of five days, and at none of the recorded interviews was a solicitor present. It was during the fourth interview that Raghip admitted witnessing the attack on Constable Blakelock [see statement 2 above, page 77; at the fifth interview, he told police that he had a broom handle as a weapon, but could not use it effectively because of the crowd.

It was only later that Engin Raghip, in his defence, claimed that these admissions had been 'put to him' by the police, and under pressure he agreed to them and signed them. He now said they were *not* a true record of events, and his reason for signing was that he thought it was usual to do so. He had at first denied any involvement, but claimed he was eventually worn down into agreeing with what officers 'suggested' happened.

On this evidence, the prosecution claimed, Raghip was placed at the scene of the murder, with the *intention* of attacking the victim – it was never suggested that he tried to kill PC Blakelock. He was found guilty of 'aiding and abetting', of 'having a common enterprise' with those who did kill the officer. What the jury was quite unaware of was the mental capacity of Engin Raghip, and consequently the unreliability of any statement he might make.

It was after the trial, and in pursuit of an appeal, that Raghip's lawyers commissioned an examination by forensic psychologist Dr Gisli Gudjonsson. The resulting report revealed that the subject had an extremely low IQ (74), placing him 'on the border of mental handicap' – in Raghip's case a mental age of ten or eleven; he was also virtually illiterate. It was Dr Gudjonsson's belief that his subject was, in circumstances such as police interrogation, unlikely to be able to cope, not least because his personality revealed an extraordinary degree of suggestibility and compliance, making him more likely than not to agree to, or with, anything 'put to him'.

In fact, Engin Raghip had been assessed psychologically before the trial, though the examining specialist had failed to appreciate the full implication of the test results, which had led to Raghip being described as of 'average' intelligence. This psychiatrist now agrees with the findings of Dr Gudjonsson, but neither of them was invited to give evidence before the Court of Appeal, and Raghip's leave to appeal was denied.

Mark Braithwaite

In the case of Mark Braithwaite, too, the court was only hearing half the story. He was arrested four weeks after the death of PC Blakelock, and like Engin Raghip was implicated only by the uncorroborated evidence of another youth – who has since emphatically stated that he made the story up because police were pressuring him to give names.

Also like Engin Raghip, Braithwaite had been held for a number of interviews without the benefit of legal advice. During his fifth interview he confessed to being at the scene of the murder [see statement 3 above, pages 77–8]. Mark Braithwaite subsequently withdrew his confession, claiming, again like Raghip, that it was made under great pressure. However, even if we were able to accept Braithwaite's own word for his guilt, it is still emphatically *not* PC Blakelock that he describes attacking. Indeed, subsequent forensic evidence is clear that there were no injuries on the dead officer's body consistent with Braithwaite's description.

Mark Braithwaite has never denied that his signed statement was a correct record of what he said during the interviews. What he insists is that the story was fabricated simply in a desperate bid to get out of his cell by seeming to 'co-operate'. He chose to describe an 'iron bar' as his weapon because, he said, it was the one weapon that he had not heard mentioned in connection with the attack. It was Braithwaite's naive belief that if he told an improbable story it would later be proved to be a lie and he would have succeeded in the more immediate need to get out of custody. Quite why this was so desperately important to him was not revealed until recently – Mark Braithwaite has been diagnosed as claustrophobic. Defence lawyers arranged for detailed examinations to be carried out by a specialist in phobias, who reports that Mark's state of panic was likely to have resulted in an inability to cope with the situation of being locked up, and render him more suggestible and eager to say or do anything which would secure his release from a tiny, hot, dark, airless cell; information not available either to the police or to the court at the time of Mark Braithwaite's trial.

Winston Silcott

The fact that Silcott was well known to the police, and that they already had him in mind as one of the likely ringleaders of the riot, makes it unsurprising that his name should have cropped up when they interviewed other youths in connection with the affray and murder. Silcott was also a well-known figure around the Estate. However, despite the fact that a number of juveniles claimed under questioning that they saw Winston Silcott during the rioting, their descriptions of his clothing and personal appearance, even where he was located, were at such variance that not a single one could reliably be called by the prosecution to give eye-witness testimony in court.

One of these young 'witnesses' was Jason Hill, who was to cause such problems with his own 'confession', and who was one of the juvenile defendants in the trial. Initially, Jason was taken into custody suspected of looting – an offence which he did not deny. While he was being interviewed, he began to tell a series of preposterous stories, including the one about putting a policeman's head on a pole [see statement 1 above, pages 76–7]. It earned him a share of the murder charge, and during the trial his apprently crucial eye-witness account, implicating Winston Silcott as the 'ringleader', was read out to the court.

It transpired that Jason had been making the story up (so he later maintained, under police pressure). Fortunately for him, Mr Justice Hodgson was not so easily led by the account, which he dismissed as bordering on fantasy, a story wildly at variance not only with the medical evidence of PC Blakelock's wounds, but also with reports made by police and fire brigade officers at the scene of the riot. In dismissing Jason Hill's evidence, His Lordship also sharply criticized police interview methods.

None of this exchange, however, was heard by the jury, who had been removed from the court during the judge's deliberations. All they were aware of was Jason Hill's statement, not its unreliability. When they returned to court, the jury were told formally to dismiss the case against Hill for 'reasons that did not concern them' [see statement 5 above, page 80].

So all the prosecution had now was what was contained in the interview between Silcott and the police [see statement 4 above, page 78] – a statement that was unsigned and contested. In fact, it was not even a confession, far from it. Silcott has consistently denied any part in the attack on PC Keith Blakelock.

And there it stands; a case where the sole evidence against six defendants consists of their own contested statements made in police custody; three of them were declared inadmissible evidence.

Furthermore, none of those statements were made in the hearing of an independent witness or with the benefit of legal advice, in itself quite contrary to the spirit of the Codes of Practice of the 'Police and Criminal Evidence Act, 1984' (revised 1990).

The appropriate paragraphs of the code relating to 'The detention, treatment and questioning of persons by police officers' reads:

6. *Right to legal advice*

6.1 Subject to paragraph 6.2, any person may at any time consult and communicate privately, whether in person, in writing or on the telephone with a solicitor.

6.2 The exercise of the above right may be delayed only in accordance with Annex B to this code. Whenever legal advice is requested (and unless Annex B applies) the custody officer must act without delay to secure the provision of such advice to the person concerned.
. . .

6.4 No attempt should be made to dissuade the suspect from obtaining legal advice.
. . .

Of course, everything relies upon the interpretation of 'Annex B' in the light of prevailing circumstances, and it must be repeated that Detective Chief Superintendent Melvin did cite the provisions of the Annex in defence of withholding legal advice. 'Annex B' reads, in part:

DELAY IN NOTIFYING ARREST OR ALLOWING ACCESS TO LEGAL ADVICE

A. *Persons detained under Police and Criminal Evidence Act 1984*
1. The rights set out in sections 5 or 6 of the code or both may be delayed if the person is in police detention in connection with a serious arrestable offence, has not yet been charged with an offence and an officer of the rank of superintendent or above has reasonable grounds for believing that the exercise of either right:

(i)   will lead to interference with or harm to evidence connected with a serious arrestable offence or interference with or physical injury to other persons; or

(ii)   will lead to the alerting of other persons suspected of having committed such an offence but not yet arrested for it; or

(iii) will hinder the recovery of property obtained as a result of such an offence.

. . .

Update

As this book was being prepared for press at the beginning of 1991, the case of the 'Tottenham Three' had still not been resolved one way or the other. However, what started as a family protest has grown to include the support of church leaders, a bevy of Members of Parliament and Lords (among them Lord Scarman), trade unionists and media representatives such as the redoubtable Mr Ludovic Kennedy. Following the release of the so-called 'Birmingham Six', the following collective letter was published in *The Independent* newspaper on 18 March 1991:

Sir: Now that the innocence of the Birmingham Six has finally been established in court, the whole world is asking how these men could have spent 16 years in jail for a crime they did not commit. We, however, would like to pose a slightly different question.

The police and the courts have apprehended and convicted innocent men. That is an established fact. But how many more times must this be demonstrated before the release of the Tottenham Three is publicly re-examined?

In March 1987 these three men – Mark Braithwaite, Engin Raghip and Winston Silcott – were sentenced to life imprisonment for the murder of PC Keith Blakelock during the civil disturbances in Tottenham in 1985. Aside from their own self-contradictory and ambiguous statements, there has never been any evidence to connect them with the killing. The three men have maintained their innocence from the beginning.

Like the Guildford Four, the Tottenham Three were convicted on confessional evidence alone. Like the Birmingham Six they were tried in a blaze of publicity amid widespread outrage. Like both the Guildford Four and the Birmingham Six, they are the victims of a terrible miscarriage of justice which grows worse with each passing day.

The Home Secretary has ordered an Appeal Court to re-examine Engin's conviction in the light of 'new material' relating to the reliability of his alleged confession. He is currently reviewing similar evidence concerning Mark Braithwaite.

We are deeply concerned at the length of time which these young men have already spent in prison, and at the slow pace with which the wheels of justice are turning. Moreover, we believe that the review process itself – conducted in private by civil servants – is seriously flawed. To restore confidence in our system of justice, we believe it is essential that there is an immediate public review of the convictions of the Tottenham Three. Justice must be done and be seen to be done.

Yours faithfully

Diane Abbott, Anthony Barnett, Tony Benn, Gerry Bermingham, Geoffrey Bindman, Ron Brown, Harry Cohen, Robin Corbett, Jeremy Corbyn, Bob Cryer, Jake Ecclestone (Nat. Union of Journalists), Harry Fletcher (Nat. Association of Probation Officers), Gifford, Ken Gill (Manufacturing Science and Finance Union), Mildred Gordon, Bernie Grant, Phillip Harvey, David Haslam (British Council of Churches), Ken Livingstone, Marjorie Mowlam, Dave Nellist, Bob Parry, Barry Sheerman, Dennis Skinner, Chris Smith, Soper, Steven Twigg (Nat. Union of Students), Patrick Towe (Broadwater Farm Clergy Group), Bob Woffinden.

The Tottenham Three Families' Campaign for Justice
London, N15
17 March 1991.

Finally, we owe it not only to the three young men over whose guilt there continues to hover an atmosphere of doubt; we also owe it to Police Constable Blakelock's colleagues who face the daily possibility of violence on the streets; we owe it to Mrs Blakelock and her three sons, whose courage and strength have been a model to all other police wives, husbands, parents and children, who cannot fail to feel anxiety whenever members of the family go out on The Job. Because if Engin Raghip, Mark Braithwaite and Winston Silcott did not kill a policeman, there is somebody out there who did. We need to be very sure.

SOLE-CHARGE COP
The Case of Richard Lakich

A 35-year-old New Zealand police constable was savagely bludgeoned to death, his head and jaw smashed with his own truncheon on the night of 26 May 1990, after stopping a youth in connection with an armed robbery. Constable Peter Umbers had been called out from his one-man station in Ranfurly, Central Otago, in response to a call from the proprietors of the Poolburn Hotel. George and Joy Dundas were woken from a deep sleep and robbed at gunpoint of money and cheques. Dundas found the one telephone that had escaped ripping out by the thief and summoned Umbers; Umbers, after alerting officers from the Armed Offenders Squad in Alexandra, had set off in pursuit alone. The constable made contact just once, radioing in from his car at 12.16 am the news that he had stopped a vehicle on the Wedderburn straight on State Highway 85, west of Ranfurly. Less than an hour later Peter Umbers's body was found by a passing ambulance driver who noticed the shattered back window of his patrol car.

By 5 o'clock in the morning more than 100 police had been drafted in from surrounding areas to hunt for the officer's killer. A squad of armed police from Cromwell set up a road-block on the Lindis Pass road near Nine Mile Creek; just ten minutes later they pulled over a stolen Toyota Hilux in the rear of which was a small arsenal of guns – including Constable Umbers's .38

calibre police-issue pistol. The car's driver, a nineteen-year-old farm labourer from Ranfurly, was arrested and charged with murder, aggravated burglary and unlawfully taking a motor vehicle. Later that same evening, he was remanded in custody at a special sitting of the District Court at Alexandra to appear before the the court at Dunedin. On the following day, the young man named as Richard Thomas Lakich made a twenty-second appearance, handcuffed to a police officer. Lakich, who was remanded in custody until the following month, did not plead to any of the charges.

In a heartfelt tribute to the slain policeman, Minister of Police Prebble later reminded a grateful community that 'it brings home to us in a very sad way the fact that police are so often faced with violent incidents but never hesitate to carry out their duties, no matter the personal danger they must face at times'.

This theme was echoed by Police Commissioner John Jamieson when he added that the incident underlined the dangers faced by officers going about their duty. The Commissioner said that over the past year there had been an alarming rise in the number of occasions on which armed offenders needed to be tackled.

One of the worrying circumstances exposed by the tragic loss of Constable Umbers was that as a 'country cop' he was, like many of his rural colleagues, singly responsible for what was known as a 'sole-charge district' – one officer on call twenty-four hours a day. A Police Association spokesman blamed staff cuts for the situation, and said it was the fear of every sole-charge policeman that he might one day face a life or death situation with no back-up.

Sergeant Trevor Marshall said that he was determined to press the Police Association to demand the reintroduction of the death penalty for the murder of police, traffic and prison officers: 'The majority of Association members prefer that step to arming as a form of deterrent. If an offender who has just done an armed robbery is confronted by a cop then he knows he's got the option of two or three years in jail or the hangman's noose if he shoots him.'

A New Zealand Roll of Honour

The unorthodox death of Constable Peter Morris Umbers did, however, highlight the fact that compared with many countries in the world – indeed, compared with many cities – New Zealand has an enviably low level of police fatalities. Although it will be little comfort to his widow and children, Constable Umbers was the first officer to be killed on duty for fourteen years, and one of only seventeen since 1890.

1890 – Constable Neil McLeod; shot near Dargaville.
1910 – Sergeant John Patrick Hackett McGuire; shot in Palmerston North.
1919 – Constable Vivian Dudding; shot in Wellington investigating a domestic disturbance.
1921 – Constable James Dorgan; shot in Timaru by a burglar.
1934 – Constable Thomas Heeps; shot by a murder suspect near Morrinsville.
1941 – Sergeant William Cooper and Constables Edward Mark Best, Frederick William Jordan and Percy Campbell Tulloch; shot by Eric Stanley Graham at Koiterangi.
1951 – Sergeant William Shore Hughes; shot in Otaki investigating a domestic dispute.
1963 – *January* Detective Inspector Wallace Chalmers and Detective Sergeant Neville Wilson Powers; shot in the Waitakere Ranges when called to subdue a mentally disturbed gunman.
        February Constables James Thomas Richardson and Bryan Leslie Schulz; shot in Lower Hutt while attending a domestic dispute.

[As a result of the alarming number of firearms incidents in 1963, a special armed police unit was formed in 1964.]

1966 – Constable Donald Richard Stokes; attacked and killed by two prisoners.
1976 – Constable Peter William Murphy; shot by an armed intruder in a shop at Invercargil.

'I SHOT THE COPPER . . .'
The Case of Mark Gaynor

Unlike his United States counterpart, the British policeman is statistically very unlikely to find himself being shot at. Our customary weapon of attack is the knife, which is more cumbersome to use, and the need for close physical contact affords the well trained officer an above-average chance of escaping at least with his life. Not that a policeman's lot is entirely free from danger; more than 19,000 police officers were attacked during 1989–90, two of them fatally. Since 1980, 21 policemen and women have been unlawfully killed on duty, an average of around two a year, except for the large, but thankfully isolated, rise to five in 1982. This average is consistent as far back as the 1960s.

What made the cold-blooded murder of PC Laurence Brown so futile, so completely unfathomable, is that he was shot dead without the slightest motive or the slightest provocation – not by a dangerous criminal cornered – where the gun is the only way out; not by a crook desperate to retain his booty; not by some terrorist or political assassin, but by a punk kid with a grudge against the world at large because his girlfriend threw him over.

The afternoon of Sunday, 27 August 1990 was a big occasion in West London, and visitors from the whole of the capital, not to mention from around the world, had flocked to the small area around Notting Hill to enjoy the annual carnival. Among the revellers were twenty-year-old Mark Gaynor and his girlfriend Leander. Later that evening, the couple returned to her home in Hackney and she broke the news that Mark had been replaced by a new boyfriend. Which young man has not experienced that pain, felt that rejection, that sense of emptiness? Strangely, Mark Gaynor expressed very little emotion, and at about 11 o'clock calmly left and walked to his own home near by. That apparent sang-froid masked feelings of anger and revenge that already were eating away at Gaynor's reason. Under cover of darkness, the youth unearthed two sawn-off shotguns, loot from an earlier burglary, from their hiding place under a flower-bed, and loading his weapons and his pockets with cartridges he walked out into the infant morning, an assassin looking for a victim.

The 999 call was logged by police at just before 2.20 am; a young man in a public telephone box had reported witnessing a Vauxhall Cavalier car being broken into at Pownall Road. Police constables Laurence Brown and Peter Townsend were on panda car patrol – Brown, ironically, was only on duty because he had volunteered to work overtime to cover colleagues. The two officers arrived at the location, checked the parked Cavalier and found it undamaged. As they turned back to their own vehicle, Brown and Townsend saw the head and shoulders of a young man appear over a four-foot-high wall, grin at them, and then duck back down as if running away. Instinctively, the policemen separated to approach the wall from both directions, PC Townsend going to the end in which the figure seemed to run, Laurence Brown following the wall until he found a gap. At that point, their quarry stepped out and levelled a shotgun at PC Brown's chest, and as the officer backed off, gunned him down point-blank from a distance of two feet. As a near solid ball of shot ripped into his victim's right side and he fell mortally wounded, the man who would later be identified as Mark Gaynor was making his escape – to dump the guns and ammunition into a canal where divers would later find them, and then to seek refuge in a nearby block of flats.

Within minutes of PC Townsend's call for assistance, a squad of twenty officers were despatched to the scene of the crime to track down a cop-killer, thought still to be armed. It was Constable Gerrard Healey who found Gaynor 25 minutes later, skulking on the tenth floor of a tower block. Placed under arrest, the youth bragged: 'Okay, you got me. I did it. I shot the copper. I blew your copper away because my girlfriend blew me away . . .'

Later, while in custody at Hackney police station, Gaynor said in a recorded statement: 'I was going to jump in the river, but I didn't. I was in love with this girl – do you think I am cracked? I just done that for the girl. I would do anything for her. The first thing that came into my head was to shoot a policeman . . . I was going to shoot myself. I rung the police. I could have handed the gun to them, but when they came I just shot one of them . . . I said I was going to get a copper. I could have gone down to the carnival today and got a few of you, but I didn't bother . . . I set him up you know. I got him to come there. I shot him good. I could have got the other one as well.'

It was not the kind of statement calculated to endear Gaynor to the police (one of whose colleagues he had just wantonly murdered, leaving behind a widow and baby daughter), and the judge's comments at Gaynor's trial paid tribute to the 'restraint' shown by officers. Nor was it the kind of statement that wins the hearts of juries.

In fact, the trial opened at the Old Bailey before Mr Justice Tucker just as this book was being prepared, at the beginning of 1991. Mark Gaynor, through his defence counsel Mr Patrick Back QC, pleaded not guilty to murder on grounds of diminished responsibility, which, if accepted, would have carried with it an automatic conviction on the lesser charge of manslaughter. In support of this defence, Mr Back called consultant psychiatrist Dr Kim Fraser, who had examined Gaynor while he was on remand in Brixton prison. Of the defendant's attitude towards policemen, Dr Fraser explained: 'He believed all police were robots. He said he wanted police on the scene. At the moment of the shooting he thought he was shooting at a robot, and he was surprised to see the blood coming from the wounds. He told me it seemed this had stopped him from shooting the other policeman.'

Earlier, the proceedings had been held up when Gaynor stepped into the dock bleeding from superficial, self-inflicted cuts on both sides of his neck: he was bundled back down to the cells and patched up with sticking plaster, leaving his embarrassed attorney to explain to His Honour and the court: 'I have given him a good talking too. He asked me to say he is very sorry for what he realizes is silly exhibitionism.'

Referring to his client's antecedents, Mr Back told the court that Gaynor, 'together with three others carried out a mugging which went wrong and one of the four stabbed the victim and caused his death. The defendant was found not guilty of that murder [in 1987], but merely of conspiracy to rob.' He had received four years for his part in the murderous attack, and was released on parole late in 1989.

This incident was in many ways characteristic of Mark Gaynor's lacklustre life. He was the fourth of five children, but unlike the others, Mark's father had been white, and the obvious difference in his pigmentation caused him to feel an outcast in the family from an early age. He had never met his father, nor would his mother speak of him, and in the end the boy claimed that if he did ever meet his father he would probably want to kill him. The family was split up when Mark was small, his two sisters and elder brother being taken into care. At school he was aggressive and disruptive, settling in the end for a life of truancy enlivened by petty crime. After his release from prison in 1989, Gaynor had planned to travel to the United States to seek work, but in the end depression got the better of his spirit and he remained unemployed in London. During this period, uncharacteristically, he slipped into drug taking. Mark had always had difficulty with relationships, particularly of the romantic or sexual kind, and it was this more than anything which had made rejection by his first real girlfriend on 27 August seem so devastating. On that night he wrote two suicide notes before going out on to the streets, armed and extremely dangerous.

Despite Dr Kim Fraser's expert testimony that he considered Mark Gaynor possessed of a personality disorder as well as a psychotic mental illness at the time he shot and killed PC Brown, this evidence was refuted by the psychiatrist brought to the stand to present evidence for the Crown. Dr Michael Brown agreed that Gaynor had an unstable personality, but attributed the alleged 'psychotic mental illness' to the misuse of drugs. The defendant had, according to Dr Brown's evidence, told him that he had been regularly abusing substances during the summer in which the murder was committed: 'Some "drove him mad", others "made him feel like Superman".' On the day he shot Laurence Brown, Gaynor claimed he had been sniffing lighter fuel. It is fair to say, however, that a blood test at the time had shown no trace of alcohol or drugs.

It was an obvious reflection of the jury's horror at such a crime that they found Mark Gaynor guilty of murder as

charged; an abhorrence which was reflected in Mr Justice
Tucker's sentencing. Recommending that he serve no less than
25 years of a life sentence, the judge told Gaynor: 'The sentence
is intended to reflect the public's outrage, and it is also to protect
police officers carrying out their duty and to deter other men and
women from attacking them. The police protect the public and
are entitled to expect the protection of the courts. Police will
receive protection from me.'

UNFIT TO PLEAD

INTRODUCTION

Enshrined in the British concept of Justice, and indeed the legal systems of most of the world, is the provision that a person cannot be punished for actions committed while in a state of mental incompetence or unbalance. This protection is encountered most frequently in a defendant's defence plea in court, and can take one of several forms:

Diminished Responsibility

Here the defendant will, through his legal representatives, assert that he was, at the time of his offence, suffering from such abnormality of mind that his responsibility was impaired. This comparatively new defence to the charge of murder was introduced into English (and Welsh) law by the Homicide Act of 1957 (Scotland has its own distinct legal system). A successful plea will result in an automatic conviction on a charge of manslaughter.

The relevant section of the legislation is

'Part I

Amendments of Laws of England and Wales as to the fact of Murder . . .

. . . 2.(1) Where a person kills or is a party to the killing of another, he shall not be convicted of murder if he was suffering from such abnormality of mind (whether arising from a condition of arrested or retarded development of mind or any inherent causes or induced by disease or injury) as substantially impaired his mental responsibility for his acts and omissions in doing or being a party to the killing.

(2) On a charge of murder, it shall be for the defence to prove that the person charged is by virtue of this section not liable to be convicted of murder.

(3) A person who but for this section would be liable, whether as principal or as accessory, to be convicted of murder shall be liable to be convicted of manslaughter.

(4) The fact that one party to a killing is by virtue of this section not liable to be convicted of murder shall not affect the question whether the killing amounted to murder in the case of another party to it. . . .'

Not surprisingly, a finding of diminished responsibility accounts for some 20% of the annual homicide figures for Great Britain.

In practical terms, the plea puts the burden of proof on the defence and, as in the case of insanity, the proof need not be 'beyond reasonable doubt' but 'on a balance of probabilities'. Medical evidence must obviously be presented on the defendant's behalf as to his state of mind, but it is for the *jury* and not expert witnesses to decide whether the abnormality amounts to diminished responsibility.

Historically, Ruth Ellis, the last woman to hang in Britain (in 1955), would have provided a prototype for the plea had it been available to her counsel.

Ruth was the unremarkable, rather brassy manager of a London drinking club. In 1953 she met David Blakely, a good-looking if somewhat degenerate youth with a generous spirit and an above average appetite for drink. They were instantly attracted towards each other, and for nearly a year all seemed to be going about as well as such a match could be expected to go. Inevitably perhaps, relations began to sour; Blakely started to see other women, Ruth started to object. Blakely planned his escape. He moved in with friends for a few days, and when Ruth tracked him down she smashed all the windows in Blakely's car parked outside the house. Two days later, on 10 April 1955, in a fit of jealous rage, Ruth Ellis intercepted her former lover coming out of the *Magdala* public house in Hampstead and emptied the chamber of a Smith and Wesson handgun into his body. Unable to advance a plea of provocation by jealousy, Ruth made little attempt to defend herself, and was convicted of murder. Even at the time there was considerable controversy over the result of the trial, it being strongly felt that in another European country the shooting of David Blakely would have been treated as a *crime passionnel*, and Ruth would have faced a reduced charge of manslaughter.

The defences of Diminished Responsibility and of Insanity (see below) are rarely encountered outside murder cases, for except in sentences for murder, indefinite and possibly life-long confinement to a secure hospital such as Broadmoor is infinitely worse than the standard punishment for the crime.

In one of the most spectacular homicide cases of the past decade, Dennis Andrew Nilsen, responsible for the murder and dismemberment of fifteen young men in London, attempted to prove a defence of diminished responsibility. At the end of October 1983, a packed No. 1 Court at the Old Bailey heard Mr Ivan Lawrence, acting for Nilsen, open his defence by declaring that it was his intention not to prove that his client was insane, but that at the time of each of the killings he was suffering from such abnormality of the mind that he was incapable of forming *the specific intention to murder*. Dr James McKeith of the Bethlem Royal Hospital testified that Nilsen had difficulty in expressing emotions and exhibited signs of maladaptive behaviour – their combination, he believed, was 'lethal'. It was a conclusion sharply opposed by the Crown prosecutor, Mr Alan Green, who reminded the court of Nilsen's calculation in killing and disposing of his victims, and the cunning way in which he had sought to establish insanity by lying; in other words, 'he was a jolly good actor'. In the end Dr McKeith was unwilling to describe the defendant's responsibility as diminished because that was a legal and not a medical definition. The second psychiatric witness for the defence, Dr Patrick Gallwey, fared little better in trying to get the court to accept what he called 'Borderline False Self As If Pseudo-Normal Narcissistic Personality Disorder' – as unwieldy a concept as it was a title.

When the defence had wound up its case, the Crown was allowed to call to the witness stand its own 'rebuttal' psychiatrist in order to contradict the expert testimony of Drs Gallwey and McKeith.

Dr Paul Bowden, after declaring himself unable to find any abnormality of mind such as described in the 1957 Homicide Act, went on to state that, in his opinion, Dennis Nilsen simply wanted to kill people – a condition which was lamentable, but in no way excusable on psychiatric grounds: 'In my experience, the vast majority of people who kill have to regard their victims as objects, otherwise they cannot kill them.'

As for the opinion of the trial judge, Mr Justice Croom-Johnson, it was clear from his summing up of the medical evidence that he considered Nilsen not insane but thoroughly evil: 'There are evil people who do evil things. Committing murder is one of them'; and 'There must be no excuses for Nilsen if he has moral defects. A nasty nature is not arrested or retarded development of mind.'

With which sentiments ten of the twelve jury members clearly concurred. On 4 November 1983, they found Dennis Nilsen guilty, by a majority, of six murders and two attempted murders. He is now confined in Wakefield Prison, Yorkshire, from which there is little prospect of release.

Insanity

There are in fact two 'insanity' defences:

1. That, because of a disease of the mind, an offender does not know the nature and quality of his act; and
2. That even if he did know the nature and quality of his act, because of a disease of the mind he did not know it was 'wrong'.

As in pleas of diminished responsibility, it is for the defence to establish a defendant's insanity 'on a balance of probabilities'. It is for the jury to decide, and the guidelines for their use are embodied in the McNaghten Rules[1] which, in part, state: 'Every man is presumed to be sane, and to possess a sufficient degree of reason to be responsible for his crimes, until the contrary be proved to [the jury's] satisfaction.'

The defence of insanity is notoriously difficult to establish, and some forensic psychiatrists, such as the American Dr Ronald Markman, believe that it is impossible to find a method for

[1]For an explanation of the McNaghten Rules see Appendix 1

objectively evaluating criminal insanity that is acceptable to all psychiatrists.

It is a dilemma that is further complicated when a cunning killer attempts to fake insanity; although this is less likely now that the supreme penalty for murder is not death. One outstanding example from the past is the case of John George Haigh, the English 'Acid Bath Murderer', who attempted, in 1949, to establish a defence of insanity with preposterous confessions to drinking the blood of his victims (see also page 135). This was a particularly transparent piece of guile in the light of previous conversations Haigh had with police officers, during which he pointedly asked, 'What are the chances of anyone being released from Broadmoor?'

An unusual situation arose in the case of Peter Sutcliffe, the English serial killer called 'The Yorkshire Ripper'. Sutcliffe claimed that his murderous attacks on women whom he believed to be prostitutes were in direct response to instructions from God which he had heard emanating from a grave in Bingley cemetery. In an unusual collaboration, the Ripper's defence attorney, the Crown prosecutor and the Attorney-General agreed that Sutcliffe was suffering from paranoid schizophrenia and sought to have the trial averted by placing him immediately in a special hospital. It was the trial judge, Mr Justice Boreham, who insisted that the trial proceed, that the jury be the final arbiters of Peter Sutcliffe's sanity. In fact, the jury found him sane and guilty of thirteen murders and seven attempted murders. Ironically, just three years after his life sentence began, Sutcliffe had to be moved from the top security wing at Parkhurst Prison on the Isle of Wight and moved to Broadmoor – his mental stability having deteriorated to such a degree that psychiatric treatment was imperative. The Yorkshire Ripper is now, if he was not at his trial, legally insane.

In Britain the success of an insanity defence will require the special verdict 'not guilty by reason of insanity', and the prisoner will be committed to hospital until such time as the Home Secretary directs otherwise.

Automatism

Certain disorders may so disturb a person's state of consciousness that they behave 'automatically', and cannot be held responsible for their actions. Automatism may result from psychomotor epilepsy, sleeping, sleepwalking, concussion, hypoglycaemia, or other dissociative states.

Of these, by far the commonest cause is epilepsy, which was one of the strongest considerations in drafting the amendments incorporated in the 1957 Homicide Act (see above).

Epilepsy

It is a well-known medical phenomenon that subsequent on an epileptic fit, the patient may enter a state known as 'epileptic automatism' in which, as the name suggests, he behaves quite automatically, without rational premeditation, and with either no, or very imperfect, recollection of his actions. If it can be established that a crime was committed by the patient in this state, then a defence can be made that the accused was not responsible for the consequences of his actions.

In fact, it is only rarely that this defence is advanced in a case of murder; for it is not sufficient to prove (and the burden of proof here lies with the *defence*) that the prisoner *is* an epileptic, but also that the act of killing was performed in a state of automatism. However, there is a basic connection between epilepsy beyond an expected numerical percentage. Drs Denis Hill and Desmond Pond, during research at the Maudsley Hospital in South-East London, observed that of 105 murderers in a sample, eighteen of them exhibited symptoms of epilepsy. Given a normal population percentage of 0.5, this figure represents a staggering 32 times the expected incidence.

What may be more important is that, aside from the observable fits and subsequent automatism, the possibility of a complete personality change should be allowed for; we can see from encephalogram tracings that a fit involves a massive discharge of energy from the brain cells, producing appropriate responses from whichever part of the brain it derives.

It may help to identify the three main clinical categories of what are collectively called epileptic fits:

Major epilepsy (called *Grand mal*); this is the most commonly encountered type of fit, and begins in the patient with an overpowering sensation that envelops the body, and can take the form of a burst of sound, or of light or of heat. This is followed by loss of consciousness, and then the characteristic rhythmic 'convulsions', possibly accompanied by a foaming at the mouth and holding the breath. When consciousness returns, the patient feels tiredness, usually accompanied by headache and confusion.

Minor epilepsy (called *Petit mal*); these are the minor losses of consciousness of which the patient himself may not even be fully aware. He may suddenly stop in the middle of speaking, or drop something that he is carrying; the eyelids and facial muscles may twitch slightly.

Psychomotor (or *Temporal Lobe*) *epilepsy*; this has been very adequately described in connection with a celebrated American murder case,[2] by Dr D.T. Davidson Jnr and Dr William Lennox:

The behaviour of a person during an automatism, or automatic seizure displays the greatest variety. He may appear to be fully aware of his surroundings and act as a normal person would, or he may be clumsy, speechless, or appear confused, act inappropriately or become surly or belligerent, or display excessive muscular activity such as violent running. In deciding as to whether a paroxysmal brain disorder is responsible for sudden and temporary abnormal actions, what the person did is not as important as whether he remembers what he did.

The person's inability to remember what he did during this period may have three explanations: First his reputed amnesia may be simply feigned. The individual tries to dodge responsibility for his actions by saying he has no recollection of them. A plea for clemency is often based upon the false claim of amnesia. Such a lie may be exposed by indirect methods; a lie detector may be useful. The brainwave tracing should be normal.

Secondly, the amnesia may be real, but hysterical based on some emotional disturbance such as the necessity of forgetting some horrible experience or escaping from an unpleasant dilemma. The person is not confused, but acts rationally and retains knowledge acquired in the past. He does not commit any major crimes in this state. Memory of events may often be recaptured under partial sedation with drugs or by hypnosis. The brainwave tracing taken during as well as before and after such episodes should be normal.

[2]In May 1950, in Massachusetts, a man named Elwell stabbed and bludgeoned to death his aunt, wrapped her body in a sheet, loaded it into the boot of his car and drove out to a swamp to dispose of it. Arrested by the police, Elwell had but a fragmentary recollection of the events and was proved to have acted in a state of psychomotor epilepsy.

The third type of amnesia is based on pathological rather than on psychological disturbance of brain function. Amnesia for events may attend such conditions as brain concussion, delirious states, complicating high fever, alcoholic intoxication or (in diabetics) an overdose of insulin. Such conditions are readily recognized.

In addition, recurrent temporary periods of amnesia may occur in persons who are otherwise mentally and physically healthy, except for possible brainwave disturbance. These episodes may come without warning and without apparent cause. As already stated, actions may be extremely diverse.

These periods of amnesia and attendant actions come suddenly without premeditation or warning. They may last for half a minute or many hours or even days. They are therefore termed seizure phenomena. The only laboratory examination that possesses significance is the finding of paroxysmal disturbance in the electrical rhythms of the brain. However, such abnormality may not be demonstrable always, because the electrical disturbance may not be continuously present or may be brought out only by means of sleep, by hard breathing, or by injections of metrazol, a convulsive drug.'

Unfit to Plead

The above pleas are all available to a defendant before he stands trial. But there is a further category of 'insanity' that excuses an accused even from the process of the law. In this instance he is not advancing a defence, but stating that he is too mentally ill to stand trial.

As most people charged with homicide are remanded in custody, assessments of the offender's mental state are usually carried out at the hospital section of the prison in which they are detained. If psychiatric disorder is suspected, opinions will be sought from independent specialists outside the prison medical service.

The decision as to whether or not a prisoner is fit to plead is made by a special jury. Before the start of a trial, either the prosecution or the defence may enter a plea of unfitness, and the special jury is empanelled to judge the psychiatric evidence – often conflicting – of the doctors who have assessed the defendant. If the jury finds the accused unfit, then the court advises the Home Secretary who will make an order for hospital confinement under the Criminal Procedures (Insanity) Act, 1964. If he subsequently recovers, an accused may be put on trial.

In the United States the modern principle of 'Competency to stand trial' was established by the precedent *Dusky* v. *United States* (1960), and with minor variations in wording is accepted by all States to define competency to stand trial.

In the *Dusky* case, it was held by the Supreme Court that:

'It is not enough for the district judge to find that 'the defendant is oriented to time and place and has some recollections of events' but that the test must be whether he has sufficient present ability to consult with his lawyer with a reasonable degree of rational understanding – and whether he has a rational as well as factual understanding of the proceedings against him.'

The problem initially was that too few of the psychiatrists who carried out the assessments (usually employees of the state mental hospitals where evaluations were carried out) were competent to assess matters of law as it related to competency. In large measure, this has been remedied over the past decade with more extensive training programmes for psychologists.

The issue of competency may be raised at any stage of the criminal process, and if the court agrees that a genuine doubt exists it will order a formal evaluation of the prisoner.

Once this evaluation has been completed and a report submitted, the findings may either be accepted both by the defence and the prosecution attorneys, in which case no hearing on the matter is necessary; or, if it is felt necessary, a court hearing may be called to decide the issue. The evaluation of competency rests *entirely* with the court which is not obliged to accept the assessor's recommendations.

When the matter of acceptance or rejection has been resolved, the case against a defendant found competent will be proceeded with, and the trial of a prisoner found incompetent to stand will be postponed until either competency returns or charges are dismissed and he is made the subject of a treatment order.

Assessing Competency

Most methods of assessment now place less weight on mental health judgements than on a purely functional evaluation of the defendant's ability – in other words, his capacity for understanding and participating in the legal process.

One American state (Florida) has formalized this into eleven requirements:

1. Understanding of the charge.
2. Appreciation of the extent and nature of the possible punishment.
3. Understanding of the broad nature of legal process.
4. Ability to explain the facts surrounding the charge to his attorney.
5. Ability to relate to an attorney.
6. Ability to co-operate in planning a defence.
7. Capacity to challenge prosecution witnesses.
8. Ability to behave in an appropriate manner in court.
9. Ability to testify relevantly.
10. Possession of sufficient motivation to help himself.
11. Ability to cope with detention while awaiting trial.

(Florida Rule of Criminal Procedure 3.21(a)(1))

One of the strongest criticisms of the 'competency to stand trial' procedure in Britain is that a defendant – quite possibly innocent of any crime – is in effect confined to an institution 'without limit of time' and it is only at the discretion of the Home Secretary that he or she will be able to stand trial and, if convicted, be sentenced to a *definite* term of confinement.

THE MAN WHO HAD TO CONFESS
The Case of David McKenzie

David McKenzie was just such an 'inmate' as we have discussed. Confined indefinitely to Rampton Special Hospital, where many of the most dangerous psychiatric cases in Britain are housed, McKenzie had been assessed by the prosecution counsel at his trial as unfit to plead: how, the court was asked, could this man be tried when he himself had no idea of whether he was innocent or guilty of the crimes with which he was being charged?

McKenzie stood accused of two horrific murders. In October 1984, 76-year-old Mrs Barbara Ann Pinder was beaten, kicked, strangled and stabbed forty-five times with a commando-type knife while at home in her flat in Battersea, south London. Her killer, in what came to be a trademark, left a knitting needle embedded in Mrs Pinder's neck.

Less than a year later, at the end of July 1985, Mrs Henrietta Osborne, a blind, almost deaf widow of 86, was savagely murdered in her small trust flat near Sloane Square, Pimlico. Neighbours had seen smoke coming from Mrs Osborne's home, and firemen later found her partially clothed body, battered, raped, strangled and, as if that were not enough, stabbed five times in the chest. A chopstick had been rammed into one eye and a ball-point pen embedded in Mrs Osborne's neck before her flat was set on fire.

By 1986 David McKenzie had acquired the Press *nom-de-*

guerre 'The Saturday Night Slaughterer', he had been picked up by the police, charged with the two murders, and had readily confessed to them.

The problem lay in McKenzie's previous history of 'confessing' to things. He had already been charged with the misdemeanour of wasting police time by admitting to a crime for which he was clearly not responsible. Now he was not only confessing to the Pinder/Osborne murders but another six or seven besides. And in most of these other crimes there was no reason to suspect McKenzie's involvement – he himself was unable to produce any convincing proof to establish his guilt. In yet other cases there is no evidence that a crime was even committed.

Questioned as to whether he really knew he committed the murders, McKenzie was emphatic that he did not – simply that there was such a strong 'bad' feeling of guilt inside him that he felt compelled to confess. In one instance he was convinced that he had raped and murdered a young woman named Tessa Howden in 1987; it is absolutely impossible for McKenzie to have been implicated in the crime, for it was committed by a man named Gary Taken – at a time when McKenzie was an in-patient at a hospital. What *is* significant is that McKenzie subsequently shared a prison cell with Taken, and heard first-hand the details of a murder which he later claimed as his own.

It was McKenzie's extraordinary suggestibility that enabled him not only to confess to crimes with which he was entirely unconnected, but to provide details in support of his claims. He himself seemed quite aware of the process going on, but powerless to control it: 'I might read something in a paper, or see something on television; then it will start fermenting in my head, I will start thinking about it. Then in about four or five weeks I'll be convinced I did that crime and say to them: "Look, I've done this crime." I'll give them details of the crime.'

Early in 1990, David McKenzie, despite still suffering from serious mental disorder, was considered fit enough to stand trial on the charges of murdering Mrs Pinder and Mrs Osborne. Nevertheless, McKenzie himself – even though he was to plead guilty – wondered whether the minutiae of his confession might not result from being at the time of his arrest in the company of policemen who would quite naturally have been discussing the details of the crimes: 'They used to stop for tea and have an unofficial chat, and what they were doing was talking about the crime. Then when the tea-break stopped they carried on [with the interview] and said, "Can you tell us about this?" I must have overheard them because I was able to tell them things I didn't even know . . . I'm not saying it was done intentionally, but that's what must have happened.'

At the Old Bailey, on 1 February 1990, David McKenzie's story – true or not, for there was no evidence other than his confession – was believed by a jury and he was subsequently returned to Rampton for an indefinite period.

However, there is still one of McKenzie's clutch of confessions that does raise a doubt. There is one outstanding modern mystery that remains unsolved by the police and that is the murder of Mrs Hilda Murrell.

The body of 78-year-old Hilda Murrell was found on 24 March 1984, on open ground at Moat Copse, some half-dozen miles from her home in Shrewsbury; she had been repeatedly stabbed and then left to die. As well as being an internationally celebrated rose grower, Mrs Murrell was well known as a vociferous opponent of nuclear energy, and her murder began to take on a distinctly mysterious appearance when it was revealed that although her house had been painstakingly searched, the only item stolen had been the manuscript of a paper she was scheduled to present at the public inquiry into the construction of the nuclear power station Sizewell B. Once the suggestion of a conspiracy was on the wind, other things came to light; like Mrs Murrell's potentially embarrassing knowledge (through a nephew in naval intelligence) on the subject of the *General Belgrano*, an Argentinian cruiser controversially sunk during the Falklands War of 1982. Although there was never a shortage either of theories or of suspects, the death of Hilda Murrell remained a perpetual mystery.

Then David McKenzie confessed, and some serious consideration had to be given to details which McKenzie has of the murder and, if one accepts his guilt of the Pinder/Osborne killings, of the similarly brutal way in which Mrs Murrell died.

But it is notoriously difficult (whatever reason one gives for this difficulty) to get a case officially reopened, and despite McKenzie's confession and in the face of a report sent by the West Mercia police to the Director of Public Prosecutions recommending that he be put on trial for the

Murrell murder, McKenzie was not charged. It was a decision which met very strong opposition, and Sir Patrick Mayhew, the Attorney-General, was asked to explain the apparent inconsistency in accepting the Pinder/Osborne confessions, but rejecting McKenzie's consistent admission to the Murrell murder.

THE MAN IN BLACK
The Case of Robert James Sartin

'It seemed a relatively idyllic life, a happy contented landscape. But underneath a very dark river had flowed unsuspected for years. That river broke through and burst into terrible reality in that quiet community. What caused it we may never know.'

(David Robson QC, at Robert Sartin's trial)

Spree killing is mercifully rare in Britain, though like other forms of multicide it is showing an uncomfortable increase. It was probably not until 1987 that the full horror of the phenomenon became evident. On 19 August that year, a 27-year-old single man named Michael Ryan pursued a reign of terror in the small Berkshire village of Hungerford. Dressed in a camouflage combat uniform and armed with a 9mm Beretta pistol, an M1 carbine and an AK-47 Kalashnikov semi-automatic assault rifle, Ryan first confronted Susan Godfrey and her two young children in Savernake. It is thought that he may have considered rape, but as Mrs Godfrey broke free and attempted to escape, her attacker cut her down with a burst of fire from the Kalashnikov. Ten minutes later, Ryan was driving into Hungerford; between 12.42 pm and 6 pm, fourteen people had been shot dead, including his own mother. Michael Ryan then holed up in a room of the school which he attended as a boy while armed police surrounded the building. Rather than surrender, Ryan put the pistol to his head and died by his own bullet. The 'Hungerford Massacre' was over.

In every important ingredient, the crime of Michael Ryan was a text-book 'spree' killing:

1. Characterized by a number of victims being slain over a comparatively short span of time – hours, or at most days.
2. Killings are committed in two or more locations as part of a 'continuous' action.
3. Victims are typically selected by chance and will be attacked or not on the momentary whim of the killer.
4. Spree killers frequently conclude their crime by killing themselves. (This may take the less obvious form of behaving so recklessly that armed officers are obliged to open fire.)

Although he had no way of knowing it at the time, Michael Ryan would attract a fan-club of at least one member: a young man whose pilgrimage to the village of Hungerford preceded his own shooting spree.

The date was 30 April 1989, a quiet Bank Holiday Sunday in the seaside suburb of Monkseaton, Tyne and Wear. Kenneth Mackintosh, the father of two young children and an enthusiastic member of the local St Peter's congregation, was delivering church leaflets along Windsor Road. From the opposite direction the slight figure of a young man approached, wearing dark glasses and a pony-tail and dressed entirely in black, with a combat knife strapped to one thigh and a shotgun held straight out in front of him. As Mr Mackintosh looked up, the assassin fired off both barrels of the weapon, sending his victim reeling to the pavement. Reaching up his hand, begging the gunman for help, for mercy, Mackintosh heard: 'No, it is your day to die!' before the contents of two more cartridges blasted their way into his chest from point-blank range. He was dead before the man in black had turned and walked on.

It was only later that the story of Robert James Sartin's twenty-minute rise to notoriety was fitted into the context of what became known as the Bloody Sunday Slaughter.

Early on that dry, sunny morning, Sartin had been served breakfast of sausage and egg in bed by his parents before they left their house in Wentworth Gardens to visit friends. Robert had taken his time dressing in his favourite black – the devil's colour, he liked to think – aware, as he often was, of the voices in his head; of one voice in particular, the voice of 'Michael'. Putting on the dark glasses that kept the thoughts inside, Sartin loaded his father's shotgun into the back of his beige Ford Escort and pulled slowly away from the front of the house. At 11.55 he was seen parking the car and walking along Pykerley Road. Seconds later, Judith Rhodes, driving her car in the opposite direction along the road, found herself looking into the twin barrels of Robert Sartin's gun. Too late to avoid it, the first shot shattered Mrs Rhodes's windscreen; as she slammed on the brakes and flung herself under the dashboard, a second blast sent burning pellets into her left hand. Reloading the gun, Sartin fired a shot defiantly at the sky before turning on his heel and walking back down the street: 'Looking sharp, not nervous', as one witness recalled, 'he was turning left and right and pointing his gun.'

William Roberts was at his garden gate exchanging Sunday chit-chat with Lorraine Noble as the madman in black bore down on them. 'Oh God,' Roberts shouted, and flung himself to the ground as the shotgun's barrels levelled. There was a deafening explosion and Mrs Noble collapsed, seriously injured, to the ground.

Thirty-nine-year-old Robert Wilson, hearing the sound of shooting and fearful for the safety of his girlfriend who was out walking the dog, had just stepped out of his front door when the rain of shot tore into his face and left side of his body. As Wilson fled, heedless of his own injuries, in search of his girlfriend, Sartin took a pot-shot at neighbour Kathleen Lynch, looking out of her bedroom window at the growing scene of carnage. The next victim was at this very moment cycling towards Sartin when he saw what he thought was an airgun in his hands; two blasts that threw him from his bike and all but robbed him of his life told Brian Thomas that this was no toy. In acute pain and trailing blood behind him, Thomas made the effort that saved him and dragged himself to the security of a nearby house.

All the time The Voices. Michael's voice. A gunman out of control.

A car approached, the driver negotiating around Brian Thomas's bicycle abandoned in the middle of the road. The car's three occupants, Robert Burgon, his wife Jean and their daughter Nicola, drove through a hail of shot as Sartin opened fire, seriously injuring Mr Burgon and his wife, before turning his murderous weapon on to Ernest Carter and another motorist whose car careered out of control into a wall. As the windscreen shattered, the sound was met by the explosion of another shot as Jean Miller was hit in the stomach as she stooped to weed her front garden.

Madness taking him over. The Voices.

'What the hell is going on?' Elderly Vera Burrows had heard the noise of shooting and was confronting Sartin for disturbing her Sunday peace.

'It's me – I am killing people. I am going to kill you.'

The gun raised like slow-motion . . . aim . . . The Voices . . . the weapon lowering again . . . 'Oh, you are old. I am not going to kill you.' . . . turning . . . walking away . . . back to the car . . . driving off . . .

Robert Sartin sitting in a seaside car park as an unarmed police constable places him under arrest. It is early evening already; and back there one person lies dead and fourteen others are wounded.

Later that same day, with Robert out of mischief in a police cell, his heartbroken parents Brian and Jean were struggling against their disbelief: 'There was our gentle, quiet son who loves kids and animals; he loves people. He is so gentle. It must have been something inside him.'

It was The Voices that were inside him . . . one voice in particular.

Because for every neighbour for whom 22-year-old Robert Sartin was 'everyone's favourite son', there was a schoolfriend who remembered the 'weirdo', the boy who liked to drop the 'r' from his surname so that it sounded like 'Satan', and who always wore black clothes.

Robert and Michael

Exactly one year after he had turned Monkseaton into a bloodbath, on Monday, 30 April 1990, a jury was empanelled to assess the evidence as to Robert Sartin's sanity. In the Crown Court at Newcastle upon Tyne, Mr David Robson QC, for the prosecution, instructed the jury in their duties, emphasizing that Sartin's fitness to plead went beyond whether or not he could say 'guilty' or 'not guilty', but whether his mental state permitted the defendant to understand the charge that was made against him, instruct his legal counsel and, if necessary, give evidence on his own behalf: 'You are not here to decide the issue of guilt or innocence. The whole of justice is held in the balance. On the one hand there are the victims of crime and the public interest that they should be protected; on the other that real justice is done and a man is not put on trial when he has no ability to defend himself.'

Mr Robson went on to describe the schizophrenia that had been developing over a number of years, and Sartin's conviction that his mind was being controlled by another. He recalled for the jury Sartin's statement to the police when he was taken into custody: 'I know I was arrested because I shot people, but I wasn't thinking about it . . . I don't feel anything for them now. I remember hearing people scream, I wasn't bothered if I hit them . . . I was not taking proper aim at anybody. Every time I fired I think I was shooting both barrels – the cartridges would just eject and I would put in the next ones. *It was as if it was not me inside myself.*'

Then the jury discovered who it was that possessed Robert Sartin, the voice that made him kill. It was Michael.

From childhood, Sartin had been obsessed with the macabre, with the occult, to such an extent that other children went in fear of him. In youth this unhealthy preoccupation found expression in Satanism and a morbid fascination with Moors Murderers Ian Brady and Myra Hindley, and the mad poisoner Graham Young. Eight months before his own rampage, Robert Sartin had visited the scene of Michael Ryan's Hungerford Massacre. Above all there was the influence of Michael. Michael Myers.

Home Office psychiatrist, Dr Marion Swann, explained to the court: 'He hears more than one voice, and one of them is Michael. Initially he didn't know who this person was, but then he watched the video of [the film] *Halloween* and came to realize Michael [Myers, the film's teenage psychopath who hacks his family to pieces] was the voice he had been hearing. He describes the ability to actually see Michael and many of the drawings he had were of Michael . . .' In conclusion, Dr Swann argued: 'He is so sick and mentally disturbed that he needs treatment for this condition as a matter of urgency.'

Robert Sartin was not in court to hear this most intimate evaluation of his psyche, he had been confined to Moss Side Special Hospital, near Liverpool. The jury, predictably, passed the only humane and just verdict possible – the verdict of 'unfit to plead'. Whether Robert Sartin will ever be considered well enough to stand trial is doubtful.

THE PROBLEM OF THE
MISSING CORPSE

AS SEEN ON THE NEWS
The Case of Michael Kyte

In all 'historic' cases of murder it is easy, with hindsight, to piece together the many small pieces of information, discard the red herrings, and present a clear narrative; background, events, conclusions and consequences can all be neatly wrought into a coherent story. Some of the crime reports in this book, because they deal basically with a single year, cannot be so tidily parcelled. Tragedies like murder rarely conform to a convenient chronology; nor is its detection as easy as it may seem to the sleuths of fiction.

All this is true of the disappearance of 33-year-old Ruth Stevens. It began at the end of 1989, charges were brought during 1990, but it must be left to 1991 before the final facts are clear. Until Ruth's killer comes to trial we will not know the full extent of the police inquiry, what information they have and what evidence will be presented in court. This is complicated by the fact that if a plea of 'unfit to plead' or one of 'guilty' (either to murder or to a lesser charge of manslaughter) is entered, the full case may never be heard in court.

Uncharacteristically in this sequence of corpseless crimes, the body of Ruth Stevens *was* eventually found in its sad, makeshift grave. What is important is that the lack of tangible remains did not prevent the arrest of a suspect and his being charged with Ruth Stevens's murder

The media (through whom the police speak), and we its watchers, saw the case in the rather fragmented form in which it is presented below, with the advantage that the bracketed [] commentary could be added later to put some of the information into perspective.

12 December 1989: Between leaving her evening class in the town of Warminster, Wiltshire, and her planned appointment to meet fiancé Patrick Kelly at the bar where he worked in Westbury, about four miles away, 33-year-old Ruth Stevens literally disappeared. An assistant in a chemist shop, Ruth was an active member of the local Red Cross and had enrolled in business studies classes on Tuesday nights; she had last been seen getting into her silver-grey Vauxhall Viva after the class. The car was also missing.

13–14 December 1989: The police, as is common in such cases, issued the registration number of Ruth Stevens's car – JBK 195P. Detective Chief Inspector John Spiller, at the head of the investigating team, appealed: 'We desperately want the public to contact us if they have seen Ruth or her car.' A huge search involving more than 100 officers was already under way in the area around where the young woman had disappeared, and a police helicopter was brought in to cover the search from the air. [What the public did not know until the following day was that the police had already detained a man who they would hold for questioning for thirteen hours about Ruth's whereabouts.]

15 December 1989: Heartbroken Pat Stevens and her husband added their personal appeal to that of the police for news of their daughter. Mrs Stevens pleaded: 'Wherever you are, Ruth, please come home.' Less optimistically, the police were expressing grave concern for Ruth Stevens's safety. News also emerged of the man 'helping police with their inquiries'. Still unnamed [he was in fact Michael Kyte] the man was described as a '48-year-old divorcee' who was subsequently released on bail. [People close to Ruth Stevens and the investigation will already have linked the man to Ruth's former boyfriend with whom she had previously lived for some time, and who had apparently still been pestering her despite her imminent marriage to Patrick Kelly.]

20 December 1989: Sooner or later the break has to come in any case. For the most part there are no instant miracles, no Sherlockian drama in the investigation of murder – just painstaking routine police work, in the field, in the office, in the laboratory; the time-consuming addition of clues each to the others to build a solid case. Ruth Stevens's car – a major piece in the puzzle – was found abandoned on the sprawling Barnsbury council estate in north London. Speculation was now rife in certain parts of the press, and tales emerged of Ruth's 'toyboy', who apparently lived in the King's Cross area of London near where the car was found. It allowed the tabloids to introduce a new dimension: 'Detectives piece together the jigsaw of Ruth's tangled love life.' Meanwhile the police were dragging the muddy waters of the Regent's Canal near the spot where the Viva had been abandoned. The likelihood was that dumping the car in London was a red herring to distract the attention of police from an answer nearer the victim's Wiltshire home; nevertheless, in police work nothing can be 'assumed', it must be carefully investigated before it is retained or eliminated. The canal yielded nothing.

31 December 1989: With the Christmas festivities over, and the press back to a less frivolous mood of reporting, news was announced that the meticulous forensic examination of Ruth Stevens's car had produced positive results. Despite the vehicle having been thoroughly cleaned, experts were able to detect minute traces of blood inside it. The implication was as sinister as it was obvious, and only served further to convince detectives that some serious harm had befallen the car's owner. Detective Inspector Spiller is reported as commenting: 'I cannot believe that Ruth would disappear of her own accord. One must assume that she either met with a nasty fate or is being held against her will.' One Sunday newspaper clearly thought that the investigation team needed a little help, and published a list of clues with the appeal to its readers: 'Now help us solve this crime.'

8 January 1990: A Wiltshire police spokesman announced that 'a man was arrested shortly before 8 o'clock this morning in connection with the disappearance of Ruth Stevens and is being questioned'. The questioning, which took place at Devizes Police Headquarters, lasted more than six hours, after which the man, 'the 48-year-old divorcee', was charged with Miss Stevens's murder [his name was Michael Kyte].

9 January 1990: Michael Kyte, in accordance with legal formality, was brought before magistrates at Warminster accused of murder. Described as an electronics engineer from Westbury, Kyte was remanded in custody. [The search continued for Ruth's body, but it was clear that the Crown Prosecution Service had sufficient confidence in the strength of the police evidence to proceed without it. Officers of the Wiltshire police force will continue issuing pleas to the public to be on the lookout for signs of 'disturbed ground' around the Westbury/Warminster area of the county.]

20 June 1990: A woman's decomposed body recovered from a shallow grave at Wellow Hill, Combe Hay, was identified as that of Ruth Stevens. Combe Hay is just south-west of the city of Bath, not a dozen miles from the victim's home in Westbury, and that of the man charged with her murder.

24 July 1990: As the due process of English law moves slowly but surely forward, Michael Kyte is summoned again before the magistrates to be committed to stand his trial.

Stop Press

7 June 1991: As the proofs of this book were being read the trial of Michael Kyte was taking place at Winchester Crown Court, Hampshire. The verdict of guilty came as no surprise, and Kyte, described as a 'cold-blooded, calculating killer' was sentenced to life imprisonment for the murder of Ruth Stevens.

CORPUS DELICTI . . .

There is a popular misconception, perpetuated in the main by pulp crime fiction, that a charge of murder cannot succeed without a corpse.

The root of the problem is a misinterpretation of the legal term *corpus delicti*. The term properly means the 'body' of the case, the *essence* of the case. By translating the word *corpus* literally as a 'corpse', it follows that without a body there is no case.

It was this simple misunderstanding that gave Britain's celebrated 'Acid Bath Murderer', John George Haigh, the confidence to confess to the police: 'Mrs Durand-Deacon no longer exists, and no trace of her can ever be found again. I have destroyed her with acid. You will find the sludge that remains at Leopold Road. Every trace has gone. *How can you prove murder if there is no body?*'

Very easily, as it turned out, and Haigh's reward for his cock-eyed belief was an appointment with the hangman. But if his interest in other people's crimes had been a fraction of his commitment to his own misdeeds, he would have read how James Camb had been convicted of murder less than eighteen months previously, despite the absence of his victim's mortal remains.

The truth of the matter is this; that to establish the *corpus delicti* of a murder three facts must be established:

1. That there has been a death;

2. That the deceased can be identified as being the person to have been killed; and
3. That death was due to unlawful violence.

The only question then is 'Who did it?'

The Case of Thomas Joseph Davidson

The first important case to establish the credibility of a conviction without a body was *Rex* v. *Davidson*. In September 1934, Davidson, a 34-year-old poultry farmer, stood in the dock of the Old Bailey charged with the murder of his son, eight-year-old John Desmond Davidson. John had disappeared during the previous December, and although his body, or any part of it, was never found, Thomas Davidson made three separate admissions to killing the child. First in a letter to the police, then in a signed statement, and finally in a letter to his wife. He had, Davidson admitted, drowned the boy in a canal and dumped his body on a smouldering refuse tip at Yiewsley, Middlesex, where the charred remains were subsequently buried beneath thousands more tons of waste.

By the time of his trial before Mr Justice Atkinson, Davidson had retracted his confession and in his defence argued that he had found the child *already drowned* in the canal. The jury chose not to believe his new story, and the defendant was sentenced to hang.

Before the Court of Criminal Appeal it was argued that in cases of homicide where the victim's body had not been recovered, evidence independent of that of the defendant himself should be presented in order to establish that a crime had been committed. However, the judgement of the court under the Lord Chief Justice, Lord Hewart, maintained that in this instance it was reasonable for the jury to conclude that little John Davidson was dead, and to choose to believe the earlier of the father's statements to the effect that he had murdered the child. The appeal was dismissed, though Thomas Davidson's sentence was later commuted to life imprisonment.

The Case of Edward Ball

One of the most interesting examples of the way in which

circumstantial evidence was built into a convincing murder prosecution in the absence of the deceased occurred in Ireland in the year following Thomas Davidson's reprieve.

James Rafferty, a newspaper man on his delivery round in the Shankhill district of County Dublin on the morning of 18 February 1936, had his attention drawn by an unoccupied Baby Austin car parked on a patch of ground at the end of Corbawn Lane where it leads to the seashore.

Rafferty alerted a Mr Margetson, who lived in the last house in the lane and who recalled seeing the car in question and several others on the previous night.

The car turned out to belong to Mrs Lavinia, or Vera, Bell, 55 years old, the estranged wife of a prominent Dublin physician.

At 6.30 pm, police called at Mrs Ball's home at 23 St Helen's Road, Booterstown, where they were received by nineteen-year-old Edward, youngest of the Balls' two sons, and despite a shiftless nature an intelligent, likeable boy. He told Chief Superintendent Reynolds that he had last seen his mother at about 7.45 the previous evening when she drove off saying she would be spending the night with a friend. Edward, so he claimed, had been at home reading until retiring to bed at around 11 o'clock.

A search of the house revealed that Mrs Ball's room was locked, and that Edward's contained a bundle of soggy, blood-stained linen and a pair of wet, muddy shoes. When Mrs Ball's door was forced, the room was in darkness, and unbearably hot. When the light was switched on, police realized that the source of the heat was an electric fire placed so as to dry a large wet stain on the carpet. Mrs Ball's wardrobe was open, though her maid, Lily Kelly, swore that none of her clothes was missing.

Interviewed again about his movements on the 18th, Edward Ball told the truth – or most of it. What he forgot to mention was that he had left a suitcase in the care of a friend's wife, explaining that it contained dirty clothes and he would be back for it in a couple of days. In fact, the suitcase was recovered by the police and opened in Edward's presence. It did indeed contain soiled clothing – shirts, a lady's coat and underslip, bed-linen and towels – extensively soiled with blood. Meanwhile, a minute examination of the house at St Helen's Road was revealing widespread blood-staining, particularly around the area of Vera Ball's bed. The trail led down the stairs, along the outside path and into the garage.

On 21 February, Edward Ball was arrested and charged with matricide. He replied, 'I do not feel like saying anything at the moment.'

Charging Ball with murder had presented a number of difficulties, not least the fact that despite extensive police and military efforts, Mrs Ball's body had not been found – has never been found. And to prove a charge of murder it is clearly necessary to prove that a death has occurred.

Mrs Ball's apparent disappearance, in combination with the copious blood-staining in her house and car, was certainly suspicious in the extreme. But if Edward Ball had stuck to his original statement to the police that his mother was simply missing, and that he had no idea of her whereabouts, there might not have been a case to answer.

It was an unwise Edward Ball who had made a second statement, in which he spoke of his mother's deepening depression, a depression so profound that she had often spoken of suicide. And then on the night of her death, so he claimed, Vera Ball had again complained that life was hopeless and she wanted to die. On her way up to her room, she had tearfully begged her son: 'I want you to do all you can to prevent people thinking I am a coward.' Expecting his mother to come downstairs again when she was more composed, Edward became anxious when she did not. When he went up to her room to offer Mrs Ball some filial comfort, Edward was horrified to find his mother lying on the bed, blood pouring from a wound in her throat, with a double-edged razor blade by her side. Ball's first impulse was to rush for help; then he remembered his mother's last words: 'Prevent people thinking I am a coward.'

Which was why he dutifully carried her body downstairs and into the car. When he reached the spot where the vehicle was later found abandoned, Ball found he was not alone on that isolated patch of ground looking out to sea; it was a favourite haunt for courting couples who enjoyed their romance played out before the backdrop of a silver moon reflecting off the Dublin Bay. Edward Ball waited; waited for four hours until the cars around him had all departed; four hours sitting with the dead and bloody body of his mother beside him, at times, to avert suspicion, putting his arm round the corpse as a lover might.

Beneath the shroud of night, Ball half carried, half dragged his burden down to the water's edge, their movement across the strand and the regular lapping of the sea breaking the otherwise silent dark.

But was that *exactly* the way it happened? Certainly the second part of the story was true – the Garda had painstakingly searched the route from bedroom to seashore, finding clues to corroborate it.

It was the suggestion of suicide that the prosecution contested at Edward Ball's trial. Dr John McGrath, State pathologist, had been experimenting with blood. In his evidence Dr McGrath compared the relatively minor amounts of blood estimated to have been shed on the bed – between a fifth and a tenth of a pint, with that which stained the carpet – about three or four pints. This led him to only one conclusion – that Mrs Ball had died there on the floor.

Furthermore, the pathologist cast doubt on the efficacy of suicide by cutting the throat with a razor blade. It would, he told the court, require several determined cuts in order to hack through to the jugular vein. It was far more likely that Mrs Ball had met her death from a number of savage blows to the head with the blood-stained hatchet found in the garden of her home; a hatchet, the prosecution contended, that had been wielded by her son.

Edward Ball did not enter the witness box on his own behalf, and his defence, if the suicide theory was not accepted, was to be one of insanity. Ball's instability was attested by two eminent psychiatrists – one from Dublin, the other first called from London by Edward's father in 1932 when he became concerned about his son's mental health. Dr Ball himself gave a moving account of Edward's unhappy childhood in a broken home, and even the judge, Mr Justice Hanna, summed up in Ball's favour.

After a long and complicated deliberation, during which the jury asked for witnesses to be recalled to clarify some points, Edward Ball was found guilty but insane, and sentenced to be detained during the pleasure of the Governor-General.

The Case of James Camb

Camb's victim met a similarly watery grave to Mrs Ball's when he raped and murdered 26-year-old actress Gay Gibson and pushed her body out of a ship's porthole. The Union Castle's liner *Durban Castle* had departed Cape Town on 10 October 1947, bound for Southampton. At 3 o'clock on the morning of the 18th, the night watchman was summoned by the ship's bell system to attend first class cabin 126 – occupied by Miss Gay Gibson. When he arrived, Frederick Steer knocked on the cabin door, part opened it, and had it slammed in his face. But in that brief moment, through that thin crack, Steer saw a face he recognized – James Camb, the 31-year-old promenade deck steward whose colleagues called him 'Valentino' on account of his success with the lady passengers. Clearly feeling that he was intruding on a personal matter, the watchman left the occupants of cabin 126 to whatever it was they were doing.

It was only later in the morning, when Miss Gibson had missed breakfast and a thorough search of the ship had failed to reveal her whereabouts, that the events of the early hours took on a dark significance. When Captain Patey confronted Camb with his nocturnal visit to the missing passenger's cabin, he flatly denied being there.

By the time the *Durban Castle* had steamed into Southampton docks, and James Camb had been deposited with the local police, he had clearly had time to reflect on the seriousness of his position, and on the futility of his previous denials. For one thing, an examination by the ship's doctor, at the captain's insistence, had revealed a number of what looked like fingernail scratches around the steward's neck and wrists. Furthermore, an inspection of cabin 126 had shown its occupant's bed-linen stained with blood-flecked saliva and urine.

When he reached the dock of the Winchester Assizes in March 1948, the amorous steward was telling a much different story. Yes, he confided to the jury, he *was* in Gay Gibson's cabin; in fact she had invited him there. They sat drinking and chatting for a while, and then 'there was a certain amount of preliminary love play, and then sexual intercourse took place'. During the course of this activity, according to Camb, Miss Gibson went 'limp'. When it was apparent she was dead, Camb panicked and pushed the body out through the porthole before scuttling back to his own cabin.

Gay Gibson's body was never recovered from the cold waters of the Atlantic, but what bodily traces she had left behind were enough for pathologist Donald Teare to deduce an entirely different scenario. Teare, giving evidence for the Crown, maintained that the blood-flecked saliva left on the bed-linen was entirely consistent with manual strangulation; and in situations of abject fear such as Gay Gibson must have felt as the hands of her killer closed round her neck, it is common for the bladder to open – accounting for the extensive staining of the bed.

On 23 March 1948, James Camb was found guilty of murder.

The Case of John George Haigh

We have already encountered John Haigh, the man who misunderstood *corpus delicti*. In fact so enamoured was he of the concept of 'no corpse – no conviction' that during his time as a guest of His Majesty's prison service he acquired the nickname 'Old Corpus Delicti'.

As it turned out, Haigh had enjoyed a very successful career as a murderer, killing and disposing of five people in baths of acid before his arrogance let him down. When Haigh told Detective Inspector Albert Webb, on 28 February 1949, that 'every trace has gone' of his latest victim, Mrs Olive Durand-Deacon, he could not have been more wrong. Indeed, although it was his proudest boast, Haigh was one of the many killers whose victim's corpse proved his downfall. When he bragged that 'you will find the sludge that remains at Leopold Road', he had overlooked what the 'sludge' might mean to a brilliant forensic pathologist. It was just Haigh's bad luck that Professor Keith Simpson was assigned to the case. To Simpson this was not merely sludge, it was incontrovertible proof that, as required by law, 'the deceased can be identified with the person alleged to have been killed'.

It was the professor's meticulous work at the scene of Mrs Durand-Deacon's murder, a small workshop outside Crawley in Sussex, that revealed among the sludge three gallstones ('Women of Mrs Durand-Deacon's age and habits – 69 and fairly plump – are prone to gallstones'), and the greater part of the bones of a left foot, later cast in plaster and found to fit the dead woman's shoe. In addition there was a set of dentures which Mrs Durand-Deacon's dentist identified as having been made for her patient; here Haigh had made a fundamental mistake in not allowing the extra time required by the acid to break down the acrylic resin from which the false teeth were fashioned. The same miscalculation resulted in the survival of the victim's plastic handbag and a number of its contents.

All told, Haigh could not have been proved more guilty if his victim had risen and pointed a finger at him!

The Case of Michael Onufrejczyc

The continued disappearance of Stanislaw Sykut from the farm in Cwmdu, Wales, which he ineffectually husbanded with fellow-Pole Onufrejczyc, might have aroused less suspicion if the remaining partner had not been so surly, abusive and uncooperative. Perhaps he, too, felt over-confident in the notion of 'no corpse – no conviction'. One certain thing is that since Monday, 14 December 1953, nothing has been seen of the unfortunate Sykut – or any part of him.

It was well known that the two partners had not got on – either with running the farm or with each other. Indeed, Stanislaw had on one occasion felt constrained to summon help from the local police after Onufrejczyc had set about him with fists flying. It was no secret that Sykut had visited his solicitor and that as a result Onufrejczyc had been ordered to refund his compatriot's £600 investment and dissolve the partnership. It was shortly afterwards that Stanislaw Sykut vanished. Or rather, he had left just a little something behind, for when the team from the forensic science laboratory made a thorough search of the farmhouse, they were able to identify more than 2000 tiny dark spots of blood on the kitchen walls; blood that proved to be human in origin regardless of Onufrejczyc's explanation that he had been killing and gutting rabbits.

Despite the slender evidence against him and the continued absence of a body, Michael Onufrejczyc stood trial at Glamorgan Assizes on 19 August 1954. During his summing-up, Mr Justice Oliver reminded the jury: 'At the trial of a person charged with murder the fact of death is provable by circumstantial evidence, notwithstanding that neither the body nor any trace of the body has been found, and that the accused has made no confession of any participation in the crime. Before he can be convicted, the fact of death should be proved by such circumstances as render the commission of the crime morally certain and leave no ground for reasonable doubt. The circumstantial evidence should be so cogent and compelling as to convince a jury that upon no rational hypothesis other than murder can the facts be discounted.'

Still protesting his innocence, Onufrejczyc was convicted of murder and sentenced to death. But it was not the hangman that finished him; the Polish farmer's sentence was commuted, and after serving ten years of a life sentence, Onufrejczyc was released, only to be killed in a traffic accident the following year.

And Stanislaw Sykut? The most convincing explanation was given by ex-Detective Superintendent David Thomas – that Sykut had been chopped up and fed to the farm's pigs.

The Case of the Brothers Hosein

A few years after the untimely death of Michael Onufrejczyc the headlines were proclaiming yet another 'Case of the Missing Body'. This time the innocent victim was Mrs Muriel McKay, wife of the deputy chairman of the *News of the World*. Mrs McKay had been abducted from her home in Wimbledon on 2 December 1969, and ransom demands were made shortly afterwards. The whole kidnap had been bungled from the start: the intended victim had been the wife of millionaire businessman Rupert Murdoch. Then the demands were for a large amount of money: 'We are from America – Mafia M3. We have your wife . . . You will need a million pounds by Wednesday.' It was later agreed that the amount could be paid in two instalments.

In all, eighteen telephone calls of an equally farcical nature were made to an increasingly anxious Alick McKay before, on 22 January, he received a ransom note accompanied by two letters written by his wife in which she admitted that the ordeal was causing her to 'deteriorate in health and spirit'. Having followed the bewilderingly complex instructions for delivering the money, during which a police officer posed as Mrs McKay's son, the kidnappers failed to collect the suitcase. 'Mafia M-3' could hardly have failed to notice the extraordinary police presence of about 150 officers in various disguises and some 50 unmarked cars.

A second attempt to deliver the money proved to be a burlesque, when a young couple came across the suitcase full of money where it had been left on a garage forecourt. Good citizens that they were, the Abbotts called in the local force thinking that somebody had mislaid their luggage. But the police, under the experienced leadership of Detective Chief Superintendent Wilfred Smith, had laid their plans well, and when a dark blue Volvo saloon driven by two coloured men began cruising back and forth around the dropping point, they were sure they had their kidnappers.

The owner of the car, traced through its registration number XGO 994G, proved to be 34-year-old Trinidad-born Indian Arthur Hosein who, with his younger brother Nizamodeen, worked the ramshackle Rooks Farm at Stocking Pelham.

A painstaking search of the farmhouse provided sufficient clues for investigating officers to link the Hoseins with the kidnap, and by the time they reached the dock of the Central Criminal Court in September 1970, the scientific evidence against the brothers was overwhelming. Apart from indisputable fingerprint evidence that proved Arthur handled the ransom notes, a handwriting expert demonstrated to the court how the ransom note written in an exercise book found at the farmhouse perfectly matched the indentations on the following page.

Both the Hoseins were found guilty of murder and kidnap; on the former charge they were sentenced to life imprisonment and on the latter to additional lengthy terms of imprisonment.

Although every inch of Rooks Farm was meticulously covered by police searchers, not the smallest trace of Mrs McKay was ever found. Among the suggestions made was that the victim had been cut up and fed to the Hoseins' herd of Wessex Saddleback pigs. Whatever the truth, an undiscovered body can only deepen the sense of loss felt by family and friends deprived of even a last resting place at which to mourn.

The Case of Leonard Ewing Scott

Evelyn Scott was a woman of some financial means just emerging from her fourth divorce when she met Leonard Scott in 1949. Scott was a bully, and aside from showing his wife physical violence it was not long before he had commandeered her money and her investments under the pretence of 'looking after her affairs'.

On 16 May 1955, Mrs Scott disappeared from her home at Bel Air, California, and was never seen again. Inevitably, friends began to ask embarrassing questions – like 'where is Evelyn?' – and Scott was obliged to concoct a series of excuses to the effect that she had been unwell and had gone away for treatment. It was anybody's guess why he added, 'I'm just going to wait until she has gone seven years and then she'll be declared legally dead.'

It was a year later, when Evelyn's false teeth and spectacles turned up in a neighbour's garden, that the finger of suspicion began to point unwaveringly at Leonard Scott. Still he might have been able to stick it out had the fraudulent business affairs not come to light and Scott was forced to flee from an indictment for forgery and theft. When the law eventually caught up with him in Canada in April 1957, there was more on Scott's charge sheet than forgery – in fact, that was the least of his worries. He now stood charged with the murder of his wife, no matter that the body was still missing.

Although the evidence against him was necessarily circumstantial, it was probably the strong financial motive that persuaded the jury in favour of a conviction. Leonard Ewing Scott was still protesting his innocence when he was led from the court to begin a life sentence. He persistently refused parole on the grounds that to accept would be to admit his guilt; and it was only when he was offered unconditional release in 1978, at the age of 81, that Scott accepted and walked from prison a free man.

Bizarre as the prison episode was, it was by no means the conclusion of the Scott case. There was a more sensational ending yet to come.

In 1984 Leonard Scott confessed to author Diane Wagner that he had bludgeoned his wife to death and buried her in the Nevada desert outside Las Vegas.

The Case of Kingsley Ignatius Rotardier

At his trial in London's Central Criminal Court in January 1988, 46-year-old male model and composer Kingsley Rotardier stood accused of the murder of the former head of the Greater London Council's chairman's office, Dr David Napier Hamilton.

Hamilton, an old Etonian and for some years Rotardier's homosexual lover, disappeared on a night in November 1985 from the flat they shared in Brixton Road, south London.

No trace of him has ever been found, and it is alleged that Rotardier killed David Hamilton in order to lay hands on his money; he then dismembered the body and burned it piecemeal in a garden incinerator. With a grim irony, the killer is said to have used Hamilton's own credit card to purchase the bone-saw and butcher's meat cleaver with which he decimated the corpse. Rotardier then went on a spree, spending his former lover's money freely and selling off his possessions to raise more cash; he even had the audacity, according to Crown evidence, to engage a solicitor to try to secure Dr Hamilton's redundancy compensation when the Greater London Council was abolished in 1986, plus the £6000 a year pension that went with it.

During the whole of the five months between Dr Hamilton's disappearance and his neighbours voicing their suspicions to the police, Rotardier had been inventing ever more elaborate deceits to explain his absence. He announced that his friend had contracted Aids, and in an attempt to secure relief was travelling variously in Germany, France and Malaysia to seek treatment. When friends wrote letters to the missing man it was Kingsley Rotardier who replied. This was, as it turned out, a mistake, for even given the understandably shaky hand of a man who had just learned he has Aids, the deception was no match for document specialist Dr Christopher Davies, who discovered that not one of the twelve handwritten and fourteen typed and hand-signed letters dated after 18 November, 1985, was genuine.

Despite the lack of his victim's body and Rotardier's denial of murder, he was convicted by a jury and sentenced by Sir James Miskin, the Recorder of London, to life imprisonment with a recommended minimum of twenty years.

THE CULTS

DEATH BY FAITH
The Twitchell Trial

A case that could have far-reaching consequences for the continued inviolability from prosecution of cults of faith and religions under the United States Fifth Amendment was heard in the Suffolk County Courtroom, Boston, during April and May 1990. On trial were the fundamental beliefs not of some marginal hippie sect, but of the powerful Church of Christ Scientist, and in the very city of its establishment at that.

On the night of 8 April 1986, two-year-old Robyn Twitchell died from a bowel obstruction. It was a tragic death that could easily have been prevented if at any time during Robyn's five-day illness his parents had bestowed the benefit of medical treatment. Extraordinary as it seemed to the shocked city of Boston, David and Ginger Twitchell had offered their child nothing by way of relief but prayer.

Devout Christian Scientists, the Twitchells – undoubtedly loving and caring parents – were following a teaching as important to them as their Bible, a Christian Science manual on *Parents, Children and God's Omnipotent Care*, which instructs: 'Christian Scientists turn resolutely to God, as the Master [Jesus Christ] did, to effect the needed healing . . . disease hath no basis in God's kingdom.' In other words, 'Harmony is the fact . . . and sickness a temporal dream.'

So instead of a doctor, David Twitchell and his wife summoned the Practitioner, a Christian Science 'specialist' in prayer who, after a mere two weeks' training, is qualified to offer his or her services as a spiritual healer for a remuneration. They also availed themselves of the services of a Christian Science Nurse, whose entitlement to that status ends with the name. Neither the Practitioner nor the Nurse have any training in medicine or even in the most rudimentary anatomy. As one Practitioner explained: 'Anatomy to a Christian Science Practitioner is a very different thing than for a medical practitioner; the anatomy of man as his spiritual being comes into play. The completeness and the wholeness in the way that God made him; yes there is anatomy, but not the physical body; we do not turn to that to define man totally.'

Nevertheless, so strong is the Christian Science lobby in America that medical insurance companies like Blue Shield and Blue Cross are obliged to meet the costs of Christian Science Practitioners and Nurses who, furthermore, enjoy protection from malpractice suits.

So David and Ginger Twitchell found themselves sitting in a tense, crowded courtroom facing a charge of manslaughter relating to the death of their infant son. On the face of it, it was just two calm, sincere Christians who sat attentively in the dock; effectively, it was the whole of their religion that had been put on trial.

There was no dispute as to the facts – the child had died as a direct result of the failure to treat medically a condition which had not, in itself, been life-threatening. What was in question was whether parents were constitutionally immune to prosecution for, in the simplest terms, 'sacrificing' their children to their own religious beliefs.

In common with another 47 states in America, Massachusetts retains a statute on its books, passed in 1971, which ensures that: 'A child should not be deemed to be neglected or to lack proper physical care for the sole reason that he is being provided remedial treatment by spiritual means alone in accordance with the tenets and practice of a recognized church.'

However, in the interpretation of District Attorney Flanagan, responsible for presenting the prosecution case to the court, the statute applies only to child *abuse*: 'The parents are being tried for manslaughter; it is up to the jury to decide if there are sufficient facts to find that the parents' failure to get medical care for their child was wilful, wanton and reckless conduct

. . . We are not going to allow parents to make their children martyrs.'

It was obvious that the case was set to become a landmark for the Church of Christ Scientist, and one that would have a potentially far-reaching influence on its recruitment drive. A massive publicity campaign was therefore launched around America through the medium of double-page advertisements in the major newspapers asking: 'Why is prayer being persecuted in Boston? Selective prosecution of Christian Science is of grave concern. Today it is the prayers of Christian Scientists, tomorrow it may be the prayers of the established religions – perhaps *your* religion.'

As for the Twitchells themselves, having lived not only with the sorrow of losing their child, but also having endured four years of uncertainty leading up to their trial, the couple were reticent in talking to the media, and had gone so far as to move home to a secret location in order to avoid unwanted publicity. Nevertheless, David Twitchell has, throughout his ordeal, publicly maintained that he was *not* careless of his son's life: 'Our spiritual understanding of God's laws told us we were behaving in an acceptable manner. It has been tough; some people might call it a severe test of your faith. There will be some people who will say we didn't care enough, but what is neglect? We used extreme measures to try to save Robyn – extreme Christian Science measures.'

This defence would be elaborated in court by the couple's lawyers led by Rikki Klieman. Ms Klieman would emphasize the legal and statutory aspects of her clients' rights, and attempt to dispel the emotionally charged atmosphere that must inevitably obscure the situation where a child is apparently left to die unnecessarily: 'The first and most important issue is whether the Constitution permits parents to be subject to criminal prosecution if there is a statute that explicitly allows for the care and treatment of a child through spiritual healing. The second issue is whether we will permit or tolerate the commonwealth to place itself in a very special relationship between a parent and a child, and to substitute its own judgement for the parents' judgement.'

From the 'other side' of the court it would be argued by observers like Wendy Mariner of the Boston University of Public Health: 'The issue of First Amendment rights for religious freedom does not extend to the freedom to endanger the life of someone else. You are allowed to believe anything you want, but you cannot allow your kids to die for the sake of your religion.'

And that, for most Americans at least, was what this trial would be about.

A Judicial Dilemma

When the trial opened in April 1990, the events leading up to Robyn Twitchell's death were presented to the jury as a pathetic chronology. On 5 April 1986, the Twitchells were aroused in the middle of the night by their son's evident pain and distress, though they had no clear idea at that time what the symptoms might indicate. The parents' automatic response was to pray, and, so David Twitchell testified, the child began to improve. Over the following four days and nights Robyn alternated between extreme discomfort and apparent recovery, indicating to the parents that their prayers were beginning to produce some beneficial result – that it was working so slowly and intermittently they took as a celestial criticism of their own weakness of prayer. Twitchell further testified that it was only on the first night that Robyn had been in what he would call 'severe' pain. On the second day of the child's illness, Ginger Twitchell called in the Practitioner, who began the process of 'healing' by prayer, which included praying with the child, with its parents, and in isolation. This treatment was reinforced by the assistance of the Christian Science Nurse, whose responsibility was to assist in the practical – though non-medical – comfort of the patient and family. Questioned as to whether at any time he considered the necessity of summoning medical help, David Twitchell insisted: 'We are not against calling medical doctors, it is just that what we have been taught and what I have experienced is that turning to prayer, turning to God, is a better, a more complete and more thorough healing solution of a problem than turning to other systems . . . If I didn't think prayer was the better solution, if I didn't think it was *safer* for my children and myself, I'd turn to medicine.'

Which was strange; because it would later be revealed that both David Twitchell and his wife had at various times sought conventional medical treatment for themselves, and had taken prescription drugs. David, for example, had visited a dentist and was given the pain-killer Novocaine; Ginger Twitchell received pain-deadening Xylocaine when giving birth to the very child to whom she later denied medical aid.

Nevertheless, when attorney Rikki Klieman presented her defence of the Twitchells, it was on the primary premise that her clients *truly believed* that their son was responding positively to healing by the power of prayer: 'These parents did not choose, or think, or consider about *martyring* their child, they didn't think about sacrificing their child, they did not think that one day they would meet their child in Heaven and therefore martyred their child. They loved their child. He was their son.'

According to Klieman, it was only on the very last day of his sickness that Robyn Twitchell took a 'dramatic turn for the worse', from which sadly he did not recover.

Quite predictably, this was to be at variance with prosecution evidence which quoted the pathologist's report that the child had been suffering from an abdominal 'twist', and although for the first few days the pain would have come and gone irregularly, at least during the last 36 hours of the child's life he would have been suffering severe cramps and frequent, if not continuous, vomiting of material that looked like faeces. In short, it could only have been, the medical experts advanced, the parents' blinding faith in the power of their own prayers that prevented them acknowledging the serious extent of their child's suffering; a total inability to recognize even the possibility of Robyn's death.

In presenting the state's case, special prosecutor John Kiernan laid emphasis on the fact that through the act of summoning the Practitioner and the Nurse, the Twitchells were acknowledging that Robyn's condition was more serious than they pretended: 'If your child is vomiting his own excrement, wouldn't you think that that child was at grave risk? If that child was screaming and clutching at his belly, isn't that child at grave risk; somebody who has not slept or eaten for five days, whose parents move into a small room to sleep next to him, obviously indicating a recognition that the child is seriously ill. Everything they did was an acknowledgement that the child was seriously ill . . . that child looked at the source of his care, his nutrition, his warmth, his love, his food, his shelter, his clothing, and he had a name for his god – and the name for his god was "mother and father"; and his mother and father abandoned him.'

Perhaps the most controversial aspect of the Twitchell trial was whether – according to the Massachusetts statute of 1971

– Christian Scientist families like David and Ginger Twitchell were exempt from prosecution. In a move for which she was subsequently severely criticized, Judge Sandra Hamlyn declined to instruct the jury on the matter, preferring instead to give her own interpretation of the law: 'The reliance on spiritual healing alone, in other words the exclusive reliance on spiritual healing alone, without medical care, may not be permitted under the circumstances the child was exposed to the risk of serious bodily injury or death.'

In effect this wholly incorrect interpretation of the statute *as it stood* left the jury little option but to find David Twitchell and his wife guilty as charged. The Twitchells, who faced a possible twenty years' imprisonment, were sentenced to ten years' probation, during which period their other three children were required to submit to regular medical examination.

It was only after conviction and sentence that members of the jury became aware through newspaper reports of the true wording of the Massachusetts law on which the defence had rested, and which was denied to the jury at the time of the trial. At least two very vociferous jury members – one their forewoman – made both public protests through the media and private representations to the judge, claiming that if they had been fully aware of the *legal* defence offered by the defendants then they would have declared them not guilty.

So what fundamental issues *were* at stake, and how, if at all, did the prosecution of David and Ginger Twitchell clarify those issues? Both sides of the case quite naturally invoke that bastion of the American Constitution, the First Amendment, which establishes the rights of freedom of speech, freedom of the press, and free exercise of religion. Their interpretations, equally naturally, were at strong variance.

The Christian Scientists and their supporters (including other unorthodox religions like the Jehovah's Witnesses) see a threat to the freedom of their religion by establishing a precedent that it is perfectly acceptable for a person to believe what he or she chooses, but not to practise it. For Rikki Klieman, the trial exhibited a clear example of religious persecution.

On the other hand, the message coming from the opposite camp – the state prosecutor's office – is that the First Amendment is alive and very much enriched by the trial and the verdict: 'It [the First Amendment] accommodates all our views . . . Our values are found there and our values include both the freedom to believe and the protection of our children . . . This is not restrictive on anybody's religion, it is just a restatement of the law, that you may believe as you wish, but when your child is at risk of death, you had better make sure you use all available means, including medical science, and prayer if you so wish.'

The Cult of Christ the Healer

The Church of Christ Scientist was founded in 1879 by Mary Baker Eddy, herself a life-long victim of frail health. It was in 1866 that Mary Eddy was walking in her native town of Lynn, just north of Boston, when she fell on an icy pavement and sustained serious internal injuries. It was while she was nursing herself through this illness, fortified by regular doses of biblical texts, that Mary Eddy devised the system of spiritual healing which, through her book *Science and Health with Key to the Scriptures*, became Christian Science.

It has grown to be a powerful organization with about 2600 churches in 68 countries worldwide. It publishes the prestigious *Christian Science Monitor*, with a circulation of 160,000, and also broadcasts its own television show. It nevertheless has a steadily declining membership with less than 150,000 in the United States, and a further 30–40,000 overseas; 120 Christian Science churches have closed in the past four years.

The most controversial of the Christian Scientists' beliefs are that people properly attuned to God's spirit are free from sin and disease. Although this is such a fundamental principle of the faith, it was not until the Twitchell case that the Church addressed itself to a systematic study of the efficacy of spiritual healing covering a multitude of physical complaints not commonly considered psychosomatic – from gangrene to glaucoma, from cancer to multiple sclerosis. The outcome of the research will, if it is positive, prove a powerful motivation to the continued reliance by the faithful upon the power of prayer alone over sickness.

ROASTED ALIVE!

The Case of Victor Castigador *et al*

It was, in many ways, a very uncharacteristic incident. The Chinese community in London is an old-established and well integrated one, and the overspill of crime from Chinatown to their hosts is negligible; what law-breaking exists within the range of the smell of five-spice powder is rarely overt.

So when two innocent security guards were burnt to death in the heart of Chinatown, it was no surprise that the press settled in to invoke the Westerners' worst prejudices against the Orient: 'Revenge of the Triads', roared one tabloid; 'Cowering victims of Terror Gang'. 'Cops Fear Flood of Chinky Mob: Triads Set to Invade London', warned another. And the attack so enraged one editor that he was constrained to demand: 'Hang These Monsters!'

The news broke on the morning of Tuesday, 4 April 1989. The approach varied between the two sections of the press: 'Roasted Alive in Pinball Alley' to the restrained 'Two Men Burnt Alive in West End Arcade', but the message was the same – something very nasty had happened in Chinatown.

The carnage was discovered at 7.55 on the morning of the 3rd, when staff of the Leisure Investments-owned amusement arcade on the corner of Gerrard Street and Wardour Street arrived for work and smelled burning and heard shouting from the basement of the building.

When police and firemen made their way to the subter-
ranean storeroom, they found four bodies lying on the floor.
As officers moved through the acrid smoke and smouldering
furnishings, it was clear that two of the victims were miraculously
alive, but so extensive was the fire damage to their bodies
that it was only afterwards, when they had been removed
to the burns unit at Queen Mary's Hospital, Roehampton,
for emergency surgery that one was identified as a woman.
This pair had been lucky. In the basement there remained
two more figures – burned beyond recognition and quite
dead.

As police scientists examined the scene of what was clearly a
murder of the kind the capital had rarely seen, the security system
installed at the arcade to provide 24-hour video surveillance was
telling the story of the beginning of the horror. It started as staff
were closing the premises in the early morning; Yurev Gomez,
the 25-year-old manager, and cashier Debbie Alvarez were
locking up and handing over to security guards Ambikaipahan
Apapayan and Kandiahkanapathy Vinayagamoorthy. As they
did so, the gang, who had earlier been posing as customers,
struck. Later testimony would complete the sequence of events
and would identify the killers as Victor Castigador, Calvin
Nelson and Paul Clinton; also along for the night's excitement
were their two girlfriends.

Castigador, armed with a plastic imitation gun, forced his four
hostages down into the basement strongroom where Mr Gomez
was ordered on pain of his life to open the safe. Then Gomez, Ms
Alvarez and the two security guards were tied up and locked in
a wire cage in the strongroom. Meanwhile, Castigador fetched a
bottle of white spirit from the adjacent store-room and poured it
over the captives while Nelson lit matches and flicked them into
the cage as the others watched.

'There was a ball of fire,' recalled Gomez. 'It was like an
oven. There was nowhere to go. I undid my hands and kicked
my way out of the cage. My skin was on fire, I could feel myself
disintegrating. I rolled on to the floor and the wall and put myself
out. I managed to get my mouth near the keyhole.' Thus Yurev
Gomez survived in agony for almost eight hours on the little
oxygen that could be sucked through his blistered mouth from
the outside.

Almost as unbelievable was the survival of Debbie Alvarez
who, with Gomez's help, managed to wriggle to the door and

lay, sustained by the small supply of air that filtered under it. Even so, both suffered terrible burns, in Yurev Gomez's case, 30%.[1]

The two Sri Lankan security guards fared far worse, being at the back of the cage, and succumbed to the most agonizing of deaths, sustaining dreadful burns before being asphyxiated by the smoke of their own burning flesh and clothing. Earlier in the attack, it was reported, one of the guards had pleaded with his captors to shoot him rather than burn him to death.

One Man's Vengeance

Given the location and circumstances of the attack, and despite immediate denials by the police, there was early speculation that the Triad gangs known to be operating in Chinatown had carried out a revenge attack. One unnamed source revealed that there had been confrontations between staff of the amusement arcade and Triad youths who had been tampering with the machines; this same source, a Chinese lawyer, added the chilling information that though the Triads' chosen weapon of assassination was the chopper, burning with petrol was common among Vietnamese gangsters. Besides, the present attack could not fail to remind the Chinese community of incidents in 1980 when two drinking clubs were fire-bombed and 37 people were burnt to death.

A shocked public did not need to wait long for its answers. Working on the perceptive theory that the robbers murdered their victims for fear of being identified, the police arrested, only days after the incident, a 34-year-old Filipino named Victor Castigador who was living in east London. On 7 April he appeared at Bow Street magistrates court charged with murder and attempted murder. Castigador (whose name, appropriately enough, translates from Spanish as 'The Enforcer') arrived in Britain from Manila in 1985, married an English woman and later worked as a security guard in the very amusement arcade

---

[1]In the classification of burn injuries, the extent of the burning is measured in percentages of the body's surface damaged. There is a broad gauge which divides the body: Head and Neck 9%; Arms 9% each; Trunk 18% front + 18% back; Legs 18% each. In a normal, healthy adult the loss of 70% of the body's surface is usually fatal.

where he committed robbery and murder. It was mainly due to his unpleasant and aggressive personality that Castigador was passed over for promotion; and when it was discovered that there was far less trouble in the arcade when he was not on duty, the small Filipino was given the sack. It was 31 March, two days before his murderous revenge. For the person who boasted that he had formerly been a hit-man for the late president Marcos in his native country, and had killed 'at least twenty people or more', his dismissal was an indignity not to be borne.

Within days of Castigador's arrest his accomplices were picked up and detained – 19-year-old Calvin Nelson and 17-year-old Paul Clinton, along with their two girlfriends.

At first all five defendants pleaded not guilty to the charges brought against them – of murder, attempted murder, and in the case of the two women, robbery (which Nelson and Clinton admitted). On the first day of their trial at the Old Bailey, 19 February 1990, Victor Castigador changed his plea to guilty, and sentence on him was deferred to the end of his accomplices' trial.

Jean Southworth QC, for the Crown, described Castigador as 'the main villain of the piece . . . he is a Filipino who obviously sees himself as a tough guy and frequently bragged to his friends of his earlier life in the Philippines where he said he had been in the commandos and the secret police'.

Even Castigador's own counsel, James Mulcahy, was obliged to admit to the judge: 'It would be very surprising if you had not come to the conclusion, having read the evidence and seen the witnesses, that Castigador was a ruthless, callous and inhuman monster.'

It was obviously a description which met with His Lordship's approval, for when the formality of conviction was complete, Mr Justice Rougier passed sentence on Victor Castigador using much the same terms of reference: 'I find it almost impossible to understand the workings of a mind as twisted and evil as yours. You condemned your victims to an agonizing death without one shred of pity or mercy. You have an uncontrollable murderous desire and you are a danger to everyone. You have forfeited the right to walk free. Some may say you have forfeited the right to live, but unlike you, we in this country do not go to those lengths.'

Castigador was sentenced to life imprisonment with Mr Justice

Rougier's recommendation that he should serve no less than 25 years.

As for the rest of the gang, Calvin Nelson was sentenced to life imprisonment in a young offenders' unit; Paul Clinton to be detained during Her Majesty's pleasure; and the two women were sentenced, one to three years' youth custody, the other to three and a half years' imprisonment, both for robbery.

As appalling as the crime had been, the residents of Chinatown had one consolation – at least it had not been the start of an open Triad war.

In the major cities of the United States, gang-wars among the Chinese are more firmly established, and few weeks pass without some new outbreak of frequently fatal violence.

The situation has been aggravated in recent years by the emergence of Vietnamese gangs, and typical of the feuds between the two Asian groups were the events of October 1990 on the streets of New York City.

It had really started the previous July, when a man believed to be the deputy leader of the Vietnamese gang calling themselves 'Born to Kill' was assassinated by a member of the rival Chinese 'Ghost Shadows'. Compounding the insult, a Chinese mob opened fire on mourners at the victim's funeral.

On 2 October, David Chiu, former member of the Ghost Shadows, was shot through the head on Manhattan's Reade Street in retaliation for the funeral incident. Two weeks later, at around 3 o'clock on the morning of 15 October, three men were shot dead at the back of a car park on Reade Street, only a few blocks from City Hall.

The victims were all in their twenties, and identified by documents in their pockets and by the tell-tale 'BTK' tattoos on their arms as members of Born to Kill. They had all been shot in the head and their bodies piled in a heap. The gang's members, mostly young Vietnamese-born immigrants, specialize in armed robbery and extortion characterized by extreme violence. The heavy interest shown by the police in their activities have caused a number of members to defect to the older-established Chinese gangs, causing bitterness and resulting in reprisals.

The Triads in Britain

Although the Gerrard Street arcade incident turned out to be free from the mark of Triad involvement, there is every reason to believe that over the next half decade or so the Chinese gangs will become increasingly territorial in Great Britain.

The main reason is that in 1997 Britain hands back control of the colony of Hong Kong to the Chinese, and the Triads, fearing the severity of Chinese Communist rule (and their tendency to large-scale executions of criminals), are already beginning to spread their activities at an accelerating rate to other major cities of the world.

In Britain, urgent confrontation of the problem is necessary if we are to avoid a repeat of the widespread problems in dealing with the Chinese mafia (thought to be the largest criminal organization in the world) that have so bedevilled countries like Australia in recent years.

Among the upwards of 150,000 Hong Kong Chinese that settle in Australia every year, it is inevitable that some Triad organizers will slip through despite the stringent immigration requirements. In 1988, from aboard the yacht *Zoe*, bound from Hong Kong to Australia, Sidney harbour authority officers seized heroin worth £22 million, the largest drugs haul in the country's history. Thirty people were arrested, all of whom were later proved to be connected to the Triad gangs that are believed responsible for 90% of the Australian heroin trade – itself the biggest single threat to the country's law and order policy.

The Australian experience is beginning to repeat itself within the Chinese communities in Britain, for it is traditionally among their own people that the Triads cause the most fear, and exert the greatest power and aggression. Businessmen fall prey to extortion rackets, ordinary citizens to the pressures of loan-sharking, and illegal gambling clubs, which are popular among Chinese communities like those in London's Soho and Manchester's Chinatown, and which are the focus of much Triad activity.

There are two main Triad gangs in Britain, one is the 'Sui Fong', the other 'Wo Sing Wo'; both originate in Hong Kong, with the Wo Sing Wo dominant in Manchester, Birmingham and Liverpool, and the Sui Fong in London and Southampton.

There is a perpetual battle for new territories, and both gangs are struggling for domination in Glasgow, Belfast, Nottingham, Bristol and Cardiff.

A third gang, the '14K', is active in London, Bristol and Liverpool, and the smaller 'San Wee On' and 'Wo On Lok' exist in London's Chinatown. However, all the gangs tend to import their 'muscle', their 'hit-men', from Hong Kong – members highly skilled in the martial arts and familiar with the brutal knife and chopper attacks which characterize Triad reprisals against rival gangs and against victims reluctant to submit to extortion.

Philip Wong was one such Glasgow businessman who was attacked by three men and 'chopped' to death with knives and cleavers in a vicious demonstration of the traditional Triad death by a 'Myriad of Swords'. Although the murder sent shockwaves through Glasgow's Chinese population, Mr Wong's killers remain at liberty – indeed, it is thought that at least two of them were Hong Kong professionals now back in the colony. It is not surprising that the fire in the Soho amusement arcade should initially have been linked with the London Triads, for only a year before this incident a video distribution business owned by a Soho Chinese (himself the recent victim of a knife attack) was broken into by seven men and the security guards employed to watch the premises were savagely beaten. This almost certainly *was* a Triad attack.

The most notorious of many Chinese secret societies, the Triad, or Hung Brotherhood, is today the largest and most powerful criminal organization in the world, with its headquarters in Hong Kong and well-structured gang hierarchies wherever the Chinese have settled overseas.

It is appropriate, perhaps, that the origins of the society are surrounded by mystery and uncertainty. Some say with confidence that it is as old as the fourth century AD. There is little doubt, however, that the Triad Society started life as a religious organization which subsequently embraced political ideals and later became almost entirely criminal.

One story relates how, at the dawn of the eighteenth century, the monks of Shoulin in Fukien province were accused of treason and their monastery razed to the ground by the Manchu army. At the time there were 108 resident monks, most of whom were killed. Survivors are variously given as eighteen and thirty-six. Whichever is the correct number, five of the survivors adopted the title Triad Society and arranged themselves into lodges in five provinces, pledging vengeance against the Manchus. They were notably active in the Taiping Rebellion of 1851 which all but destroyed the Manchu dynasty.

The name Triad derives from an anglicization of its alternative name 'Three in Harmony', a reference to the old Chinese belief that perfection will only be found when Heaven, Earth and Man are in harmony; the triangle is of great symbolic importance to the Society.

The Triad has flourished in Hong Kong, Singapore and Malaysia, where it was a powerful and frightening force among the immigrant labourers in 1925 when, due to internal disagreements, the Malaysian Triad split into five smaller factions known as the 18, 24, 36, 108 and Independent groups (names reflecting the historical numbers associated with the Shoulin origins). In Singapore, too, the secret societies have been an unhealthy influence since the beginning of the nineteenth century. In 1854, Chinese riots ravaged the Republic (then a British colony) for a week, resulting in more than 400 deaths; seven years later, the migrant miners in Larut began a series of bloody massacres that left thousands dead. By the end of the Second World War, Triad activity in the South China Sea was almost entirely devoted to organized criminal activities such as extortion, illegal gambling, prostitution and drug smuggling.

Little if anything remains of the original 'honourable' motivations of the Society, though some pale fragments of the original elaborate 'religious' initiation rituals survive for the purpose of instilling fear and loyalty into the hearts and minds of new recruits.

PROPHET OF DOOM

The Case of Jeffrey Lundgren

It stands there in the middle of the small community that grew around it and called itself Kirtland, in the mid-west state of Ohio. The slightly sinister gothic revival edifice known simply as the Temple was built in 1836 by Joseph Smith himself as a celebration of his recently founded Church of Jesus Christ of Latter-Day Saints – centrepiece of the Mormon colony. In 1860 the Church divided into the old Mormons and the new, more radical Reorganized Church of Latter Day Saints, with their administrative headquarters in Independence, Missouri. Joseph Smith was by then beyond caring – he and his brother Hyrum had been arrested for conspiracy in 1844 and while they were imprisoned in the local jail they were murdered by a lynch-mob. The Temple at Kirtland followed the Reorganized branch of the Church.

In 1986, Jeffrey Lundgren, a 35-year-old member from the mother church at Independence, was appointed as a guide to visitors to the Kirtland Temple, and with his wife Alice and their four children, Lundgren took over the small house provided by the church for his use. As a guide, Jeffrey Lundgren was by all accounts an unqualified disaster, so much of a disaster that in 1987, without much ceremony, he was kicked out of house and job and obliged to rent a modest farm on the edge of town.

Not, you may think, an entirely promising start for a self-

proclaimed prophet – for that is the way Lundgren had come
to see himself, a prophet like the great founder Joseph Smith
150 years before him. Surprising as it may seem in hindsight –
that is, with the certain knowledge that Lundgren is a multiple
murderer – the prophet, or 'Father', as he insisted on being
addressed, began to attract a steady stream of converts from the
Kirtland Temple, and in no time had turned the fifteen-acre farm
into his very own religious community. Although it was clear that
Lundgren was a persuasive dominator of a weak and simple flock
desperate for leadership, still the cult grew, and in the absence of
any direct or overt misdemeanour he and his commune were left
pretty much to their own devices by neighbours and townsfolk.
Among the dozen or so families that attached themselves to the
commune were Dennis and Cheryl Avery and their daughters
Trina, Rebecca and Karen, though they did not live on the
farm.

At the beginning of 1988, the official Reorganized Church of
Latter Day Saints set in motion the procedures by which this
poacher of their flock, this usurper, would be excommunicated,
and his lay ministry credentials revoked. It was about the same
time that Jeffrey Lundgren began to receive visions and hear
voices. There was to be a great earthquake, he revealed to his
awe-struck congregation; Divine Salvation would be with them
and with them alone if on 3 May (coincidentally Lundgren's
birthday) they were to break into the Kirtland Temple, expel
the 'infidels' and sit tight there to await the imminent return to
earth of Jesus Christ.

Such a crackpot scheme could not have hoped to remain secret
for very long, and before the Day of Judgement arrived the police
paid a visit to the Lundgrens and their followers to make it clear
that their every movement was under close surveillance.

Doom did not crack on 3 May, nor did the earth quake, and
Jeffrey Lundgren did not sack the Temple at Kirtland. Instead
he set about remodelling his community more into a troop of
warriors of the Lord than a flock of His sheep; at any rate they
began to stockpile an arsenal of weapons and undergo strict
training as a paramilitary force. They also began to drink quite
a lot.

As it happened, just prior to Jeffrey's birthday on 3 May 1989,
he had another revelation, the long and short of which was that
in order for the group to be cleansed in preparation for a 'journey
into the wilderness' lives must be sacrificed. On the night of 18

April, under the watchful eyes of the local police, the commune, their goods and chattels on their backs, left the farmhouse for the 'wilderness' – or at least for Missouri and Kansas City.

What they left behind were the sacrifices – Dennis and Cheryl Avery and their three children, aged thirteen, nine and seven years. They had been herded at gunpoint into the barn, blindfolded, gagged with packing tape, shot dead with a .45 calibre handgun and buried. Kirtland had not had a murder for a dozen years – now it had five.

It was not until 5 January 1990 that seven members of Jeffrey Lundgren's sect were taken into custody by Kansas City police – six were still fugitives as the group had split apart in the previous December over undisclosed 'sexual indiscretions'. The bodies of the Avery family had been unearthed only days previously.

Among the members at large were Jeffrey Lundgren and his wife, who were indicted along with eleven others by a Lake County grand jury on a variety of murder and conspiracy charges. Lundgren himself faced five counts of aggravated murder.

On Sunday, 7 January, agents of the Federal Bureau of Alcohol, Tobacco and Firearms, in collaboration with members of the San Diego Sheriff's Department, arrested Jeffrey Lundgren and his family at the Santa Fe Motel, in National City. Officers had been keeping the motel under surveillance since Saturday night to make sure the fugitives did not slip across the nearby border into Mexico. As well as Lundgren, Alice Lundgren and 19-year-old Damon Lundgren, who were placed under arrest, three younger children were taken into protective custody. Federal agents seized from the motel room an AR-15 assault rifle, three handguns, assorted knives and survival equipment; from a locker used by Lundgren, they removed three more handguns and a quantity of smokeless powder.

On 31 August 1990, a jury in the Lake County Common Pleas Court deliberated for three hours and fifteen minutes before returning verdicts of guilty on five counts of murder and five of kidnapping against Jeffrey Lundgren. Two days earlier the same court had convicted Lundgren's 19-year-old son Damon on four counts of murder and four of kidnapping. Mrs Alice Lundgren had already been sentenced to five consecutive life terms for the murders, which she had consistently blamed on her husband. She gave evidence during her trial that Lundgren had criticized the Avery family for their lack of zeal in pursuing the cult's beliefs and regretted that they might have to be disposed of.

At his sentencing trial on 21 September, 40-year-old Jeffrey
Lundgren showed no sign of emotion as Judge Martin O. Parks,
acting on the jury's recommendation, sentenced him to death.
The execution was scheduled to take place on 17 April 1991, but
mandatory appeals will delay the execution perhaps for many
years; besides, the state of Ohio has not executed anybody since
1963 – Lundgren will simply join the other 100 prisoners on Death
Row.

THE YAHWEHS
The Case of Yahweh Ben Yahweh

On 7 November 1990, Yahweh Ben Yahweh, who claims to have risen from the dead to be the Messiah to members of a black American tribe of Israel, was arrested along with twelve of his followers on Federal racketeering charges.

The 'lost tribe' which call themselves 'Yahwehs' face a huge 25-page indictment which includes fourteen killings and two attempted killings. Yahweh Ben Yahweh (born Hulton Mitchell, Jnr) gave himself up in Atlanta, while his deputy, Judith Israel, was picked up driving a group of the faithful to a meeting in Texas; other members of the sect were arrested around Miami. The cult claims to have thousands of followers waiting to be led out of the wilderness of white domination.

However, the sect is nothing if not businesslike, and since it opened its 'Temple of Love' in Miami a decade ago, the Yahwehs have accumulated businesses and real estate worth in excess of $9 million; in fact this extraordinary enterprise was rewarded recently by Miami's mayor declaring a 'Yahweh Ben Yahweh Day'.

The string of murders on the indictment include several members who disagreed too publicly with the sect's administration – one man was decapitated. Other cases resulted from an enthusiastic response to Yahweh Ben Yahweh's chilling instruction to his flock to 'kill me a white devil and bring me an ear!'

In one incident, acting on the Yahwehs' behalf, a former professional football player murdered two tenants in a housing complex who had refused to move out when the sect wanted to purchase it. It is in great part due to the testimony given by this repentant sportsman that other crimes came to light and charges were brought. A future *Update* will report on the trial of the Yahwehs, and any other developments within the Lost Tribe.

THE MULTICIDE

THE MAN WHO RETURNED
The Case of Arthur J. Shawcross

For ten weeks, cable television station WGRC was drawing huge audiences from its subscribers in homes in Rochester, a city of 241,000 souls in New York state, for one of the biggest attractions in recent years. Not a game show, not a chat show, no Hollywood celebrities here, but one of the longest, most expensive and most macabre trials in Monroe County's legal history.

From within the teak-panelled courtroom of the County Public Safety Building came talk more gruesome than any *Night Gallery* – talk of murder and mutilation, cannibalism and sexual abuse. Yet still the proceedings, either because of, or despite, the television coverage, often exuded an atmosphere of carnival. One newspaper reported the daily arrival of school trips of students, and regular courtgoers were baking cranberry bread for the prosecuting counsel. Nor were the jury unmoved by this atmosphere of jollity – on the day after Halloween they all wore identical bow ties, and at one sitting half of them wore Notre Dame football jerseys because the judge had expressed his support for that team the previous day. 'The jury has been attentive and able to keep their humour up,' commented Judge Wisner.

It might be said in mitigation that such apparently inappropriate behaviour frequently results from a sense of great relief such as that which swept almost tangibly through the Rochester area following an almost two-year reign of terror during which women's bodies were appearing regularly in the creeks and gorges around the Genesee river. It was in the first days of January that police had arrested 45-year-old Arthur J. Shawcross, school dropout, three-time divorcee and Vietnam veteran. He was currently married for the fourth time to Rosemary, a woman who had corresponded with him while he was in prison, but still with enough spare time and energy for a mistress, Clara, a full-time job as a food packer, and a passionate love of fishing. He also found time in this busy schedule, according to his own confession, to murder eleven women. Not that Arthur Shawcross was any stranger to murder; in 1972 he had confessed to strangling a ten-year-old boy and an eight-year-old girl in Waterstown and had served fifteen of a twenty five-year sentence.

4 January 1990, the start of a new year, and New York state police announced that they had detained a man (not immediately identified as Shawcross) in connection with the 'Rochester Killings'. In fact the police said little enough except that they were saying nothing. It was left to Rochester's TV station WOKR to break the news that 'a 45-year-old food service worker' had been arrested near the site of one of the killings. Already this week two more women's bodies had been found, and the suspect had confessed to ten murders while in custody.

On the following morning, police officials jubilantly announced that they had arrested Arthur J. Shawcross and that he had been accused of only eleven out of sixteen murders, which was consistent with detectives' claims that there were two killers at large in the area. At least they had reduced the number by 50%, so they had every reason to feel relieved.

It had, police elaborated, been a chain of circumstances arising from the two recent murders of 2 and 3 January that had led to the arrest. It had been around midday on the 3rd that state troopers on helicopter surveillance spotted a body on the ice of Salmon Creek under a bridge on Route 31 through Northampton Park. Sitting in a car on the bridge had been Arthur Shawcross, returning, it now appears, to the scene of his earlier crime. Alerted by the helicopter team, police patrol cars tailed Shawcross to the nearby nursing home where his wife worked and he was interviewed briefly.

The following day a hunter reported to police that he had found a body among some foundation rubble at the edge of

Northampton Park – prostitute Felicia Stephens was a missing person no longer. Again Shawcross was questioned, and this time he not only confessed to eleven murders, but gave directions to locations where two more victims – Maria Welch and Darlene Trippi, prostitutes like most of the other victims – were found buried in woodland near the towns of Greece and Clarkson. One of the women had been missing since the previous 6 November, the other since 15 December. The case was solved. But what of Arthur J. Shawcross?

Cookery and Fishing

After he had been paroled from Green Haven state prison in Duchess County on 30 April 1987, Arthur Shawcross had gone to live in a hostel at Binghampton. That is until the local newspaper got wind who he was and published his story front-page. Run out of town by angry residents, Shawcross moved on to Delhi, a town 40 miles west of Binghampton, where residents felt no more inclinded to make him welcome, and fearing an eventual confrontation, the police began, if not to 'lean' on him, then at least to make it clear to Arthur Shawcross that his movements would be very carefully monitored for any indication of transgression. 'We would,' said the local police chief, 'make sure he knew we were there.' Enduring this treatment for a month, Mr and Mrs Shawcross moved into an apartment on Rochester's Alexander Street, close to the centre of town. Here he seems to have blended into the anonymity of city life and took a regular job preparing food for a wholesaler who supplied hospitals and schools. In his spare time, Arthur Shawcross took up fishing and made a particular favourite spot of the banks along the Genesee River which flows through Rochester, and which would begin to attract a sinister reputation shortly after he moved to town. In all, seven bodies were going to be found along or near the river gorge over the next year or two; most were prostitutes working the area, most were either strangled or asphyxiated, and many – according to his confession – had ridiculed Arthur's sexual performance. One of the women was a friend of Mr and Mrs Shawcross – 58-year-old Dorothy Keller – who had committed no greater sin than to push Arthur Shawcross while they were swimming together in the Genesee. Her skeleton was later found on an island in the river gorge.

While the police were congratulating themselves and each other, Arthur Shawcross was appearing before Judge John M. Regan at the Municipal Court, arraigned on eight charges of murder; he pleaded not guilty and was returned to custody. Neighbouring Monroe County District Attorney, Howard Relin, announced that the three remaining murders committed outside Rochester city limits would later be put before grand juries in Monroe and Wayne Counties.[1]

Of the five remaining Rochester murders not claimed by Shawcross, a police spokesman said: 'They're considered co-incidental cases that occurred during the same time period. The investigation of them is continuing.'

In what was to prove the understatement of the year, Police Chief Gordon Urlacher gave as his opinion of Arthur Shawcross: 'It's very difficult to get inside the head of someone like this.'

While the self-confessed serial killer remained out of harm's way in Monroe County jail, this was a time for police, legal representatives and media to attempt that difficult task of getting into Arthur Shawcross's head. The picture they got from friends and neighbours in Rochester was that of a thoroughly nice man. He was quietly spoken and considerate, and if he was a little short-tempered, he was also more than generous with his time and with what little money he had. He was known to have befriended a number of his elderly neighbours, paying them small attentions and sometimes bringing modest gifts of chocolate or cigarettes; and on special occasions, pies and cookies that he had baked himself. And while he was cooking Christmas goodies and buying gifts for his many friends in those few weeks before his arrest, he was also murdering more prostitutes.

As a leading criminologist said of some serial killers: 'They are not glassy eyed lunatics. They have jobs, they have families, and they kill part-time as a hobby.'

Experts on the mentality of multicides found that Shawcross fitted neatly into one of several prototypes, and considered the warm, generous, charming personality by which he was known entirely consistent with the type of serial killer for whom this

[1]On 11 January, Shawcross was charged by the Wayne County grand jury with the murder of 29-year-old Elizabeth Gibson, whose body had been found in woods the previous 27 November.

gregariousness was a simple act, played without a shred of feeling: 'Underneath there's no affectional ties to anyone, no emotional pain, no sense of blame or of right or wrong, and no development of conscience.'

Multiple Personality, Multiple Killer

The trial of Arthur J. Shawcross opened in Rochester in the summer of 1990 before Judge Donald J. Wisner. The defendant pleaded not guilty by reason of insanity to the ten murders with which he was charged, namely: Dorothy Blackburn (aged 27), Anna Marie Steffen (28), Dorothy Keeler (59), Patricia Ives (25), Frances Brown (22), June Stott (29), Felicia Stevens (20), Maria Welch (22), Darlene Trippi (32) and June Cicero (54). For the eleventh killing he will later be tried in neighbouring Wayne County where the victim's body was found.

Despite Shawcross's confession, his lawyers claimed that he was suffering what they elaborately called 'multiple personality disorder, brain damage, and post-traumatic stress syndrome', and should not be held responsible for his actions.

Calling as an expert witness Dr Dorothy Otnow Lewis, the defence had her show the court a videotape taken of Shawcross, purportedly under hypnosis, dramatically reliving a scene from his childhood in which he claimed he had been sodomized by his mother with a broom handle. Almost as though he knew he would get a sympathetic audience, Shawcross then drifted first into one of his *alter egos*, a thirteenth-century English cannibal named Ariemes, who initially introduced him into the delights of eating human flesh, and then changing to a high-pitched female voice to become 'Bessie', who he claims guided him during his murderous attacks. Little wonder, perhaps, that the prosecution observed: 'This is not psychiatry, it is a performance!'

On 13 December 1990, Arthur J. Shawcross sat, apparently unmoved, as the Jury's foreman rejected on their behalf the prisoner's defence of insanity. As each of the ten victims' names was read out, the foreman responded: 'Guilty of murder in the second degree.'

Shawcross faces a possible 25 years to life on each of the convictions, though he will not be sentenced until 1991. In the same year he is also due to appear in Wayne County Court facing an additional charge of murder.

In one of the most curious postscripts to any case, Arthur Shawcross's defence attorneys asked the trial judge to declare a mistrial because their own leading witness, the controversial Dr Dorothy Otnow Lewis of New York University Medical Center, had 'sabotaged' their case. Dr Lewis, who had given lengthy evidence as to the defendant's sanity, had reportedly caused the court to break into laughter several times. Her rambling answers and her seeming inability to locate important documents among her large untidy pile of papers had been widely noted by the media. It was also revealed that Dr Lewis herself had in turn sent a note to the judge during her testimony complaining that she was not getting full co-operation from the very lawyers who were employing her skills.

Nevertheless, whatever the rights and wrongs of the legal/medical wrangle, Dr Lewis's performance on the witness stand was described by one juror reported in the *Rochester Times Union*: 'If she could have kept her feet on the floor instead of in her mouth, she would have been OK. The more she talked the worse it got; it's just too bad she didn't leave after she read her qualifications.'

The professor's own view of her testimony was that 'I refused to just answer yes or no. I tried to say "wait, this is more complicated; this is what is wrong with this man". But the questions were yes or no.'

A poetic final word on the subject was offered by Monroe County's First District Attorney when he observed: 'What happened to Dr Lewis sometimes happens to witnesses: witnesses sometimes self-destruct on the stand.'

But it was not all carnival time and good-humoured banter for the state authorities. Already the Parole Board, whose decision it was to release Arthur Shawcross, was coming under scrutiny, and one District Attorney was reported confessing: 'Every prosecutor in New York State can recount three or four horror stories about people who should never have been paroled and were.' Also in the firing line were parole officials who were overseeing Arthur Shawcross; it emerged that they had on a number of occasions casually raised his name as a possible suspect for the Rochester Killings, but quickly dismissed them because he seemed to be integrating well, and besides, Arthur rode a bicycle while most of the murdered prostitutes were picked up in a car. Nobody bothered with the fact that Shawcross had a well-known habit of borrowing cars from whoever would lend him one. Nobody bothered when one of the dead women was seen just before she disappeared walking with a man pushing a bicycle.

But it is easy to see fault in hindsight, and there really was no reason why parole officials, mental health consellors who were meeting with him regularly, or the police should have been alarmed by anything in Arthur J. Shawcross's modest lifestyle.

But that, surely, is a lifestyle shared by many multiple killers.

Stop Press

It was on 1 February 1991 that Arthur Shawcross was sentenced to ten consecutive terms of 25 years imprisonment. Gallantly, having put the state to great expense already, Shawcross pleaded guilty to the eleventh murder – that of Elizabeth Gibson – thus saving Wayne County the cost of his trial.

MURDER UPDATES

THE LONG MEMORY OF THE LAW
The Case of David Lashley

Thirteen years to the month after 24-year-old Australian heiress Janie Shepherd was murdered, her killer was led through watertight security into the dock of St Albans Crown Court in the county of Hertfordshire. For the police it was the culmination of an inquiry that had seemed insoluble; for Janie's parents it was the final act of a nightmare they thought would never end.

Statistically, Janie Shepherd was very unlikely ever to have become involved in murder, least of all be its victim. She was the step-daughter of British Petroleum's Australian Chairman, John Darling, had left the family home in Sydney for England in 1971, and was living with her cousin Camilla and her husband Alistair Sampson in a luxury apartment in Clifton Hill in the St John's Wood district of north-west London. Like many girls born into the wealthy middle-class, Janie was in receipt of a generous allowance from her father, and had chosen to work despite the lack of need. And like many girls who choose rather than need to work, she found herself involved in the cultured atmosphere of the small commercial art gallery. In Janie's case it was the Caelt Gallery, a specialist in modern unknowns with premises in London's Westbourne Grove.

When she left the gallery on the evening of Friday, 4 February 1977, Janie drove straight back to the flat in St John's Wood, changed quickly, threw a few 'essentials' into her red shoulder bag and by 8.40 was back behind the wheel of her dark blue Mini-Cooper. She had planned to spend the weekend with her boyfriend Roddy Kinkead-Weekes. The couple had met eighteen months previously in the autumn of 1975, and had since become almost inseparable, 'perfectly suited', it was said, Kinkead-Weekes complementing Janie's good breeding with his own Eton-educated, merchant banking background. He had telephoned the gallery earlier that evening and suggested they spend a quiet evening together at his flat in Lennox Gardens, Chelsea. She offered to pick up a snack on the way over and stopped in at the Europa Supermarket in Queensway, where she bought smoked trout, tomatoes and chicory, and yoghurt.

When Janie failed to arrive by 9.30 pm after her three-mile journey, Kinkead-Weekes checked with her cousin that she had left home. He rang again at 10.00 and at regular intervals until midnight. Then Roddy Kinkead-Weekes, Camilla and Alistair Sampson rang around the local hospitals to see if Janie had met with an accident. All the replies they received were comfortingly negative, but even so Janie had to be *somewhere*, and with increasing alarm both the Sampsons and Kinkead-Weekes reported her missing to their respective local police stations.

At 3.15 am on Saturday, 5 February, Janie Shepherd became an 'official' missing person, and her description and that of her car were prepared and circulated. Janie would never again be seen alive, and it would be ten weeks before her decomposing body was found by two schoolboys on a patch of open land in Hertfordshire.

The blue Mini, registration number KGM 300P, was easier to find. Just four days after her disappearance Janie Shepherd's car was found spattered with mud and with a collection of parking tickets under the windscreen wiper on a yellow line in Elgin Crescent, Notting Hill. The parking tickets dated back to the morning of 7 February, but witnesses were found who would testify to seeing the car parked there as early as 1.10 am on Saturday the 5th – even before its owner had been reported missing.

The state of the car left police with little optimism for Janie's safety; it was clear that a fierce struggle had taken place in the vehicle which resulted in two deep slashes in the soft sun-roof. The girl's boots had been left in the car, as had the red satchel bag, without its usual contents, but with two recent till receipts: one was for the groceries bought on the evening of the 4th at the Europa foodstore, the other from a petrol station near the supermarket where Janie had topped up the seven-gallon fuel tank of her car. Given the amount of petrol left in the tank, police scientists estimated that the car would have been driven on a roughly 75 mile round trip. That the journey had been through muddy countryside was obvious from the state of the tyres and bodywork, but exactly where within that 45 mile radius around Notting Hill was anybody's guess, and would traverse a possible four counties.

By this time Detective Chief Inspector Roger Lewis, head of CID at St John's Wood police station, was convinced that his local missing person inquiry – which, given the girl's background, could have been a kidnap for ransom – was now a national murder hunt. As a consequence, it was entrusted to Detective Chief Superintendent Henry Mooney of Scotland Yard's Murder Squad to coordinate the police operation covering three forces – the Met, Hertfordshire and Thames Valley.

Mooney was certainly no stranger to murder; with twenty years experience in the force he had been notably responsible, alongside Inspector Leonard Read, for the arrest and conviction of east London gangsters Ronnie and Reggie Kray for the murders of George Cornell and Jack 'The Hat' McVitie. Only this time Henry Mooney was working with a big handicap – he had a full-scale murder investigation under way, but no corpse.

The Missing Body

The hunt for Janie Shepherd was relentless. Police helicopter teams made aerial searches over the area that might have been covered by the car, and for the very first time in a British murder inquiry dogs trained to sniff out dead bodies were used in the ground search. The customary 'Appeal for Assistance' posters were distributed, asking the general public for sightings of Janie or her car, while the press carried descriptions and photographs of models in similar clothing to that worn by her when she disappeared.

Meanwhile, on 9 February, Janie's mother and step-father arrived in England and set about their own personal search of the fields and hedgerows, woods and lanes in locations that were consistent with forensic matches of the mud on the recovered Mini. In addition, more than 50 officers under the direction of DCI Roger Lewis were engaged in similar intensive routine searches.

Back at Scotland Yard, DCS Mooney had begun the painstaking task of searching records at the Yard and at Notting Hill police station for similar offences against women, and discovered that in July 1976 a young woman had been raped in her own car less than half a mile from where Janie Shepherd's Mini had been abandoned in Elgin Crescent. The woman was parked outside her flat in Chesterton Street when a man came up to her and asked the time. As she glanced down at her watch he opened the car door and forced her at knife point into the passenger seat and drove to an isolated spot where he raped his captive twice, tried to strangle her and then, before jumping out of the car, slashed one of her wrists with the knife. Miraculously, the woman survived her ordeal to give a description of her assailant and to help construct an Identikit portrait of a black man with a noticeable scar on his face. Although police routinely searched their files for possible suspects, they dismissed the most likely one because his record made no mention of a scar. The man's name was David Lashley, a van driver who in 1970 had been convicted of a series of five rapes of young women in cars, and sentenced to twelve years' imprisonment. At the time of the Chesterton Street offence, Lashley had recently been released on parole.

If his predecessors had overlooked the obvious connection, it did not escape Henry Mooney, and on 17 February 1977, Lashley was picked up at his current address in Southall, north London, and taken in for questioning on the Chesterton Street rape and the disappearance of Janie Shepherd. At an identity parade 'Miss A', the Chesterton Street victim, positively identified David Lashley as her attacker – he had the distinctive scar on his cheek. According to Mooney – though Lashley has consistently denied it – the prisoner confessed to the attack on Miss A; Mooney was equally certain that Lashley had abducted and murdered Janie Shepherd. However, no amount of forensic investigation could link Lashley with Janie's car, and despite their continued search, Roger Lewis's team had not produced a body.

It was not until 18 April, Easter Monday, that Janie Shepherd's rustic grave was discovered – and then not by police searchers, but by ten-year-old Neil Gardner and eleven-year-old Dean James, two schoolfriends who were out cycling on the common known as Nomansland, near Wheathampstead in Hertfordshire. The lads had found what they at first thought was a bundle of rags nestling in a hollow not 50 yards off the B651 road from Wheathampstead to St Albans.

The Case Collapses

It was then that an extraordinary piece of police procedure – now thankfully obsolete – robbed Henry Mooney of the case which he had so meticulously, so single-mindedly, pursued for the past two months. Until a change of law in 1984, it was a Home Office requirement that a murder investigation became the responsibility of the force in whose jurisdiction a body is found. So the case of Janie Shepherd was given to Hertfordshire's Detective Chief Superintendent Ronald Harvey. Whether the outcome would have been more successful, more quickly, if Mooney had been given the corpse is arguable. As it was, the work done by Scotland Yard had, in effect, to be repeated by officers from the Herts force – statements rechecked, witnesses reinterviewed, evidence reviewed, and so endlessly on. On top of this, David Lashley, incarcerated in Brixton Prison awaiting trial on a charge of attempting to murder Miss A, was exercising his right to refuse to speak to officers investigating any other crime.

As soon as the body had been found and preliminary on-site examination and photography carried out, the sad remains of Janie Shepherd were removed to the St Albans mortuary for forensic post-mortem. In charge of the medical examination was pathologist Professor James Malcolm Cameron, an illustrious (though sometimes controversial) recipient of the legacy of British forensic brilliance that has been handed down through Sir Bernard Spilsbury, John Glaister, Francis Camps and Keith Simpson. At the time, Cameron was Professor of Forensic Medicine at the London Hospital Medical School and consultant to the Home Office. Like Henry Mooney, Professor Cameron had played his part in helping to smash the protection gangs of the 1960s, and was engaged on the medical investigation into the gangland shooting organized by the Kray twins against two of south London's most notorious gangsters, the brothers Charlie and Eddie Richardson, at Mr Smith's Club in Catford.

The body of Janie Shepherd was fully clothed in her jeans and striped socks (the boots she had been wearing when she left home were found abandoned in her car), and a black sweater with bright green cuffs and a scarlet neck. This last fact was remarkable since Janie was last seen wearing a shirt, polo-necked jumper and patterned cardigan – the black and coloured sweater had been taken along as a change of clothing for the weekend. Beneath the clothing Cameron found a ligature around the left ankle and a mark on the right that indicated the feet had been bound; there were also ligatures on the upper arms. Extensive bruising on the upper part of the body suggested that Janie had put up a courageous fight for her life. Cause of death was established as asphyxia on account of congestion of the heart and lungs, and Professor Cameron gave his opinion that Janie Shepherd had died from 'compression of the neck'. The extent of putrefaction of the body made it impossible to confirm that the victim had been sexually assaulted.

Since a post-mortem examination is conducted as much for the purpose of establishing identity as to determine time and cause of death, Cameron was joined by Bernard Sims, a forensic dentist experienced in the identification of badly mutilated human remains by means of dental features. Using a post-mortem dental chart and comparing it with that kept by Janie Shepherd's dentist of treatment carried out over the years, Sims was able to prove – almost like a fingerprint – the uniqueness of the victim's teeth.

On 22 April, almost three months after she had been reported missing, a coroner's inquest was held into the death of Janie Shepherd. But this was by no means the end of the matter; coroner Dr Arnold Mendoza formally opened and then immediately adjourned the hearing, anticipating further information. By 24 October the police were in no better position to offer the coroner's jury any concrete evidence at all. Despite the six-month-long inquiry nothing could be added to Professor Cameron's autopsy report or to the previous police statements. Still Janie Shepherd's killer remained unidentified. The inquest jury returned the only verdict they could, that of murder 'by person or persons unknown'.

The case file, it seemed, was all but closed, and the police officers actively pursuing the murder drastically reduced. In December 1977, David Lashley was sentenced to fifteen years' imprisonment for the attempted murder of Miss A. About Janie Shepherd he would say nothing. Nothing to the police, that is. When he did decide to talk it was by way of an arrogant boast.

In the end it was not Detective Chief Superintendent Mooney (who had retired, on schedule, in June 1987), nor his successor

Detective Chief Superintendent Harvey (who became Commander of Scotland Yard's Serious Crimes Squad before the Shepherd case was over); it was not Inspector Roger Lewis and his seemingly inexhaustible team of investigating officers – as willing to wade ankle-deep in icy mud as to pound the streets on house-to-house inquiries. Nor was it the collection of almost 1000 witness statements. It was a man unknown, but for his criminal activities, who finalized the case of Janie Shepherd. His name was Daniel Reece – not his real name as it turned out, but the one which he had been given along with a new identity after giving evidence as a 'supergrass' in an armed robbery case and putting his safety at risk. His own crimes included a thirteen-year sentence for rape and buggery.

Confession and Conviction

For reasons never adequately explained, the Shepherd/Lashley inquiry was rejuvenated in July 1988, when Detective Superintendent Ian Whinnett of the Hertfordshire force assembled a team of seven officers to reassess the evidence and make further inquiries. It is possible that the imminent release of David Lashley – in February 1989 – led senior police officers to make every attempt to keep the man with an undisguised hatred of women and policemen, and who had spent the whole of his eleven-year term as a Category A (dangerous) prisoner, on the inside for as long as possible.

Whatever the reason may have been, it meant once again going through the statements, tracing witnesses for requestioning, and all the tedious paper-work involved in reopening an investigation. It was also part of Ian Whinnett's job to receive and analyze reports from prison staff about the behaviour and demeanour of David Lashley.

It was at this stage that the police are believed to have become aware of David Reece's claim that Lashley had confessed to the Shepherd murder. Both Lashley and Reece had been fanatical body-builders while in Frankland Prison, and spent much of their free time weight-lifting in the prison gymnasium. This and perhaps their mutual commitment to rape and violence threw the two men as close together as such bizarre personalities ever can be. Lashley, according to his confidante, had boasted of grabbing a 'nice-looking blonde' in her Mini car (he even recalled the 'For

Sale' notice that Janie Shepherd had recently stuck on her rear window), threatening her with a knife, and slashing the sun-roof to show that he meant business. Then Lashley drove her to a secluded part of Ladbroke Grove where the rape and murder took place. At this point Lashley began to reveal details that could only have been known to the police and the killer; Lashley demonstrated to Reece, for example, exactly how he had killed Janie – holding her neck in one hand and pressing the fist of his other into her windpipe – as Professor Cameron had observed, she died of a 'crushed throat'. Another detail that had puzzled the earlier investigation was why Janie Shepherd's body had been found dressed in her *spare* set of clothes. This Lashley obligingly explained, saying he had slashed the clothing she was wearing with the knife, and had needed to redress the body in order to drive it out of town, strapped into the passenger's seat, to where it was dumped. In as fine an example of the pot calling the kettle black as it is possible to imagine, Daniel Reece decided that Lashley was a menace to womankind and too dangerous to be released! Hence his brief moment of good citizenship in reporting Lashley's conversation to the prison authorities – and without Reece's testimony in court it is very unlikely that the police, new enquiry or not, would have been able to make out a watertight case against David Lashley for the murder of Janie Shepherd.

At 7 o'clock on the morning of 17 February 1989, David Lashley was released from Frankland Prison. He was a free man for just half a minute before Detective Superintendent Whinnett and Detective-Constable Mick Farenden placed him under arrest charged with the Shepherd murder, and escorted him in a waiting security van to St Albans police station. By the time Lashley had worked his way through the obligatory magistrates' hearings and their consequent remands in custody, others of Lashley's fellow-prisoners had begun to tell tales; tales of his confessions to killing a woman in a car and dumping her body in some woods. One of them was Robert Hodgson, who had shared a cell in Wakefield Prison with Lashley; Hodgson was later to give evidence at his cell-mate's trial.

Thirteen years to the month after Janie Shepherd left her home in London, never to return, her killer was finally brought face to face with justice. On Tuesday, 7 February 1990, David Lashley stood in the dock of St Albans Crown Court; he pleaded not guilty to murder. Also in the court, for this final episode of their waking nightmare, were Janie's parents, recently arrived from Australia.

As chief witness for the prosecution, Daniel Reece was given the opportunity to recount in public Lashley's gaoltime confession. It all began, he said: 'In the middle of 1987; he [Lashley] was reading an article about a man who was sent to prison for life for rape. He was furious, he said the man should have killed the woman because he could not have been given a longer sentence. He said the man should have killed the girl like he killed Janie Shepherd.' Reece continued: 'He said there was a "For Sale" notice in the window of the Mini; he said he used this as an excuse to talk to Janie . . . [Lashley] said to me he ripped Janie Shepherd's clothes from her. He made her talk to him and made her say she was enjoying what he was doing. He said he was choking Janie Shepherd as he was raping her. He put one hand behind the back of her neck and put his fist on her windpipe. He said she was choking and he crushed her throat.' Later, according to Reece, Lashley described putting the sweater from Janie's bag on her dead body and strapping it into the passenger seat of the car: 'He thought it was funny because when he went round a corner or a bend in the road, the body would sway from side to side.'

As a final piece of hard fact, the prosecution was able to introduce a piece of forensic evidence impossible to imagine when Lashley first came to the notice of the Shepherd inquiry team. In the rear of Janie's abandoned car, scene-of-crime experts had found a semen stain. In 1977, technology had not advanced to the level of being able to make identifications from these body fluids, but the sample had been kept. The intervening years had seen the development of DNA profiling – the genetic analysis of body secretions – and from the stored sample it was now possible to identify the source as an A-secretor. David Lashley was an A-secretor.

In Lashley's defence, Ms Helen Gringrod QC told the court that her client pleaded not guilty to the charge of murder on the basis of an alibi. She stated that the defendant was in Leicester with a girlfriend during the day of the Shepherd abduction, and had returned to his aunt's house, where he lived, at around 7.00 pm; he spent the evening watching television and went to bed complaining of feeling unwell at 9.30. Mrs Eurtha Smith confirmed her nephew's story under oath.

After a three-week-long trial, the jury retired to consider their verdict on Monday, 19 March, 1990. After two hours and fifteen minutes they returned with an unanimous verdict of Guilty. Amid cheers of delight that the court usher had difficulty subduing, Mr Justice Alliot, the trial judge, began to address the prisoner, and in sentencing Lashley to life imprisonment, remarked: 'In my view you are such an appalling, dangerous man that the real issue is whether the authorities can ever allow you your liberty in your natural lifetime . . . The decision is such that whoever is responsible must have careful regard before you are allowed your liberty again.'

David Lashley is confined in a British prison which has not been named to ensure his personal safety.

HEROES AND VILLAINS
The Case of Ronald and Reginald Kray

There can be few people who have not heard of Ronnie and
Reggie Kray, the terrible twins who stepped out of London's
East-End gangland and into a nation's mythology via two
gruesome murders and a police investigation led by the legendary
Detective Inspector Leonard 'Nipper' Read.

Notorious for their activities during the 1950s and 1960s, the
Krays were finally arrested on 8 May 1968. They had made a
very lucrative business out of 'protection' which, on account of
their naturally aggressive personalities, was administered with
extreme violence. But these were the minor indictments against
Ronnie and Reggie when they appeared for their Old Bailey trial.
Heading the charge sheet were the murders of George Cornell
(an adherent of the rival Richardson gang who was shot through
the head in the Blind Beggar public house in March 1966) and
Jack 'The Hat' McVitie (stabbed to death in October 1967).
There was also the matter of the disappearance of escaped
convict Frank Mitchell (known as 'The Mad Axeman') whom
the Krays had sprung from Dartmoor in 1966.

Police had been hampered throughout their investigation into
the gang's activities by the blanket of fear that the twins seem
to have cast over the East End. For years the tenacity of
investigating officers had been hampered by a conspiracy of
silence. Once the brothers and their heavies had been placed

in custody, however, people began to come forward with information. Even members of the Krays' own gang were exchanging evidence for immunity from prosecution.

After a trial lasting 61 days (then the longest trial in British legal history), during which the disclosed catalogue of crime and violence beggared imagination, Ronald Kray was sentenced to two life terms for murder, his brother Reginald to life for one murder and ten years as an accessory to the other; the judge's recommendation was that they both serve not less than 30 years. Other members of the gang, including brother Charlie Kray, were sentenced to various terms of imprisonment.

After the trial the twins were separated for the first time in their lives – Ronnie was confined to Durham jail, Reggie to Parkhurst on the Isle of Wight. In 1972 they were briefly reunited at Parkhurst before Ron's increasing mental problems necessitated his transfer to Broadmoor. As for Reg, he has been shuffled around the prison system, serving time at Brixton (on remand), Wandsworth, Parkhurst, Gartree, Lewes and Nottingham.

That, however, was not the end of the Krays, or of the legends into which they have grown, for since their conviction in 1968 hardly a year goes by – sometimes, it seems, hardly a month – without some new story emerging in the popular press. When Mr Justice Melford Stevenson told the twins in sentencing: 'I think society deserves a rest from your activities', he could not have been more wrong. Society has been lapping it up.

Part of the reason for this clearly lies in the perceived personalities of the Krays themselves, and there is a tendency to consign to history the twins' more gruesome activities in favour of their bizarre sense of humour. Ronald, for example, who was always fond of snakes, named their two pet pythons 'Nipper' and 'Gerrard' after Inspector Read and his partner on the Kray investigation, Detective Chief Superintendent Frederick Gerrard. In the end, as we know, the Yard had the last laugh – but you cannot keep a good joke down.

Any more than one could remain unaware of the almost childlike, but obviously genuine desire of the twins to be popular. Their clubs became open houses for a galaxy of established and rising show business stars – Barbara Windsor, Diana Dors and her husband Alan Lake, Judy Garland, Barbra Streisand, Lita Roza, George Sewell, Victor Spinetti, George Raft, Sophie Tucker and Winifred Atwell, among others; and sports personalities like the boxers Freddie Mills, Billy Walker

and Sonny Liston. Then there was all the time unstintingly
given in support of various London charities, particularly youth
clubs – an interest which both Ron and Reg still maintain,
frequently sending examples of their paintings to be sold at
charity auctions.

In short, Ronnie and Reggie Kray have become, in the popular
imagination, caricatures of gangsters, and rather as Hollywood
has fictionalized its hoodlums like Al Capone, Pretty Boy Floyd
and John Dillinger, the sanitized image that has emerged is of
the 'loveable rogues', the 'rough diamonds'. But if Ron and Reg
have become caricatures of themselves, it was not without a lot of
help from the world of entertainment. In the past couple of years
alone, two talented contemporary comedians – Norman Hale
and Gareth Pace – have developed a highly popular act based on
two sinister, dinner-suited toughs called 'The Two Rons'; and the
award-winning *Spitting Image* team has created a series of strange
anthropomorphic creatures, including two menacing black birds
named Ron and Reg Crow.

Publicity and Parole

Recently, the situation has become rather more serious. It has
been felt for some years that, despite the obvious gravity of
the Krays' offences, their sentences have become a little out
of proportion by comparison with contemporary sentencing
practice. The circumstances have been complicated by Ronald's
continuing poor mental health, and it may be that this will
preclude the possibility of his release in the near future. Reggie,
however, looks forward optimistically to a comparatively early
release, and the popular press (whose polls among their readers
show firmly in favour of his freedom) have been fuelling
speculation for the past eighteen months.

The hype really began in the latter months of 1989. The
twins, at Reg's suggestion, took on an organization which called
itself Progress Management and announced itself as acting as
'Publicity Agents for the Kray Twins and Peter Gillett'. (Gillett
is a singer and former cell-mate and close friend of Reggie Kray.)
It is from Progress's Crawley, Sussex, headquarters that the Free
Reggie Kray Campaign has been masterminded.

The campaign's activities, announced Progress Management
chief Nicky Treeby, would include concerts, sponsored runs and

intensive petitioning of Downing Street on his client's behalf. To mark the launch of the campaign, and to help with necessary finances, a new portrait of the twins had been painted by artist Paul Lake, and prints of it, signed by Ron and Reg, were sold at £199 each.

Ironically, David Bailey's 1960s sequence of photographs of the Krays have long been regarded as fine examples of portrait photography, and a family group comprising Ronald, Reginald and brother Charles was included in the major exhibition 'The Art of Photography' at the end of 1989. It gave spectators the eerie experience of seeing three of London's best known hard-men gazing down from the walls of the capital's Royal Academy of Art.

It was at this time that Reggie Kray himself started talking about his plans for the future and of a life without prison walls. Although his recommended sentence was 30 years, it is the customary practice to review sentences with a view to recommending release on licence (see Appendix 2), and there is a strong likelihood that when the Parole Board eventually sits on the case of Reggie Kray it will make a favourable suggestion to the Home Secretary. As Reg pointed out: 'With the exception of Harry Roberts who killed three policemen [in 1966], my seventeen years as a Category A [dangerous] prisoner is a record in English penal establishments.'

At the same time details were announced of Ronald's imminent marriage to a young woman named Kate Howard, and on 6 November the couple wed in Broadmoor. One newspaper reported Kate saying: 'It feels great to be Mrs Kray . . . and Ronnie said he felt brilliant.'

But 1990 was to develop into more than the year of Ronnie's romance. It was the year in which the brothers Kray were to be immortalized on film, and that film – *The Krays* – would go on to win the *Evening Standard* newspaper's award for the best film of the year.

Already, in 1988, the twins (with a little help from veteran journalist and television presenter Fred Dinenage) had put together their version of the events of the Fifties and Sixties in the autobiographical *Our Story*.[1] The book became, unsurprisingly,

---

[1]*Our Story*, Ron and Reg Kray with Fred Dinenage. Sidgwick and Jackson, London, 1988.

a huge best-seller and was republished in paperback. The following year the abridged text was put on to audio cassette [2]with the brothers' parts being read by Roger Blake and Jim McManus.

Now it was the turn of a new face on the scene, writer and artist Philip Ridley (who had the advantage at least to hail from Stepney, even if he was only seven years old when the Krays were put on trial). Whatever the merit of the final script (and there was intensely felt opinion both for and against), Ron and Reg Kray were well enough served by the two young men chosen to depict them – the twins Gary and Martin Kemp (Ron and Reg respectively) – better known until then as members of Spandau Ballet, a rock band who emerged around 1983 and enjoyed such hit records as 'True' and 'Gold'.

The film was lightly sprinkled with mindless violence – albeit stylishly portrayed – but then, so were the lives of its subjects, and thus it was no more than anybody should have expected. The question on everybody's lips then, as now, is whether the film tended to glamourize that violence – in other words, were the twins being further elevated in their cult status? In the main, and this is simply a personal opinion, it neither did nor did not. Those for whom the Krays were already anti-heroes had their opinion reinforced; those who considered Ronnie and Reggie to be a couple of dangerous thugs had their worst prejudices confirmed as well.

What was never in doubt was the high quality of the film-making, and a nostalgic attention to details of Fifties and Sixties life and artefacts. Less certain is the writer's deliberately vague use of facts and chronology – not least that the two murders central to the Kray gang's downfall are portrayed as occurring on the same night, when in reality they were separated by almost eighteen months.

Meanwhile the news press – and not only the tub-thumping tabloids – were asking about the large sum of money that the Kray brothers were reportedly making from the film that bore their name (some mentioned £255,000). This book is not the correct place to enter into a debate on the rights and wrongs of 'cheque book cinema', but it does conveniently lead us back

[2]*Our Story*, Ron and Reg Kray with Fred Dinenage. EMI 'Listen For Pleasure', 1989.

to Mr Nicky Treeby, Progress Management and the possibility of release for Reggie Kray. For following in the wake of the alleged payment for the film came news from Reggie's agent that a television company had offered, according to one newspaper, the sum of £500,000 for Kray's first interview on his release.

Reginald Kray's Parole Board is due to sit in the spring of 1991,[3] and in common humanity it must be hoped that he receives a sympathetic hearing. Over the years there have been several bogus justifications for his release (among which the most spurious is that 'We never hurt any members of the public, it was always our own kind', which ignores the Kray gang's contribution to the general atmosphere of fear and violence on the capital's streets), but the reality is that the law must by now have revenged itself for the years of frustration when it seemed that nothing would stop these two leery lads from Stepney laughing in the face of authority. By now, as John Pearson suggests in his *The Profession of Violence*, 'Reggie's menace is confined to history.'

We are unlikely to have heard the last of the Kray twins, but perhaps we can share Reggie's hope that the next time the newspapers have a story to lead it will be under the headline 'Reg Kray Free After 23 Years'.

[3]See Appendix 2 for a note on 'Life Sentence and Release on Licence.'

IN THE BELLY OF THE BEAST
The Case of Jack Henry Abbott

When Jack Abbott first came to the attention of American author Norman Mailer, he was 37 years old. Of those 37 years, he had spent more than 21 in prison – 14 in solitary confinement. In 1966 he stabbed a fellow-prisoner to death and was sentenced to an additional 14 years. During this time Abbott engrossed himself in an intensive programme of self-education, becoming familiar with most of the major branches of philosophy, in the end specializing in Marxism. Mailer was at this time engaged on writing *The Executioner's Song*, an analysis of the life and crimes of convicted double-murderer Mark Gary Gilmore. When Abbott learned of the Gilmore project through a newspaper article, he wrote a letter to Mailer offering the benefit of his own experience of violence in prisons; it was his contention that only a person who has endured a decade or more of incarceration can fully appreciate the principle and practice of institutional violence.

The result was an extraordinary series of letters in which Mailer recognized 'an intellectual, a radical, a potential leader, a man obsessed with a vision of more elevated human relations in a better world that revolution could forge'. These letters were to constitute the basis of the best-selling autobiography *In the Belly of the Beast*. As a result of this success, and Mailer's conviction that he was 'a powerful and important

American writer', Abbott was released on parole. He worked for a brief period as Norman Mailer's researcher, and enjoyed the attentions of the New York literati; but the years of institutionalization had ill-equipped Jack Abbott for a life outside prison.

In the early hours of the morning of 18 July 1981, Abbott became involved in an argument with 22-year-old Richard Adan, an actor and playwright then working as a waiter at the Bini Bon diner on Second Avenue, New York. Abbott had taken strong exception to being told that the men's lavatory was for staff use only, and reacted in the only way that seemed natural to him – he stabbed Adan to death. After two months on the run, he was arrested in Louisiana and sentenced to be confined in the maximum security prison at Marion, Illinois.

On 5 June 1990, Jack Abbott was back in court again, not on a homicide charge this time, but to oppose the efforts of his last victim's widow to sue him for $10 million.

Abbott, now aged 45, neat in a brown tweed sports jacket and jeans and wearing steel-rimmed spectacles, declined the offer of legal aid and claimed instead his right to act as his own lawyer.

It had been in 1981, shortly after Adan's death, that his wife Ricci had begun the proceedings to extract financial compensation for the 'wrongful death' and 'pain and suffering' caused to Richard Adan by his killer. In 1983, Abbott had been found liable for monetary damages, but the motion had been legally blocked by him for seven years, until this present jury was empanelled to determine the amount of those damages.

Having failed to win a postponement of the case, Jack Abbott told Acting Justice Carol H. Arber that postponements were important in criminal cases because 'they stop people from being executed'. Picking up the atmosphere of levity, Ms Arber replied, 'Don't worry Mr Abbott, we won't execute you, this is a civil proceeding.'

Black Burlesque

Under what has become known as the 'Son of Sam'[1] law, criminals are unable to profit financially from stories about their crimes. In Jack Abbott's case, the considerable income from *In the Belly of the Beast*, as well as a second book, *My Return*, and the subsequent film rights, was being held jointly by the New York County Sheriff and the New York State Crime Victims Board.

In *My Return*, Abbott discussed the Adan stabbing, and dismissed Mrs Adan's claim that her husband endured 'pain and suffering', commenting that far from it, he had benefited from a quick, painless death. Abbott also contended that because the whole argument only arose because of Richard Adan's apparent 'lack of respect', he was at least partly responsible for his own death.

A further indication of the burlesque that was in store surfaced as Jack Abbott gazed around the court to see who was present, caught sight of William Majeski, the cop who had arrested him in Louisiana, and began making obscene gestures at him.

On the following morning, 6 June, Jack Henry Abbott began to conduct his own defence, which posed certain logistical problems as well as providing light entertainment, since armed officers were obliged to shadow him as he walked about the court – addressing the jury, questioning witnesses at the stand . . . Abbott complained bitterly to the judge that the guards were damaging his image as a lawyer, but Ms Arber allowed the escort to remain pending further discussion of the matter. It was eventually resolved by the guards staying in one place so long

---

[1]During 1976–7 a wave of murders hit New York leaving six people dead and a further seven seriously wounded; the victims were all young couples sitting in parked cars. Ironically, the killer was traced through a traffic violation ticket issued to him on the night of his last murder; when police traced the car they found on the back seat a loaded .44 Bulldog revolver which had been used in previous killings. Thus the murderer who had written an arrogant note to the police some months before, claiming 'I am a monster. I am the Son of Sam', was identified as David Berkowitz.

Under arrest, Berkowitz claimed that mysterious voices had been ordering him to kill, and explained that his nickname had been taken from a neighbour's black Labrador dog which was called Sam.

In August 1977, the Son of Sam was sentenced to 365 years imprisonment, and his crimes attracted considerable media exploitation.

as Abbott gave notice and asked permission when he wanted to cross the court-room.

In a rambling cross-examination of a Mr Manuel Martin, theatre director and playwright, Abbott asked: 'Did you know the author of *In the Belly of the Beast* was highly intelligent and very talented? Did you know that it [the book] was highly publicized? Did you come to my trial?'

'No never, never. You killed a promise of a wonderful life [Adan's], I would never spend any money to read a book you wrote.'

There followed an exchange during which Abbott ridiculed the witness's Spanish accent, and Mr Martin, in an angry response claimed: 'You talk about *my* accent – I can't understand *you* because you mumble!'

It was not only Manuel Martin who was having trouble making sense of Jack Abbott's speech, even Acting Justice Arber was constrained to ask him if he could speak more clearly. 'But your honour I can't,' mumbled Abbott, and with some aplomb whisked out his false teeth and showed them around the court: 'I'm just getting used to these and they hurt.'

Sparks flew again on the third day of the trial when Mrs Ricci Adan's father, the theatre director and former actor, Henry Howard, took the witness stand to testify to his son-in-law's potential: 'He was an Adonis; he had magic and star quality.' He turned on Abbott and added, 'Then you killed him!'

In cross-examination Abbott asked Howard if he had read *In the Belly of the Beast*, and elicited the reply: 'I couldn't care less about your books or your thoughts, or anything that is so childish and moronic. You miss the point – it seems to me *you* are not in the belly of the beast – *this* is the belly of the beast right here, with guys like you sticking knives in our hearts.' Half standing in the witness box, Henry Howard pointed his finger at Abbott and concluded: 'You are nothing but a killer.'

The black humour began to creep back into the Massachusetts Supreme Court hearing on Friday, 8 June when Abbott, attempting to convince a jury that Richard Adan had suffered no pain when he was stabbed, folded a piece of paper into the shape of a knife and re-enacted Adan's death for the benefit of witness Wayne Larsen. Thrusting the 'knife' towards him one way, Abbott asked Larsen (who was appearing as an eye-witness to the incident), 'Was this the way I stabbed him or' – thrusting the paper knife in a different direction 'did you think you saw me stab him this way?'

'I don't know,' replied Larsen, 'unaccustomed as I am to stabbing people like you are.'

The confrontation the court had been waiting for took place at the end of the fifth day, when Jack Abbott questioned Mrs Ricci Adan:

'Are you under the impression I killed your husband?'

'You killed my husband. How could you do that?'

'What did I do?'

'I know you killed my husband with a knife. I know you thrust it into his chest and he died. He's dead.'

'Does nothing else matter to you than that Richard Adan died at my hands?'

'Yes. Something has to be done. There has to be some kind of a balance, some retribution for what has happened to my husband. Some kind of payback. I don't know what.'

'Did you attend my trial?'

'No I did not. I was in shock. I didn't want to see it all. I didn't want to see you.'

'So you don't know what happened?'

'I don't know.'

'Do you care?'

'Objection!' yelled Mrs Adan's lawyer.

'You don't have to answer,' responded Acting Justice Arber.

Such overtly provocative questioning, including the suggestion that her late husband's life was 'not worth a dime', soon reduced Mrs Adan to tears, a condition which Abbott berated with taunts like, 'Could you answer the question without using a Kleenex?' At the same time he sneered quite regularly at Mrs Adan's continued attempts to secure financial compensation from Richard's untimely death.

At one point towards the end of his examination of Mrs Adan, Abbott demanded that the judge declare a mistrial on the grounds that the plaintiff's tears were unfairly prejudicing the jury against him. Ms Arber declined to do any such thing.

On Friday, 15 June 1990, after six hours of deliberation and considerable use of an electronic calculator, the jury, to the apparent delight of everybody in court except Jack Abbott, awarded Mrs Ricci Adan $7.575 million damages ($5.575 million for loss of her husband's potential earnings and $2 million for the pain he suffered).

One of the happiest people in court was clearly the victim's father-in-law, Mr Henry Howard, who had crossed swords with Abbott from the witness stand: 'We now own him lock, stock and barrel,' said Howard jubilantly. 'It's delightful to know that Abbott will never earn a penny from anything he ever writes. It's the first thing we've had to smile about in nine years. If he slows down we'll send him a word processor.'

As for Jack Abbott, before he was returned to continue his sentence at Auburn state prison, he told Acting Justice Carol Arber: 'It is a little excessive, your honour, I would say.'

He is due for parole again in eleven years.

REPRIEVED
The Case of Percy Stoner

The most extraordinary and most pitiful of this year's British updates rated no more than a couple of paragraphs in the national press, but recalled a case which once held front page headlines, a case that took place before most readers of this book were born.

The facts were these. In 1935, 68-year-old retired architect Francis Mawson Rattenbury was living with his already twice-divorced wife Alma at the Villa Madeira in the refined English south-coast resort of Bournemouth. The ménage was completed by an eighteen-year-old handyman/chauffeur named Percy Stoner, whom Alma had first seduced at an Oxford hotel and had subsequently taken as a permanent lover. If Rattenbury knew of the affair (and he could hardly have avoided it), it seems not to have bothered him as long as he had his hand firmly on the real love in his life – the whisky decanter.

In the small hours of 25 March, Alma, so she claimed, found her husband lying on the drawing-room carpet, his head beaten in, but still breathing. When the doctor and the police arrived, summoned by a startled maid, they found Alma Rattenbury apparently much the worse for drink, gibbering hysterically and making what appeared to be a confession: 'I did it with a mallet . . . He's lived too long . . .' and so on. It was just the first of several admissions of guilt, most of which were aimed at protecting her beloved Percy. Percy himself had begun to make statements, too, the essence of which were that *he* was the guilty party and Mrs Rattenbury had nothing to do with the dreadful incident. By this time Francis Rattenbury had succumbed to his injuries, breathing his last at the Strathallen Nursing Home, and Alma and Percy – still confessing like mad – were facing a murder charge.

The trial opened on 27 May 1935, at the Old Bailey before Mr Justice Humphreys. By now, Alma Rattenbury had been persuaded by her counsel to stop protecting Percy Stoner, and reluctantly she did so. Percy, with a show of dignity beyond his years, upheld his confession (though he uttered not one single word throughout the trial). Despite attempts by the prosecuting counsel and the judge himself to implicate Mrs Rattenbury in 'leading Stoner astray', she was acquitted. On 31 May, Percy Stoner was convicted of murder and sentenced to death. Heartbroken, Alma Rattenbury committed suicide three days later.

Then Percy began to talk; giving notice of appeal, he claimed that he had been innocent all along, that it had been Mrs Rattenbury who killed her husband. Stoner was reprieved and served just seven years of a life sentence before being released in 1942 to join the armed forces fighting World War II. Percy survived the war, married, and settled down to a quiet life in the town one might have thought he wanted to forget – Bournemouth.

This classic English *crime passionnel* has received periodic attention over the succeeding 45 years, with the debate continuing over who *really* killed Francis Rattenbury. Despite his excellent health and longevity, Percy Stoner has remained silent on the matter.

On 28 September 1990, newspapers reported that Percy Stoner, now 73 years old, had appeared before the Bournemouth magistrates. He pleaded guilty to a sexual attack on a twelve-year-old boy in public lavatories near his home. Stoner had been arrested after police found him in the conveniences wearing only a hat, shoes and socks. He was put on probation for two years.

SELF-PRESERVATION
The Case of David Pagett

The law, and the agencies that enforce it, like any other complex system, are subject to development if not exactly by trial and error, then by a process of learning from mistakes and closing loopholes as they are seen to appear. It is a great sadness that this gradual refinement so often results from deep personal tragedies.

Such a tragedy was suffered by the Wood family of Birmingham in July 1980, but it was only a decade later that the shortcomings that led to the death of seventeen-year-old Gail Kinchin resulted in improved police procedures in the matter of firearms use.

The background to this recent development was a unique siege situation which developed during the early morning of Thursday, 12 June 1980. Gail Kinchin had moved out of the home she shared with her mother Josephine and stepfather Eric Wood in the Kings Heath district of Birmingham and moved in with 31-year-old David Pagett to his council flat in Rugely.

Pagett turned out to be a thoroughly nasty bit of work – at least as far as Gail was concerned – much given to the pleasures of women and drink; he was also handy with his fists. With Gail now for all practical purposes in his clutches, Pagett, a man already known to be a bully, began to be driven by the blind belligerence that accompanied his increased dependence upon alcohol, and his behaviour towards Gail deteriorated into violence and paranoia.

Inevitably, Gail Kinchin became pregnant, and equally predictably, Pagett made her condition the excuse for further indignities – often forcing her to spend nights sleeping on the draughty floor. If she complained, or made to leave him, there were the very believable threats to the life of Gail's mother.

But of such desperation, desperate means are born, and if for no other reason than the safety of her unborn child, Gail Kinchin, with her mother's help, courageously made plans to flee the flat on the afternoon of 11 June 1980, travelling via her mother's home to that of a friend.

Pagett was furious, of course, and, the worse for drink, he loaded himself and a double-barrelled shotgun into his car and made for the Woods' home in Kings Heath. Here he smashed his way into the house, shotgun raised, to confront Eric Wood who, fearing for his own and his wife's life, made a desperate dash for the door to summon assistance. The burning pain in his legs cut short that bid for freedom as the blast of lead shot tore into his limbs and felled him. Pagett now turned his violent attentions on Mrs Wood, who was bundled screaming at gunpoint, terrified, into the waiting car. All Pagett wanted was an address!

When he had similarly snatched Gail from her 'safe' house in Masefield Square, Pagett kicked and pushed her into the car to join her mother and drove off at a reckless pace towards Rugely, skilfully evading the road blocks set up by police in the wake of Eric Wood's wounding and his wife's kidnap. It was while Pagett was negotiating one of these that Josephine Wood, thinking quickly, managed to flee the madman's clutches. Not that Pagett seemed to care, even if he noticed; he had what he wanted, a trembling, fearful Gail back in his evil power. He would teach her a lesson she would never forget!

It was only minutes after David Pagett had reached the safety of his flat, barricading himself and Gail inside, that armed police officers began to surround the block.

Detective Sergeant Thomas Sartain and Detective Constable Gerald Richards, both carrying police issue Smith and Wessons, entered the building. Hampered by the darkness imposed by broken landing lights, the two officers positioned themselves outside Pagett's door. Before long they heard a rattling of bolts, and in the flash of unaccustomed light from the now open front door they could see the fugitive, a shotgun in one hand and Gail Kinchin grasped with the other as a human shield.

Obviously feeling securely above the law, Pagett rejected all appeals for him to surrender his weapon and in total defiance forced the two officers to retreat up the stairs behind them; to their horror the policemen found themselves trapped – behind them was a solid wall, in front of them was a madman with a shotgun and a pregnant hostage. There was a momentary scuffle in the darkness below, and then with a deafening roar the shotgun exploded in a flash of fire. Miraculously the deadly spray of lead missed the crouching officers and in what they must at the time have considered their only means of self-preservation, Richards and Sartain returned fire. Pagett loosed off the other barrel of his weapon and again the detectives returned his fire. This time, a body crumpled and fell. Gail lay bleeding on the floor, her baby was dead inside her, killed instantly by a bullet. Despite emergency treatment in hospital, Gail Kinchin died before the month was out.

To sustain a *murder* charge against Pagett, it had to be demonstrated at his trial that he had used the girl as a shield in the full knowledge that when he first fired the shotgun at the detectives they were likely to shoot back and could maim or kill his hostage. It was a complex and unique prosecution which divided the jury, who eventually returned a verdict of manslaughter. On the lesser charges which Pagett faced – three of attempted murder (of Mr Wood and the two police officers), and two of kidnap (Mrs Wood and Gail Kinchin) – he was found guilty. Sentencing Pagett to seven concurrent twelve-year terms of imprisonment, Mr Justice Park observed: 'The use of a hostage by a desperate armed man to achieve safety for himself – and by that use to cause the death of the hostage – is a very grave offence, falling only just short of murder . . .'

Nevertheless, the victim's family have remained far from happy with the way in which the police conducted the siege, a discontentment that was not relieved by the fact that due to the conduct of the trial much evidence concerning the shooting was never heard. It has been Mr and Mrs Wood's consistent view that the police should have been prepared to shoulder a great deal more of the responsibility for the outcome of the incident.

Consequently, in 1990, Josephine Wood decided to sue the West Midlands Chief Constable at the time of the shooting, Sir Philip Knights, for negligence over the death of her daughter. In October the case was heard before the High Court at Birmingham, during which the Woods' counsel, Mr Malcolm

Lee, advanced the accusation that Gail Kinchin might not have died if correct police procedures had been followed. This fault in procedure, as outlined in the court, was that the two officers entrusted with the unenviable task of confronting Pagett were not senior enough to make the decisions required in such a potentially dangerous situation. Indeed, Mr Colin Greenwood, a firearms expert and former police instructor, is reported as giving his opinion that the officer whose bullets hit Gail Kinchin 'appears to have made command decisions he was not qualified to make. The entire command structure appears then to have failed.' It must in fairness be added that former Detective Constable (now Sergeant) Richards defended his position vigorously, stating in support of his self-defence claim: 'A shot was fired from the shotgun. I responded by firing four shots in all from my revolver.'

Nothing will ever compensate Mr and Mrs Wood for the loss of their daughter and unborn grandson – least of all the small sum of agreed damages paid to the family. But perhaps they can console themselves that pressure such as theirs and incidents like the tragedy that claimed the lives of Gail Kinchin and her child have been instrumental in a wide reappraisal of the guidelines for the police use of firearms and the strict control by senior officers over the circumstances under which they are issued.

Firearms and the Police

One of the most common myths to have attached itself to the British police force is that it has always been unarmed – unarmed, that is, except for that well-known symbol of law and order, the truncheon. It is this misconception that has fuelled the passionate debate on whether or not, faced with the growing threat of terrorism and the inexorable growth of violent crime on the streets, the British policeman should be armed. Visions of our bobbies patrolling their beat, gun on hip like their American and European counterparts, arouse feelings either of horror or enthusiasm.

It may, then, come as a surprise to many that it is only in comparatively recently years that the police at large have *not* been armed. In 1829, when Sir Robert Peel's first force went out on to the streets of London, they were issued with truncheons, cutlasses and flintlock pistols. Indeed, it is a little-known fact that for 50 years – up until 1936 – constables on night duty were allowed to carry a service revolver.

Today, although its individual members do not carry firearms, the police force has access, at any given time of need, to a formidable arsenal of weaponry ranging from a traditional truncheon to the Heckler and Koch 9mm MP5 (K) submachinegun; and although, rightly, there are restrictions on the employment of weapons, increasing use is being made of the specially trained marksmen of the firearms support units. The Metropolitan police have their own permanent firearms wing, designated D.11 Branch, and the use of its officers has been essential to the maintenance of law and order on the streets during recent inner-city riots, and the successful solution to the growing number of armed hostage situations.

THE MISSING TEN PERCENT
The Enigma of Ian Murray Erskine

A glance at the annual statistics will reveal a particularly high clear-up rate for homicide in Britain, a reflection not only upon the seriousness of the crime, but on the generally excellent standard of the British law enforcement system – from the humble bobby on house-to-house enquiries, through the experienced detectives who co-ordinate the major investigation incident rooms, to the forensic scientists with their bewildering arsenal of high-tech gadgetry.

As soon as a body is found in the proverbial 'suspicious circumstances', the well-oiled machinery of a murder investigation bursts into action, a multitude of different but closely interlinked disciplines that will take the inquiry from the scene-of-crime officer's first clue to the Crown prosecutor's final speech in court. Because homicides are never exactly alike, no investigation is ever exactly like another, but they are all characterized by persistence and an eye for important detail.

The success rate itself is a tribute to the system's effectiveness, but if the figure for satisfactory solutions to murder is 90%, then it follows that 10% end less successfully.

One of the most baffling unsolved cases of recent years is the murder of Ian Murray Erskine. Forty-four-year-old Erskine was known as a quiet, sensitive and cultured man holding a senior position with the Bank of England during the day and enjoying an active social life outside his profession. A great lover of opera,

Murray, as he was known to his friends, was a frequent visitor to the Royal Opera House in London's Covent Garden. He was also an enthusiast for fine wines and kept more than 500 bottles in his own collection. Erskine was also unobtrusively homosexual.

On the evening of Friday, 15 December 1989, only ten days before Christmas, Ian Erskine arrived home to his modest apartment in Norland Square, Holland Park, at 6.30. A cautious man, Erskine needed to open three locks and turn off an alarm before he could cross the threshold. If he seemed in a particular hurry that night, it could have been because he was looking forward to meeting a special friend – a man he referred to as 'the Rhodesian'; he would no doubt have been playing some of his beloved opera on the stereo as he got ready for the rendezvous.

On Monday, the 18th, Ian Erskine failed to turn up for work. This in itself was a rarity, but that he should not telephone the office with an explanation was unheard of.

By Wednesday, his friends felt concerned enough to report Erskine's apparent disappearance to the police. That same afternoon a detective paid a routine visit to the flat in Holland Park and found the occupant's B-registration blue Saab parked outside. Going down the steps to the basement front door, the officer was surprised to find that, contrary to Erskine's security conscious habits, the front door was secured only by a single lock, the alarm had not been set, and an electric light had been left burning in the hallway.

In subsequent days the police were to learn that Ian Erskine's cheque book and credit card had already been fraudulently used by a man described as 'bearded', who had entered Austin Kaye, the jeweller in the Strand, on Saturday 16 December and used the stolen Access card to buy a £200 watch. This watch, it was hoped, would be useful in the search for clues to Erskine's whereabouts and the identity of the man making free use of his bank account. It was a distinctive type of 'yachting watch', made by Seiko, of which only 340 were on sale in Britain.

On Monday the card was used again by the same hirsute man at about 11.00 am to order a vehicle from the Guy Salmon car rental company. The red Ford Fiesta was delivered to the man calling himself 'Erskine' outside the Charing Cross Hotel adjoining one of London's main railway stations. The driver delivering the car apologized to 'Erskine' for being late (almost an hour as he had first gone to the wrong hotel) and then asked for his driving licence.

Piecing together further evidence provided by the use of

Erskine's cards, detectives became aware of the possibility that two men were involved in fraudulent transactions. A second sighting had been reported at a bureau de change on the afternoon of Saturday the 15th involving the sum of $500; but the clerk's description of the man is very different from that given by the jeweller and the car rental delivery driver. A further interesting possibility was that the man (or men) using Ian Erskine's card also knew the rightful owner, as the credit limit was never exceeded.

On Thursday, 21 December, the first 'Erskine' returned the hire car, dropping it off outside the Railway Tavern in York Road, just behind King's Cross railway station. The milometer showed that the vehicle had travelled about 200 miles. And here the trail temporarily came to an end.

The Riddle Remains

It was three months later, on 25 March 1990, that two men taking a narrow-boat on a day trip down the river Cam, near Ely in Cambridgeshire, decided to investigate a large black plastic rubbish sack that was floating on the surface of the water near the river bank. Inside were the decomposing pieces of Ian Erskine's dismembered body. We know that the bag had been at that remote position on the river since at least 23 December of the previous year, when a local farmer had seen the bundle but paid no more attention to it. The site was, significantly, a 200-mile round trip from London – the mileage recorded on the hired Fiesta.

With the discovery of Erskine's remains, a missing person inquiry was dramatically upgraded to a murder hunt. The consequent painstaking forensic search of the Holland Park flat indicated that the victim had been killed there in his own home – probably asphyxiated, thought the pathologist. If this was true, it gave strength to the theory that two men were involved in the murder as the only way of removing Ian Erskine's eleven-and-a-half stone dead weight was up the awkward flight of steep stone steps leading from the basement to street level.

Meanwhile videofits had been assembled from the descriptions of the men using Erskine's credit cards, and in the process police learned an interesting fact about suspect number two – the man who had used the Access card to obtain $500. Apparently he had been seen several times the previous November in the

Norland Arms, a public house just around the corner from Norland Square. What was more, he had been drinking with the victim himself. Another significant discovery was that Ian Erskine was a homosexual with a preference for sado-masochistic practices and corporal punishment. What was more, it was his habit to satisfy his sexual requirements through the medium of advertisements in gay and other contact magazines. It transpired that some years before his death, Erskine had placed an advertisement in *Loot*, London's 'free' classified magazine. The man who answered his request for a 'top guy', a 'master', was the man known as 'the Rhodesian', and the pair subsequently enjoyed a social and sexual relationship.

Then, on 8 January 1990, at London's Liverpool Street Station, the same bearded man who had hired the Ford Fiesta, used Ian Erskine's cheque-book and card once again – to purchase £50 worth of Dutch guilders from a bureau de change, and to pay for a five-day return ticket to Holland. But by this time Erskine's bank had recognized the forgery of his signature and had put a stop on his charge card; when a man tried to make dishonest use of it in Holland, it was seized.

Meanwhile, in the absence of any rational explanation of the motives behind the murder of Ian Murray Erskine, some rather improbable theories were given an airing.

Erskine was an accountant employed by the Bank of England in Threadneedle Street in the heart of the City of London. It was a position of great trust, indeed Ian Erskine was a senior manager in one of the Bank's most security-conscious activities – investigating the finances of some of the City's most controversial institutions. In the weeks before his disappearance, Erskine had been probing the crooked business involved in 'laundering' the financial profits of illegal drug trafficking. However fanciful, was it beyond possibility that his disappearance should be somehow connected? But why? He was only one of a substantial team of accountants investigating the rackets, and his death was unlikely to silence the inquiry even if he had been made an example – and no threats were ever made to the lives of other members of the team. Nevertheless, it may have been with this at the back of their minds that Bank of England officials were persuaded to decline to offer comment on their late employee, beyond affirming that they would 'rather not talk about it'. Nor, for that matter, would Scotland Yard.

It was much later in the year, almost twelve months to the

day since he was last seen alive, that the general public – who had anyway forgotten Ian Erskine's tragic death – once again encountered news of 'the Rhodesian'. According to the police – who had most certainly *not* forgotten Erskine's murder – there *was* such a person; and he *was* Rhodesian: a former member of that country's notorious security force, the Sellous Scouts – a rather less accountable equivalent of Britain's SAS. By the end of December police were still searching for him; but with surprisingly little help from the more secretive members on the S&M fringes of the gay community, some of whom might perhaps be expected to have encountered 'the Rhodesian'. To date he remains a fugitive. The murder of Ian Erskine remains unsolved.

Although Erskine was not outwardly flamboyant in his sexual encounters, the subculture of sado-masochism can be perilous territory. Quite how hazardous was well illustrated at a brief trial in the Old Bailey a week before the remains of Ian Erskine were pulled from the waters of the Cam.

The late Leonard John Hudspith was a masochistic homosexual; he also suffered from Aids, though how much this contributed to the bravado that amounted to a death wish, he can no longer tell us. There is a spot on London's Hampstead Heath known to those who collect there as the 'orgy bush', a meeting place for homosexuals and, according to evidence given in court, notorious for its sado-masochistic activities – which is why Leonard Hudspith was there. Hudspith, a 32-year-old accounts clerk, was apparently no stranger to the spot, and on this last night of his life approached Kevin Scott and two companions and introduced himself as being interested in sado-masochism. Taking him at his word, Scott began punching and slapping him. This was to the evident delight of Hudspith who, according to the defendant, began to taunt them with 'Is that all you can do?' and 'Do you call yourselves men?' The other two had by now begun to show just what they could do and 'put the boot in a few times pretty hard'. In fact they punched and kicked him to death.

So savage had the attack been, that when Hudspith's body was found eighteen days later the only means of identifying him was through dental records. Given the victim's sexual preferences, it was accepted by the prosecution that death was the result not of premeditated murder but of manslaughter. The sentence against Scott was five years' imprisonment.

ONE THING LEADS TO ANOTHER
The Case of John Cannan

This tragic if otherwise mundane homicide, committed in 1988, has fuelled new interest in the identity of a man who has been the source of sinister speculation among both police and public since the summer of 1986; the man called 'Mr Kipper'.

As we shall see, information revealed during the investigation and the trial of John Cannan for the murder of Mrs Shirley Banks has led to a three-pronged reassessment of the case of missing estate agent Susannah Lamplugh, by the press, police and by the Lamplugh family themselves. If there is a connection between the Banks case and that of Suzy Lamplugh and the still unsolved murder of Sandra Court, then it will mean that a serial killer – thankfully one of few in British criminal history – has at last been stopped. It is only fair and proper to point out, however, that although he was convicted and sentenced for the Banks murder, John Cannan has consistently denied any connection with Ms Lamplugh or Ms Court.

The sad case of Shirley Banks began with her disappearance in early October, 1987. On Thursday the 8th, Mrs Banks, married for just four weeks and only recently returned from a honeymoon in Capri, made a late evening shopping trip to buy a new evening dress and accessories from the Debenhams store in her home city of Bristol. Shirley and her husband Richard had planned to dine out that evening to celebrate an important contract he had completed in his new job. She had come home to get ready, but decided to go out again to buy something special to wear for the occasion. Mrs Banks was driving her orange Mini Clubman estate and both she and it disappeared some time after 8 o'clock when she bumped into a work colleague as she left the store.

When his wife had not arrived home by 11 o'clock that night, Richard Banks was understandably concerned, though it was not until the following evening that he reported her missing to the police. In fact this is not as odd as it might seem, for on the morning of the 9th Banks had phoned Shirley's employers – the Alexander Workwear shoe factory, in Bristol – and learned that someone calling herself Mrs Banks had reported in sick. It was reasonable, then, to suppose that his wife had simply spent the night away from home. Although the telephone call to Alexander's had not come through to Mrs Banks's department, the friend she met at Debenhams the previous evening said Shirley was her normal cheerful self and parted with the words, 'See you tomorrow'.

Over the following several days, other telephone calls which the police described as of a 'bizarre nature' were made to Mrs Banks's relatives, using numbers from a book which had disappeared with her.

So the hunt began for Shirley Banks and her Mini Clubman, registration HWL 507N, and what became known as the 'Bride Squad' took up temporary occupation of part of the Avon and Somerset police training school.

The first major breakthrough came on the afternoon of Thursday, 29 October. A woman shopkeeper had been assaulted in a robbery attempt at Leamington Spa, Warwickshire. Later that same day a panda car picked up a man fitting the description of the attacker, and in the back of his car an excise license issued for Mrs Banks's car was found. It was not disclosed at the time, but the driver was 33-year-old John Cannan, described as a 'businessman'.

On the following day, 30 October, police recovered the car that had belonged to Mrs Banks from a lock-up garage rented by Cannan as part of an apartment in a luxury block in Leigh Woods – less than a mile from the missing woman's home. The vehicle had undergone substantial cosmetic alterations to disguise its identity: the bodywork had been crudely painted dark blue, the number plates were changed (to SLP 386S), and a cassette player had been installed in the dashboard.

Although forensic experts examined the vehicle minutely,

they could find no evidence that a life or death struggle had taken place inside the car; at the same time, search teams using sniffer dogs were equally unsuccessful in finding any trace of Mrs Banks herself in the area around the apartment block.

Pieces of the Puzzle

The man now named as John Cannan appeared before Bristol magistrates on 1 November, charged with stealing Mrs Banks's car and with the Leamington Spa shop attack. Three days later the *Star* newspaper made a front-page headline connection between the disappearance of Shirley Banks and that of Suzy Lamplugh, at the same time disclosing that an unnamed convicted rapist had been released from Wormwood Scrubs only two days before Ms Lamplugh vanished. His name, it transpired, was John Cannan.

At the same time that magistrates were preparing to hear charges against John Cannan, his solicitor, Mr James Moriarty, said his client 'denies emphatically' any connection with the disappearance of either Mrs Banks or Ms Lamplugh. 'Furthermore, I am deeply concerned that his chances of a fair trial will be severely prejudiced by reports in the press,' Mr Moriarty continued. 'I am disappointed that there are elements of the press who seem to have forgotten that trial is by jury and not by newspaper. I have no wish to gag the press on any legitimate matter of news, but I should make it clear that unattributed theories of alleged sources have not yet been dignified by evidence.'

On 10 November, John Cannan reappeared before Bristol magistrates to face further indictments. The charge sheet now read:

1. Stealing Mrs Shirley Banks's car.
2. Kidnapping Mrs Banks in Bristol on 8 October.
3. Attempting to abduct 30-year-old Julia Holman in Bristol on 7 October.
4. Assault with intent to rob Carmel Cleary at Leamington Spa on 29 October.
5. Causing grievous bodily harm to a woman at Sutton Coldfield in December 1980.

While Cannon remained in custody, the Bride Squad were

spreading their net ever wider in the search for information about his past movements. Taking a step that is only ever contemplated with extreme caution, police issued a photograph of John Cannan with a request for any member of the public who had rented property to him between January 1986 and October 1987 to come forward. At the same time the details of four numbered keys was announced for which police urgently needed to find doors. Listed were a bronze Yale-type key with the name 'Casswells' and the code 'HDIA' stamped on it, a silver-coloured mortice key marked 'Union Parkes' 'M159' for a three-lever lock, a silver-coloured key marked 'PES' that would fit a four-lever Squires padlock, and a flat silver-coloured key of the type that would fit the door of a garage.

It is rare for photographs of the accused to be released for publication before or during their trial – and *never* in a case of rape. The reason is that frequently one of the most fundamental issues at trial is identification, and to broadcast a suspect's portrait will obviously prejudice impartiality (see the 'Tottenham Three' case on page 71). In the present instance, although the photograph was published, it was simply described as being of a man 'connected with the inquiry'.

Two days before Christmas 1987, John Cannan was brought before the magistrates to have the murder of Mrs Shirley Banks 'in Bristol or elsewhere between 8 October and 30 October' added to his already impressive list. This despite the continuing absence of a body.

In the event, the Crown was not forced to proceed against John Cannan burdened by such a handicap. The last piece in this massive, and in many ways quite extraordinary puzzle was put into place in the first days of April 1988, when the badly decomposed body of Shirley Banks was found floating in a brook by an auxiliary nurse walking with her family in Somerset's Quantock Hills; at first the unlucky woman had thought it was a tailor's dummy.

While a portable headquarters was set up at Great Wood Forest, near the village of Over Stoway, to act as a central co-ordination point for police search teams combing the area for clues, the sad remains of Mrs Banks were removed to Wellington for post-mortem examination. At the inquest held before the West Somerset coroner, Mr Michael Rose, Home Office pathologist Professor Bernard Knight's report was read, attributing the victim's death to head injuries caused by being battered with a heavy rock. There were five lacerations of the scalp which Professor Knight suggested were probably inflicted while Mrs Banks was alive.

In late September 1988, almost a year to the week since she had disappeared, John Cannan was committed for trial at Crown Court charged with Shirley Banks's murder; there was also a clutch of other charges including rape, assault and abduction. It was seven more months before Cannan faced Mr Justice Drake at Exeter.

Prints and Tests

Opening for the prosecution on 6 April, Mr Paul Chadd QC told the court how, on the day before he kidnapped Mrs Banks, Cannan had tried to abduct businesswoman Julia Holman at gunpoint from a Bristol car park. Ms Holman, courageous in the extreme considering the gun barrel pointing through the door of her car, slammed the door shut and made a Hollywood getaway. The following evening, Mr Chadd contended, Cannan pulled the same trick on Mrs Banks; this time he was more successful. However, when taken into custody for the offence committed at Leamington Spa, Cannan denied knowing Mrs Banks, although her vehicle licence was found in the back of his own car, and Mrs Banks's car was found, much altered, in the garage at Cannan's home in Leigh Woods. Feigning surprise, he had told detectives that he bought it from a man outside a city car auction for £125, and had tried to disguise the car when he heard the police were looking for it. Far-fetched as the story might have sounded, it *could* have explained everything without linking Cannan with Shirley Banks. But, continued prosecuting counsel, a police forensic team had found a document in John Cannan's apartment which bore the victim's left thumbprint – proof positive that Cannan knew Shirley Banks, and that she had probably been taken to his home.

On the second day of the trial, Mr Chadd introduced the court to the case of a woman from Reading, Berkshire, who, he claimed, had been brutally raped and indecently assaulted by Cannan at knifepoint one year before the murder of Shirley Banks. The unnamed woman, a young mother, gave evidence to the court how on the evening of 6 October 1986, she had been sitting in her parked car reading a book in the Chantry Green area of Reading, when the man she identified as John Cannan approached to ask directions. As the woman turned to look for her map book, Cannan pulled a balaclava over his face, opened the car door and threatened her with a knife: 'I want sex – get in the back seat of the car.' The terrified young woman said she was then, and remains, convinced that if she had resisted he would have killed her. Forensic scientists who subsequently carried out DNA profiling tests on stained underwear gave evidence that the odds against the attacker *not* being John Cannan were 260 million to one.

Later in the trial, Cannan created a small drama of his own. It was during the evidence of a young married woman solicitor who had been conducting an affair with him, and when she broke off the liaison after a year Cannan threatened the lives of her and her family 'in a most unpleasant way'. As the woman wept at the recollection of this nightmare, Cannan rose from the dock shouting, 'I hate it! I hate it! It's time the truth came out, the whole truth. This is a play act.' He later apologized to Mr Justice Drake who pointed out that he would have every opportunity to tell *his* version of the truth if he was called to the witness stand.

On 13 April the court was hushed as pensioner Mrs Amelia Hart talked of what she witnessed on the afternoon of 9 October 1987. She had been sitting in her car close to some woods near Cannan's home in Bristol, when she claims to have heard a sound like something being hit very hard; then she saw a man who 'was beating something with his hands, and he was punching and kept running back and jumping on something'. This was followed by the sound of a female voice crying 'No, no', and the man repeating 'I warned you what I would do . . . I warned you, I warned you.' Then there was what Mrs Hart described as 'the most dreadful, dreadful screams, chilling, blood-curdling screams. Then it stopped and there was a dreadful choking sound.' Fearlessly, Mrs Hart called out to the man, demanding what was going on. In response, 'he sprang at me in the car. The window was wide open and as he came down his hands came towards my neck . . . He called me a cow.' As she sped away in the car, Mrs Hart might have contemplated that she was a very lucky woman.

Contrary to anticipation, John Cannan did not take the stand to give evidence on his own behalf, and no witnesses were called by the defence. Towards the end of the trial,

Cannan had interrupted the proceeding again, demanding: 'I want to give evidence', but after a talking to by his counsel, Mr Anthony Palmer QC, he sat down quietly. It was therefore left to Mr Palmer to present John Cannan's alibi that at the time Shirley Banks was kidnapped, he was at home watching television. 'Justice,' Mr Palmer was reported as saying, 'sometimes demands plain speaking. Whoever did murder Shirley Banks has not been proved. It has not been proved that this young woman was actually abducted or kidnapped.'

The Undisclosed Record

With so many indictments on the charge sheet, it was little surprise that the jury of eight men and four women who had been empanelled to judge Cannan's guilt found it difficult to reach conclusions. On 27 April, after five hours' deliberation, they found him guilty of the kidnap and rape of the unnamed Reading housewife, but after a further retirement told the trial judge that they were undecided on the other five counts. After a night spent in a hotel, the jury returned to court on the following morning, and after further debate returned verdicts of guilty on all charges.

In sentencing Cannan, Mr Justice Drake told him that although he was undoubtedly a charming and attractive companion to some women, having sex by force had become an obsession: 'My duty is to protect other women from you, and from the possibility that you might ever again be at liberty to commit such offences against women. You should never be again at liberty outside prison walls.'

John Cannan sat in the dock shaking his head as he was condemned to maximum terms of imprisonment on each of the charges – including three life sentences. As he was led from the court, he was heard to complain: 'Wrong verdict, wrong verdict. They haven't heard the truth.'

One thing the jury most certainly had not heard was the string of offences committed by Cannan before he was arrested in the present case; and the revelation that he had previously been convicted of raping a shop manageress in 1981 after threatening to kill her baby, reportedly brought tears to some jurors' eyes. Perhaps if they had known in retirement what they knew now, the jury's job would have been quicker and easier, but that, thankfully, is not the British way of justice. A defendant is on trial only for the offences with which he is charged, and no discussion of his past life and misdeeds should prejudice the impartiality of that trial. Only afterwards can the whole story be told.

John Cannan was born in Sutton Coldfield, near Birmingham in the English Midlands. He attended the local Riland school, which he left at the age of sixteen with the quite creditable distinction of five CSE certificates and a couple of O-level GCEs. After a spell in the merchant navy, he drifted in and out of a variety of jobs. His first violent crime had been committed when Cannan was only fourteen years old and he was put on a year's probation for attacking a girl in a telephone booth.

In 1978, after an engagement lasting seven years, John Cannan married June Vale. In 1980, he became infatuated with the manageress of a Sutton Coldfield off-licence, and despite his recent marriage, wooed her with champagne and flowers until she consented to a relationship. The affair lasted ten months, during which time the woman became increasingly uneasy about the violent streak that was beginning to reveal itself in Cannan's personality. It was in 1981 that John Cannan was sentenced to five years in Horfield Prison for the rape of a pregnant Birmingham boutique manager, and a further three years for robbing her shop of £85. Released in 1986 to find himself divorced, Cannan started up an intense affair with solicitor Mrs Annabel Rose, whom he had met while in prison. Mrs Rose would be called by the prosecution to give evidence in the Shirley Banks case. Despite this relationship, Cannan, ever the ladies' man, was dating a string of young women including a professional ice skater. In October 1986, he committed the Reading rape.

Just before his arrest in October 1987, John Cannan decided to broaden his opportunities for sex by joining a Bristol video dating agency. He paid £95 to sit in front of a camera and 'sell' himself – which he did with enthusiasm, even though much of what he said would contravene the Trade Description Act. For a start he used the name John Peterson; then he claimed to own an expensive luxury flat (he rented it), to support the Social Democratic Party (which he may well have done), and to be about to embark on a journey to the Himalayas (in fact he got as far as Horfield Prison, Bristol).

Of his later crimes – the attempt to abduct Julia Holman on 7 October 1987; the abduction and subsequent murder of Mrs Banks on 8 October; and the assault on Carmel Cleary in Leamington Spa on 29 October, the jury was well aware – and convicted accordingly.

Following John Cannan's conviction, Superintendent Timothy Bryan, who had been in overall charge of the case, summed his quarry up to the satisfaction of all: 'I can honestly say that in my 23 years' police experience, I have never met a more dangerous and evil criminal.'

On 23 July 1990, John Cannan's appeal against conviction was heard by the Court of Appeal, and rejected.

The Lamplugh Connection

A connection between the disappearance of Shirley Banks and the Suzy Lamplugh case had been hinted at by the press as early as 22 October 1987 – before John Cannan had been questioned in connection with Mrs Banks's disappearance. Speculation of a link continued during the following week, and when Cannan was initially named as the man charged with 'stealing missing bride Shirley Banks's car' and an additional kidnap attempt, his solicitor issued a strong statement claiming that his client denied ever meeting either Mrs Banks or Suzy Lamplugh.

The British legal system, quite rightly, does not allow the introduction into a case against a defendant either his previous record or irrelevant accusations – however strongly those beliefs may be held by police and prosecution service. Indeed, it was not until the jury had delivered their verdict and Cannan was being sentenced that they knew he was a convicted rapist. That said, it did not go unobserved by those who by training or inclination notice such things, that throughout the trial two members of the Lamplugh Trust attended each day.

However, the optimism with which John Cannan's name had been linked with the missing Ms Lamplugh at the beginning of the Banks case – by both press and police – was revived at the end of April 1989. Even before Cannan's appeal against conviction had been lodged, police had begun the series of interviews with him that in part led to their strong conviction – and that is all it is at present – that he was responsible for the abduction of Suzy Lamplugh.

Chronology of the Lamplugh Case

In order to appreciate the arguments made for the 'Cannan connection', it is useful to have a brief chronological guide to the complexities of the Lamplugh case based on contemporary media accounts:

1986

28 July: London estate agent Susannah Lamplugh keeps a 12.45 pm appointment with a prospective client calling himself 'Mr Kipper' to view a house at Shorrold's Road, Fulham. A man in a neighbouring house witnessed the transaction at 1.15, and was able to help a police artist create an impression of Mr Kipper. Ms Lamplugh, a former beautician aboard the QE2 liner, was using an office car which was found unlocked at 10 o'clock that night parked in Stevenage Road on the other side of Fulham – though witnesses indicate that it may have been there since before 5.00 pm. Ms Lamplugh's purse was still in the vehicle.

29 July: Convinced that Suzy Lamplugh has been abducted by the enigmatic Mr Kipper, police investigators led by Detective Superintendent Nicholas Carter issue descriptions of both the victim and the possible kidnapper. Ms Lamplugh, who lived in a flat in Disraeli Road, Putney, is 25 years old, has shoulder-length blonde hair and blue eyes. When she disappeared she was wearing a peach-coloured blouse, grey skirt and black jacket. The man police wish to interview is described as being aged between 25 and 30, about five feet seven inches tall, medium build, with neat, dark, swept-back hair, wearing a dark lounge suit. Meanwhile police frogmen search the stretch of the river Thames which runs parallel to the road in which the car was found abandoned.

4 August: Despite more than one thousand calls from the public, and the emergence of a number of 'Mr Kippers' (one of them actually engaged in looking for property in the Fulham area), police are no nearer finding the missing woman. In the hope that it might jog the memories of possible witnesses, police stage a reconstruction of Ms Lamplugh's last known movements. Dressed in identical clothing to that worn by Suzy Lamplugh when she disappeared, Police Constable Susan Long leaves the Fulham Road office of estate agents Sturgis & Co at 12.40 and drives to the house in Shorrold's Road for a

1.00 pm appointment with Mr Kipper – here played by Detective Sergeant Christopher Ball. After a few moments in the house, the couple leave in Ms Lamplugh's white Ford Fiesta (registration number B396 GAN) and drive to where the car was parked in Stevenage Road. Police officers along the route of the reconstruction question residents and stop motorists who may have remembered seeing the incidents the previous week.

20 August: Scotland Yard issue a new Photofit portrait of Mr Kipper, based on witness accounts, giving an entirely new picture of Susannah Lamplugh's last hours. Police now think it possible that she had lunch with her client after showing him around the Shorrold's Road property. A witness claims to have seen a man with Ms Lamplugh holding a bottle of champagne outside the house. Furthermore, an acquaintance of the missing woman saw the couple driving along the Fulham Palace Road in a white Ford Fiesta at 2.45 pm. Various other recent witnesses added to the description of Mr Kipper that he was wearing an 'immaculate' charcoal grey suit and light-coloured shirt and tie.

7 September: As public interest begins to wane, the Lamplugh family – in particular Suzy's mother Diana – take the opportunity to keep the case in the news by talking to the press. It is a hint of things to come when Mrs Lamplugh officially launches the Suzy Lamplugh Trust.

12 November: Suzy Lamplugh's home in Disraeli Road is sold by her parents to the couple with whom Suzy was negotiating the deal before she disappeared.

14 November: Diana Lamplugh and her family take the stage at the Royal Society of Medicine seminar to announce the foundation of the Suzy Lamplugh Trust. Said Mrs Lamplugh: 'I suppose it began as something just for myself, to pull something worthwhile out of the most horrendous experience. But now I've talked to so many people, I can see that even if Suzy walked back through the door tomorrow, the Trust would have to go on.'

4 December: Press conference held in London to announce the Suzy Lamplugh Trust. Its aim is to raise £450,000, and by means of videos, newsletters and courses it hopes to 'encourage women to be self-aware and to be aware of others – both to reduce their vulnerability and to increase their effectiveness at work'.

1987

15 January: Scotland Yard officers fly to Antwerp to interview a man whose car was found abandoned in north London. The blue BMW is registered in Belgium to a man named Kiper.

16 January: Police checking the clue of the car registered to Mr David Kiper are told by his family that the vehicle had been stolen the previous summer. Thirty-nine-year-old Mr Kiper himself, a diamond merchant, is on business in the Middle East. The car, which was found in Queen's Grove, St John's Wood, has been checked by forensic experts and no connection has been found with the missing Suzy Lamplugh.

26 January: Police issue a statement clearing Belgian Mr David Rosengarten of any connection with the Lamplugh case. Mr Rosengarten became implicated because his mother's maiden name is Kiper, and his uncle, to whom the car belongs, has that surname.

11 March: Following an odd clue given by a London accountant, Thames Valley police search historic Denham Place in Buckinghamshire. Officers leading the search for Suzy Lamplugh had been told she was being held in the house.

30 March: A new theory is being tested by the police, that Ms Lamplugh was 'moonlighting' as a private beautician with a select group of clients including men, who she visited in their homes. A qualified beautician, she once worked aboard a cruise liner.

6 May: A female estate agent is lured by a bogus purchaser to a house in Margate, Kent, where he attacks her. Police on the Lamplugh case deny there is any connection between the incident and their inquiry.

July: On the first anniversary of Suzy Lamplugh's disappearance, after one of the most exhaustive police inquiries, the team is no nearer a solution to the enigma than in the first weeks of the investigation. All that seems to have been resolved is the conviction on the part of the police and the Lamplugh family that Suzy is no longer alive.

8 October: Mrs Shirley Banks disappears while on a shopping trip in Bristol. The search for her abductor will throw up connections between this case and the disappearance of Suzy Lamplugh.

29 October: John Cannan arrested in Leamington Spa.

23 December: Cannan charged with murder of Mrs Shirley Banks.

1988

4 April: The body of Mrs Banks is found floating in a stream.

23 September: Assistant Commissioner Paul Condon of Scotland Yard issues a statement defending the reputation of

Suzy Lamplugh after a book by *Observer* newspaper journalist Andrew Stephen suggests that she had numerous lovers and was obsessed with men. The Lamplugh family had already failed in their attempt to prevent Faber and Faber publishing the book. In response, the publishers emphasize that it was originally the family which wanted an independent account, and the book was based to a large extent on correspondence and taped interviews with members of the family.

14 October: Despite having dissociated themselves from *The Suzy Lamplugh Story*, both the family and the trust have been unable to revoke the publishing contract under which a percentage of the book's royalties go to the Suzy Lamplugh Trust. The Trust's chairman says that under trust law they are obliged to accept the money.

1989

[*6 April – 28 April*: Trial of John Cannan on charges of murder, rape, abduction and assault results in him being convicted on all counts and sentenced to several terms of life imprisonment. Free from the restraints imposed by the court proceedings, the press once again reopen the question of John Cannan's connection, if any, to the Lamplugh case. Police interviews with Cannan fail to provide any further evidence and Cannan consistently denies ever having met Ms Lamplugh.]

11 May: Publication of Diana Lamplugh's book *Survive the Nine to Five*, which outlines ways in which women can avoid potentially dangerous situations at work.

1990

8 May: Publication of the Lamplugh Trust conference report *Working With the Sex Offender*, echoing current demands for dramatic change in the way the criminal justice system treats sex offenders.

[*23 July*: John Cannan's appeal is heard and rejected.]

September: Detectives studying the Cannan/Lamplugh connection have a mass of circumstantial evidence, none of which is sufficient to bring charges. Senior officers are publicly cautious, and state that in the absence of a body, forensic evidence, eyewitnesses or a confession, John Cannan must be considered, as he himself claims, innocent. However, Suzy Lamplugh's mother has stated that she is convinced the man who killed her daughter is now in jail.

Is John Cannan Mr Kipper?

So what is this mass of circumstantial evidence which is supposed to make the connection? The main points are outlined below, though no matter how convincing, no single factor or any combination of them *proves* that Cannan is Mr Kipper.

1. The Identikit picture of Mr Kipper bears a strong resemblance to John Cannan, who was known by his fellow-prisoners in Wormwood Scrubs as 'Kipper'.
2. Cannan was released from prison on 25 July 1986, three days before Suzy Lamplugh disappeared. He had told friends he was dating a girl from Fulham.
3. John Cannan was living in a parole hostel in Fulham, just four miles from where Ms Lamplugh worked and where Mr Kipper claimed he was looking for property.
4. It is thought that Mr Kipper drove a BMW car – John Cannan did drive a BMW car.
5. One newspaper report claimed that Cannan visited two bars known to have been frequented by Suzy Lamplugh – The White Horse and the Crocodile and Tears.
6. Cannan was fond of impressing women with champagne; there were reports of Mr Kipper carrying a beribboned bottle of champagne when he met Ms Lamplugh at Shorrold's Road.
7. Cannan had previously used the ploy of posing as a house buyer in order to lure women.
8. Gillie Page, a girlfriend of Cannan's, recalled him discussing bodies in concrete while talking about the Lamplugh case.
9. A woman visiting Cannan in prison reported that he mentioned Suzy Lamplugh and said he knew who killed Shirley Banks, Suzy Lamplugh and another woman [? Sandra Court].
10. Suzy Lamplugh had spoken of having a boyfriend in Bristol, where John Cannan abducted Shirley Banks and which he looked upon as his 'home town'.
11. Cannan was reputed to be obsessed by numerics, and when he put false number plates on Shirley Banks's Mini he chose SLP 3869 – it has been suggested that this represents a code for *Su*zy *Lamp*lugh and the year of her disappearance, '86.

After interviewing him, a police spokesman for the Lamplugh

investigating team said: 'He [Cannan] is a clever and convincing liar. When the dust has settled and he has had a chance to consider his future behind bars we hope he will be able to help us. We are paying close attention to the *modus operandi* of his abductions. The fact that we believe Suzy Lamplugh knew her attacker may also be important.' He confirmed that the file on Ms Lamplugh would be reopened and extra officers assigned to the investigation. Police have also said that the evidence linking Cannan with Lamplugh, while circumstantial, is 'overwhelming'. It should, nevertheless, be added that through his solicitor, John Cannan still denies the connection: 'My instructions are that he has never met the lady. What the police position may be I can't say.'

It was not until the summer of 1990, after Cannan's unsuccessful appeal, that the story resurfaced, and this time it was not only the Suzy Lamplugh connection that police were investigating, but a possible link with the case of Sandra Court, an insurance clerk who was murdered in Dorset four years previously.

Twenty-seven-year-old Ms Court had been celebrating her last day at one job before flying off to start a new one as a nanny in Spain. After leaving a Bournemouth nightclub, she was strangled. Investigating officers have now established that John Cannan arrived in Bournemouth on the same day, 2 May 1986, in a car driven by a former cell-mate at Wormwood Scrubs. On this same weekend Suzy Lamplugh was 25 years old and had cancelled a birthday date with a 'man from Bristol' – Cannan's 'home town'. John Cannan is vague about his movements over this weekend, but police investigating the Court case visited him in Wakefield jail.

A further possible avenue of corroboration may be the anonymous letter received by the police after Sandra Court's murder claiming that the death was an accident. In advance of the forensic report, the *Sunday Times* newspaper invited handwriting expert Robert Harris to compare the anonymous letter with a sample of John Cannan's handwriting. Mr Harris concluded that the anonymous letter was almost certainly written in a disguised hand, and there was a strong possibility that it was written by Cannan – he found four clear similarities between the two scripts.

In early September 1990, Mrs Diana Lamplugh, through the Lamplugh Trust, issued a report which stated: 'We are not looking for anyone else. We feel very relieved that, in our estimation, the man who killed Suzy cannot kill anybody else. The police came to see us after they interviewed him in prison and the result is that they had to tell us they cannot do any more. We agree with their assessment of the situation. It is impossible to get any further.' In the absence of finding Suzy's body to give it a decent burial, the Lamplughs hope to have a stained-glass window dedicated to her memory installed at All Saints Church, East Sheen.

Although it is unlikely that this will be the last word on the Lamplugh case, little more concrete information can emerge until either her body is found or her killer makes a confession.

OBITUARY
The Crusade of Jean Justice

On 2 July 1990, justice was deprived of one of its most imaginative and tireless crusaders when the appropriately named Jean Justice died. I first met Jean only towards the end of his life, and the biography that we planned to celebrate his life must needs be replaced by an obituary.

Jean Justice was the epitome of the single-issue fanatic, as he himself was quick to agree, engaging in an extraordinary thirty-year battle for justice in the case of James Hanratty and the A6 Murder.

At approximately 9.30 on the late summer evening of 22 August 1961, Michael Gregsten, a young married research scientist and his girlfriend, Valerie Storie, were relaxing in his car at a lay-by outside the village of Dornley on the A6 road through Bedfordshire. It was an unlikely prelude to the five-and-a-half hour nightmare that was to leave 36-year-old Gregsten dead and Valerie Storie crippled for the rest of her life. There in the quiet of the cornfield a man stepped from the darkness and tapped on the driver's side window; when Mike Gregsten wound it down he found himself face to face with the barrel of a revolver: 'This is a hold-up.'

For two hours the gunman sat nervously in the back seat of the grey Morris Minor covering his prisoners with the weapon while relating a rambling and improbable story about his recent flight from the police. At 11.30 Gregsten was ordered to start his car for the first leg of a terrifying journey along the A6 traversing three counties and finally coming to an end at the prophetically named Deadman's Hill, where Michael Gregsten was shot twice through the head at point-blank range. After compounding his savage attack with the rape of Valerie Storie, the killer bundled her from the car and fired five bullets in quick succession into her body, causing injuries that robbed her for ever of the use of her legs, and almost of her life.

Over the succeeding months, this crime – as seemingly pointless as it was tragic – meandered through an investigative maze of uncertain, unsafe and downright impossible identifications concluding with the announcement of two likely suspects – first Peter Louis Alphon, then James Hanratty, both petty crooks, both with known police records. In what was to become one of crime detections's most controversial decisions, it was Hanratty whose fate was the bewildering ordeal of the process of the law – the police stations, the magistrate's court, culminating in the then longest trial in British criminal history. At the end of it James Hanratty, who had consistently protested his innocence, was convicted and sentenced to hang.

On 3 April 1962, he wrote a final letter to his parents:

. . . I have always loved you and Dad and all of my family and I don't think there is a son anywhere in the world that loves his Mum and Dad as much as I do at this stage. Though I will never see you again, through the fault of others, I will know in my own mind, as my love for you is very strong, your love for me will be just as strong . . . I am sitting here Mum and you have been on my mind all evening. But I will be glad when morning does come . . .

The following morning James Hanratty walked with dignity on to the scaffold at Bedford Gaol.

If the British legal system has been punctuated by the tragic inevitability of occasional miscarriages, it has also been dignified by its share of those whose belief in the principles of justice make them fearless watchdogs of the law, and none so persistently, so tenaciously pursued the elusive truth behind the shootings on Deadman's Hill than Jean Justice, who was to campaign selflessly over the following three decades to free Hanratty's name from the stigma of murder. Indeed, the names of Jean

Justice and James Hanratty were to become inseparable.

On that November day in 1961, when Hanratty stood in the dock of the magistrate's court at Ampthill, his unlikely champion, lured there by the publicity of a 'major case', sat only yards away in the public gallery of the packed Victorian courtroom. The 31-year-old son of a Belgian diplomat, a man of independent means who had twice changed nationality in order to avoid national service, failed his law examinations at Oxford, and had settled to a life of decadent ease, Justice was about to embark upon a drama that was by turns a black comedy and the borderline of nightmare.

Over the course of the Ampthill preliminaries and the early part of the trial at Bedford Assizes, as James Hanratty was pushed helplessly through the painstaking process of English law, Jean Justice became increasingly, almost obsessively, convinced that the wrong man was standing there in the shadow of the gallows. Thus the crusade began for the man who, according to one sympathetic fellow-campaigner, 'badgered and infuriated almost everyone connected with the case', often exhibiting a tenacity that the less fearless among us might describe as foolhardy.

Most important, our young man-about-London turned crusader deliberately sought out and courted the friendship and affection of Peter Louis Alphon, the original suspect in the police case, an established and dangerous criminal, the balance of whose mind was already in considerable doubt. It was the start of a phantasmagoric relationship that over many, many months led Jean Justice to confront the limit of his own courage:

I used to meet him at one o'clock in the King's Arms in Shepherd Market . . .[1] He would invariably buy me a large Amontillado. Then, hands clasped in token of the deep bond between us, we would talk. Remorselessly, I used to insist over and over that what he had done to an innocent man would have to be remedied. I shall never forget the calculated callousness of his reply: "That man was expendable," he said, "had it been you, I should have taken a different course . . ." He added significantly: "If I had known you

[1]These texts in Jean Justice's own words have been taken variously from his published writing on the Hanratty case and conversations with the present writer during the last months of Jean Justice's life.

a year ago, this terrible murder would never have taken place . . ."

'From the King's Arms we used to stroll down Piccadilly and make for Fortnum and Mason, where we always ordered the soup. One day I remember, a particularly truculent waitress irritated him. His eyes blazed with anger, he suddenly sprang to his feet, and without a word of apology or explanation to me, he walked out. When I followed to remonstrate with him, I could feel his cold fury. "I would kill you now," he snarled, "but there are too many witnesses."

THE SENTENCE IS DEATH

EXECUTION USA

It somehow comes as no surprise that an Iraqi Revolutionary Command Council which is unembarrassed by executing its own military officers for failing to win battles, and similarly disposes of its political opponents after secret trials, should have a full catalogue of capital offences in the 'criminal' category, and one of the highest execution rates in the world.

Those who retain such visual images as the 'Bamboo Curtain' will be correspondingly sanguine to hear revelations that the Chinese have executed – often publicly – more than 500 'felons' during the previous year as part of an on-going campaign to reduce the crime statistics.

But it never ceases to chill the heart to learn that in the United States, the 'Land of the Free', in excess of 2000 prisoners are incarcerated on Death Rows countrywide at any one time; and that in 1990 the USA took over from South Africa as the execution capital of the Western world.

Since the introduction of more mechanically sophisticated methods of execution to replace their British inheritance of the gallows, the United States is now able to offer a bewildering selection of death machines:

The Electric Chair

Where the prisoner is strapped into a wooden chair and powerful surges of electricity are passed through his body via moistened copper electrodes attached to his shaven head and leg. First used on William Kemmler on 6 August 1890 in Auburn Prison, New York.

Kemmler's execution was under the immediate direction and

control of the prison warden, C.F. Durston, and took place in a room set apart for the purpose, in the basement of the prison's administrative building, to which the electric current was conducted by means of an ordinary electric wire. Dr Carlos Macdonald, one of the medical witnesses, left the following account:

The apparatus consisted of a stationary engine, an alternating-current dynamo and exciter, a Cardew volt meter with extra resistance coil, calibrated for a range of from 30 to 2000 volts, an ammeter for alternating currents from 0.10 to 3 amperes, a Wheatstone bridge, rheostat, bell signals, and necessary switches; a 'death chair' with adjustable head-rest, binding tapes, and two adjustable electrodes. The chair, a square-framed heavy oaken one with a high, slightly sloping back and broad arms, was fastened to the floor, the feet of the chair being properly insulated.

Attached to the back of the chair, above the head-rest, was a sliding arrangement shaped like a figure four (4), the base or horizontal arm of which projected forward, and from which was suspended the head electrode, so as to rest on the vertex, or top of the head, against which it was firmly held by means of a spiral spring. The spinal, or body electrode was attached to the lower part of the back of the chair and projected forward horizontally on a level with the hollow of the sacrum. The electrodes each consisted of a bell-shaped rubber cup about four inches in diameter, the part corresponding to the handle of the bell being of wood, through the long axis of which the wire passed into the bell, terminating in a metallic disc about three inches in diameter, and faced with a layer of sponge. The lower electrode was also provided with a sliding arrangement and spiral spring to hold it in place, while a broad strap fastened to the back of the chair and passed round the lower part of the prisoner's abdomen rendered the contact secure. The head was firmly secured by means of conjoined broad leather bands, which encircled the forehead and chin, concealing the eyes and upper portion of the face, and were fastened at the back of the almost perpendicular head-rest, while the chest, arms and legs were secured by broad straps attached to corresponding portions of the chair. The wire attached to the head electrode descended from the ceiling, and that of the lower one passed along the floor to the chair, being protected by a strip of wood.

The dynamo and engine were located in one of the prison [work] shops several hundred feet distant from the execution room; the voltmeter, ammeter, switchboard, etc., were located in a room adjoining the execution room, which contained the death chair, electrodes and connecting wires. Communication between the meter room and dynamo room was by means of electric signals.

Of the twenty-five official witnesses present, fourteen were physicians. Before Kemmler was brought into the room the warden asked the physicians how long the contact should be maintained. Dr MacDonald suggested twenty seconds but subsequently assented to ten seconds.

The preliminary arrangements having been completed, Kemmler was brought into the execution room by the warden and introduced to the witnesses who were seated in a semi-circle facing the death chair. On entering the room the prisoner appeared strikingly calm and collected. In fact, his manner and appearance indicated a state of subdued elation, as if gratified at being the central figure of the occasion, his somewhat limited intellect evidently rendering him unable to fully appreciate the gravity of his situation. He was given a chair near the death chair and, on being seated, in response to the warden's introduction, said: 'Well, I wish every one good luck in this world, and I think I am going to a good place, and the papers has been saying a lot of stuff about me that wasn't true. That's all I have to say.'

At the warden's bidding he then arose, removed his coat, and without the least display of emotion or nervousness, took his seat in the execution chair, calmly submitting to the adjustment of the electrodes and binding straps, himself aiding the proceedings by suggestions and fixing his body and limbs in the proper position. Observing the nervousness of the prison officers who were adjusting the straps he admonished them not to hurry, and to 'be sure that everything is all right'.

He pressed his bared back firmly against the spinal electrode and requested that the head electrode be pressed down more firmly on the top of his head, from which the hair had been imperfectly clipped before he entered the room, remarking at the same time that he desired to perform his part to the best of his ability. The preparations terminated with a final moistening of the electrodes, the whole occupying at most between three and four minutes. Everything being seemingly ready, the warden signalled to his assistants in charge of the switches in the adjoining room to turn the lever which closed the circuit and instantly sent the deadly current through the *prisoner's body. The instant the contact was made the body was thrown into a state of extreme rigidity, every fibre of the entire muscular system being apparently in a marked condition of tonic spasm. Synchronously with the onset of rigidity, body sensation, motion and consciousness were apparently absolutely suspended, and remained so while electrical contact was maintained. At the end of seventeen seconds Kemmler was pronounced dead, none of the witnesses dissenting, and the warden signalled to have the contact broken, which was immediately done.*

For obvious reasons, the only means of determining the question of death while the body was in circuit was by ocular demonstration; so that it can not be positively asserted that the heart's action entirely ceased with the onset of unconsciousness, though most of the medical witnesses present thought that it did.

When the electrical contact was broken the condition of rigidity noted above was instantly succeeded by one of complete muscular relaxation. At the same time superficial discolorations resembling commencing capillary post-mortem changes were observed on the exposed portions of the face. The body remained limp and motionless for approximately half a minute, when there occurred a series of slight spasmodic movements of the chest, accompanied by the expulsion of a small amount of mucus from the mouth. There were no evidences of a return to consciousness or of sensory function; but in view of the possibility that life was not wholly extinct, beyond resuscitation, and in order to take no risk of such a contingency, the current was ordered to be reapplied, which was done within about two minutes from the time the first contact was broken. The sudden muscular rigidity noted on the first closure of the circuit was again observed and continued until the contact was again broken, when the opposite state of complete muscular relaxation re-occured. The second closure of the circuit was inadvertantly maintained for about seventy seconds, when a small volume of vapour, and subsequently of smoke, was seen to issue from the point of application of the spinal electrode, due, as was subsequently found, to scorching of the edge of the sponge with which the electrode was faced, and from which the moisture had been evaporated by prolonged electrical contact. The odour of burning sponge was faintly perceptible in the room.

There was also some desiccation of the already dead body, immediately underneath the electrodes, especially under the lower one. A careful examination of the body was now made in which the medical witnesses participated to a greater or less extent. The radial pulse and heart's action had ceased, the pupils were dilated and the corneas were depressed and flaccid on pressure. In other word, William Kemmler was dead, and the intent and purpose of the law to effect sudden and painless death in the execution of criminals had been successfully carried out.

In the excitement and confusion of the moment, occasioned by the belief on the part of some that death was not complete, the second application of the current in Kemmler's case was maintained too long – nearly a minute and a half. If there was a spark of unconscious vitality remaining in the prisoner's body after the first contact was broken, it was absolutely extinguished the instant the second and last contact was made. That the man was dead, however, comparatively long before the burning of the sponge and desiccation of the tissue occurred, there is no reason to doubt.

The Gas Chamber

The gas chamber is a small, airtight room with an observation window, a chair with straps attached to it, and a bucket of acid beneath it. This form of execution was first used in Nevada in 1924 as a more humane alternative to hanging and electrocution. The victim is strapped into the chair and at the appointed moment a remote-control mechanism drops sodium cyanide (NaCN) pellets into the acid-filled bucket below the chair, causing the release of the deadly gas hydrogen cyanide (HCN).

To suffer an *almost* instantaneous, *almost* painless death, the victim must inhale the fatal gas deeply as soon as it is released into the chamber. If the instinctive reaction of self-preservation forces the prisoner to hold his breath, or take only a timid sniff, he will suffer a slow and painful end with dizziness, headache, nausea, vomiting and difficult breathing, until unconsciousness leads to final oblivion. A doctor is able to monitor extinction of life via earphones attached to a stethoscope strapped to the prisoner's chest.

Despite its claim to be a speedy death, cases like Jimmy Lee Gray, executed in Mississippi in 1983, took an agonizing, convulsive eight minutes to die. First used in California's San Quentin Prison in 1924.

Lethal Injection

Death results from the injection into a vein of the arm a succession of lethal drugs – sodium thiopental (to render the prisoner unconscious), pancuronium bromide to induce paralysis of the lungs, and potassium chloride (causing cardiac arrest).

The First Execution by Lethal Injection

The conscience-salving quest for a 'humane' method of judicial execution led to the making of legal history in the month of December 1982, when the first death was administered by 'lethal injection' (though the method had been officially adopted by the states of Oklahoma and Texas as early as 1977). The victim of this experiment was a 40-year-old black man named Charlie Brooks who had been convicted in 1976 of killing David Gregory, a secondhand car salesman of Fort Worth.

Brooks was to be the first person executed in Texas for eighteen years, and the case caused widespread controversy both on legal and ethical grounds. Brooks's partner in the shooting, Woody Lourdres, had his original conviction and death sentence overturned as the result of a legal technicality – the jury had been incorrectly selected; subsequently Lourdres plea-bargained himself a 40-year term of imprisonment. As it was unclear which of the men fired the fatal shot, there was an obvious unfairness on two different sentences for the same conviction on the same set of evidence.

The American medical profession was strongly opposed to the practice of doctors administering lethal injections and their Association issued a statement that 'The use of a lethal injection as a means of terminating the life of a convict is not the practice of medicine. A physician who accepts the task of performing an execution on behalf of the State obviously does not enhance the image of the medical profession . . . This is not an appropriate role for a physician.' In September 1981, the Secretary General of the World Medical Association issued this statement as part of a press release: 'Acting as an executioner is not the practice of medicine and physician services are not required to carry out capital punishment even if the methodology utilizes pharmacologic agents or equipment that might otherwise be used in the practice of medicine. The physician's only role would be to certify death once the state had carried out the execution.' In the end it was 'medical technicians' from the staff of the Medical Director of the Texas Department of Corrections, overseen by a doctor, who performed the first 'operation'.

Brooks was wheeled into the execution room (formerly a gas chamber) at Huntsville Prison strapped to a hospital trolley. While the prisoner was awaiting execution, his lawyers had been appealing to a judge of the Fifth Circuit Court of Appeals to reverse its earlier refusal to grant a stay. After hastily convening a telephone jury, the court reconfirmed at a few minutes to midnight that it would not grant a stay.

Just after midnight the condemned man's arm was bound to a padded board and his veins examined by the doctor to ensure that they were large enough to take the injection catheter. (This is a particular problem in subjects who have been habitual drug users where veins may be weak and scarred requiring surgery to expose a deeper vein.) The needle was inserted into his vein and attached to a rubber tube which went across the floor and through a hole in the wall to the executioner's chamber.

Among the witnesses in the death house was Brooks's girl-friend, twenty-seven-year-old nurse Vanessa Sapp, and after the couple had exchanged some final affectionate words the condemned man was joined by two Islamic priests who accompanied him in a brief Muslim service.

At 12.07 am a dose of the barbiturate drug sodium thiopental was added to the intravenous saline drip which had already been started to keep the vein open. Brooks was observed to clench his fist, raise his head and appear to yawn or gasp for breath before falling into unconsciousness. The second ingredient of the deadly cocktail was added – pancuronium bromide, a muscle relaxant used in sufficient quantity to paralyze the lungs; and the third – potassium chloride to induce cardiac arrest. At 12.16 Charlie Brooks was pronounced dead.

The claim that lethal injection provided the state with a speedy and painless way of disposing of its condemned prisoners was met with very mixed reaction from the medical profession and interested laymen from the very beginning, and experience with upwards of forty prisoners since 1982 has done nothing to allay the fears of the abolitionist lobby. The problem of finding a suitable vein in some inmates has already been mentioned and a case has been cited in Texas in 1985 where no less than 23 attempts were made to find a vein, taking 40 minutes, during which the condemned man was strapped to the trolley. Complications can also arise from the simple eventuality of the prisoner resenting his undignified end to such an extent as to struggle; in this case the poison could be injected into a main artery or into the muscle, causing considerable pain. In another instance reported by Amnesty International in its vital report *When the State Kills . . .* (London, 1989), during the execution by lethal injection of Raymond Landry in December 1988, the tube feeding the needle became detached and the poisonous mixture spurted across the room towards the witnesses. According to the Texas Attorney General, 'There was more pressure in the hose than his veins could absorb.'

In addition to these three methods unique to the United States, there are still pockets of support for hanging, and some use of what has always been the military option, the firing squad. Some states go so far as to extend to the condemned man a choice of deaths – North Carolina, for example, can offer the gas chamber or lethal injection; Utah lethal injection or firing squad.

Methods of Execution Current in the United States

Alabama	Electric chair
Arizona	Gas chamber
Arkansas	Electric chair or Lethal injection
California	Gas chamber
Colorado	Gas chamber
Connecticut	Electric chair
Delaware	Hanging
Florida	Electric chair
Georgia	Electric chair
Idaho	Firing squad or Lethal injection
Illinois	Lethal injection
Indiana	Electric chair
Kentucky	Electric chair
Louisiana	Electric chair

Maryland	Gas chamber
Mississippi	Gas chamber or Lethal injection
Missouri	Gas chamber
Montana	Hanging or Lethal injection
Nebraska	Electric chair
Nevada	Lethal injection
New Hampshire	Hanging
New Jersey	Lethal injection
New Mexico	Lethal injection
North Carolina	Gas chamber or Lethal injection
Ohio	Electric chair
Oklahoma	Firing squad or Lethal injection
Oregon	Lethal injection
Pennsylvania	Electric chair
South Carolina	Electric chair
South Dakota	Lethal injection
Tennessee	Electric chair
Texas	Lethal injection
Utah	Firing squad or Lethal injection
Vermont	Electric chair
Virginia	Electric chair
Washington	Hanging or Lethal injection
Wyoming	Lethal injection

In common with other civilized societies during the optimistic years of the 1960s and early 1970s, the United States enjoyed a respite from the uncertain benefits of judicial execution. Subsequently, although much of the rest of the world (including Britain) tended to become *more* abolitionist, the United States Supreme Court ruled in 1976 (four years after its suspension) that individual states within the union had the right to reintroduce the death penalty for the crime of 'aggravated' (usually first-degree) murder as and when they felt it necessary. Some states, like Texas and Florida, have taken the opportunity with apparent enthusiasm – Florida being the first, in May 1979, when it electrocuted John Spenkelink. Other states passed the required legislation to create the administrative machinery to process the death penalty if required, but have so far not exercised that option. The remainder have remained abolitionist in practice and principle.

Death sentence used	Law passed, not used	Abolitionist
Alabama	Arizona	Alaska
Florida	California	Hawaii
Georgia	Colorado	Iowa
Indiana	Connecticut	Kansas
Louisiana	Delaware	Maine
Mississippi	Idaho	Massachusetts
Missouri	Kentucky	Michigan
Nevada	Maryland	Minnesota
North Carolina	Montana	New York
South Carolina	Nebraska	North Dakota
Texas	New Hampshire	Rhode Island
Utah	New Jersey	West Virginia
Virginia	New Mexico	Wisconsin
	Ohio	
Since 1990:	Oregon	
Arkansas	Pennsylvania	
Illinois	South Dakota	
Oklahoma	Tennessee	
	Vermont	
	Washington	
	Wyoming	

Until the end of 1989, thirteen states had carried out a total of 120 executions since reinstatement in 1976.

During 1990 the total of executions rose to 142. Perhaps more alarming was that three more states had exercised their option to reintroduce capital punishment – Arkansas, Illinois and Oklahoma.

That the sentence of death can still be a wretched and undignified affair after exactly 100 years, when William Kemmler's execution produced smoke, it is unnecessary to look further than the appalling sight presented to witnesses at the execution of Jesse Tafero in Florida (see page 247).

Perhaps the most disturbing aspect of the death sentence in the USA – apart from its general anachronism in a civilized world – is the obvious randomness with which it is implemented. For example, given that each state is allowed to make its own choice, it follows that what constitutes a capital offence on one side of the state line may not a couple of miles over the border.

More invidious still is the vagary of execution within a single state, a single prison. With more than 2000 prisoners on Death Row countrywide and only a score or so executions, we might be forgiven for asking how these few are chosen. It is tempting to imagine that only the most cynical murderers, the most evil assassins are selected to suffer the ultimate sanction of the law. In reality it is more likely to be the poorest and least articulate that are put to death.

In a cumbersome process of seemingly endless petitions, it is possible for a case to drag on for eight to ten or more years between conviction in a state court and the point when the Federal court removes the final obstacle to execution. It is clear that in order to embark on this legal marathon, a prisoner must first have sufficient intellect and information to be aware of his constitutional rights, and also have sufficient funds to retain the services of even the most liberal and altruistic of lawyers. Few states which use the death penalty make provision for legal aid for the purpose of appealing against execution.

A condemned prisoner's only hope in many cases is to have his cause supported by one of the charitable legal organizations like the Southern Prisoners Defense Committee based in Atlanta, Georgia (a state high on the execution table and part of that southern belt of states that keeps the executioner generally busy). Often this vital function is the self-imposed responsibility of just one dedicated campaigner. Such a veteran of the appeals system is Marie Deans, who operates from a single room in Virginia, her work existing on an irregular flow of small private donations. With just a telephone and an unshakeable belief in the justice of her cause, Ms Deans tries, by a combination of cajoling, bullying and embarrassing lawyers into taking on death row appeals free of legal costs – which effectively involves them working evenings, weekends and other leisure hours to fit the cases into already heavy schedules.

Perhaps understandably – perhaps not – this self-sacrificing endeavour too often attracts abuse and obstruction. It is less the hate mail, slashed tyres and offensive telephone calls that hurt Marie Deans than the official calumny heaped on her and her colleagues in an attempt to undermine their credibility.

Charles Watson, Virginia state prosecutor, for example, has gone on record as believing that Marie Deans and the lawyers who support her 'are some of the largest perverters of the law. I sometimes question their loyalty, their motives, because most of them don't get paid for it but they do get an awful lot of publicity.

And you find in most instances its young lawyers trying to get started, and any capital case, no matter where it's at – in Virginia or anyplace else – generates a lot of publicity. They themselves perhaps feel that the man deserves to die, but they want to carry it on to see when and where they can be the first one to hit on an excuse to have the death penalty overturned in this specific case. In other words they dream up a new idea that's never been tried before – and it's worth millions in publicity.'

However true that may be, any discussion of the finances of capital punishment is bound to expose another of the system's failings – it has been calculated in some quarters that due to the huge legal costs to the state in dealing with protracted appeals, it costs as much as six times more to execute a prisoner in the United States than to keep him in prison for life.

The Politics of Death

The basic problem with reforming the capital punishment issue in the United States is that it is so large on the political agenda that few candidates could risk ignoring its negative impact on their chances of electoral success.

Indeed, so great was the crime and punishment issue during 1990, that political candidates were tripping over each other in the race to promise more vigorous application of the death penalty. In Texas, for example, Attorney General Jim Mattox, Democratic nominee for governor, advertised himself on television as the man who has 'carried out thirty-two death penalties' – not personally, you understand, but through a proxy.

That this was no throw-away macho chest-beating can be understood in the light of a recent *New York Times*/CBS News poll which found that 72% of their sample was in favour of judicially executing convicted murderers.

And it is this often exaggerated fear of violent crime, and a frustration with politicians who seem incapable of stemming its flow that has given support for capital punishment its reason. Said Governor Martinez's campaign manager: 'You cannot be against the death penalty and survive a campaign for major office in Florida.'

In California, which retains but has not so far exercised its right to execute since 1976, Democratic nominee for governor, Dianne Feinstein, is announced as 'the only Democrat for governor for the death penalty'.

The fact that crime statistics do *not* support the efficacy of capital punishment is seen from the continuing reports of the National Crime Survey which, in 1976 (the year the death penalty was restored), found one household in three reported being 'touched by crime' and in 1988 the figure had dropped dramatically to one in four. In parallel with this, according to public opinion polls, support for the capital sentence increased from 65% in 1976 to 72% in 1985, and as many as 79% at the end of 1988.

However, a cautionary note to swinging the noose on the campaign trail, so to speak, is offered by the case of former governor of Texas Mark White, who, while seeking nomination in a three-party play-off, promoted himself on Texas television strolling past rows of photographs of condemned prisoners executed during his term as governor. The fact that most of the inmates were from the ethnic minorities understandably lost Mr White the black and Hispanic vote, forcing him into third place and out of the race.

THE YEAR ON DEATH ROW

At the end of 1989, the running total of executions carried out in the United States stood at 120 since reinstatement in 1976. By the end of 1990 this figure had risen to 142. In addition, three states which had not previously carried out sentence of death joined the thirteen who had.

121
SMITH, Gerald; (2nd in Missouri)

Gerald Smith was convicted of the murder of his girlfriend Karen Roberts in St Louis. While in detention, Smith wrote a full and detailed confession in a letter to the newspapers; he explained that Roberts had infected him with venereal disease and 'I wanted her to feel some pain, so I beat her lousy little head in'. Smith added: 'If she were living now I would do it all over again.' The letter was signed 'Gerald Smith, the cold-blooded killer'. The Supreme Court voted to lift his stay of execution on 16 January and two days later he was put to death by lethal injection at Potosi Prison, Missouri.

122
BUTLER, Jerome; (34th in Texas)

Aged 54 at the time of his sentence, Butler was found guilty of robbing and shooting to death a taxi driver in Houston in 1986. He had spent a great part of his life in and out of prisons, and by the time of his capital conviction had clearly had enough, whereupon Jerome Butler instructed his attorney to stop their efforts to secure a reprieve. He was put to death by lethal injection in the state prison at Huntsville on 21 April.

123
WOOMER, Ronald; (3rd in South Carolina)

Woomer went on a rape, robbery and shooting spree in 1979 which left four people dead. In company with Eugene Scaar, he had gone out on 22 February and committed two burglaries, killing both the house owners and the mentally retarded sister of one of them. Later that day Woomer and Scaar robbed, raped and kidnapped a shop assistant; then Scaar turned the gun on himself rather than risk capture and arrest. After apologizing for his brutal crimes, Woomer was executed in the electric chair at Columbia, South Carolina on 22 April.

124
TAFERO, Jesse Joseph; (22nd in Florida)

As Tafero and his girlfriend Sonya Jacobs sat in his car parked along the Interstate Highway 95 near Fort Lauderdale, Florida, on 20 February 1976, a Florida highway patrolman and a visiting Canadian officer approached the vehicle and were summarily shot dead. Both Tafero and Jacobs were tried and convicted of the murders, but in 1981 Sonya Jacobs's death sentence was commuted to life, leaving Jesse Tafero to face the chair alone on 4 May 1990, at Starke. Described by his defence attorney as nothing short of 'torture', the execution at Florida state prison went very badly wrong when, according to a spokesman for the Correctional Department, a sponge in the headpiece caught fire as current passed through it (see 'The First Execution by Electricity', page 234). It is customary to require only one surge of electricity to immobilize and kill the condemned man, though in Tafero's case the technicians needed to switch the current on and off three times in the course of four minutes. Each time it was turned on, flames shot from the helmet on Tafero's head, and black smoke poured from beneath the mask covering his face. Only after the third attempt did the prisoner stop breathing and moving his head. An Associated Press reporter said: 'This is the first time I've ever seen visible sparks and flames coming from the head.' Governor Robert Martinez launched an immediate inquiry into the incident.

125
STOKES, Winford; (3rd in Missouri)

Executed by lethal injection at Potosi, Missouri, on 11 May, 39-year-old Stokes had been convicted of the strangling and stabbing of Pamela Benda of University City. Stokes had two previous murder convictions, one for shooting a St Louis bar-owner in 1969, the other an elderly woman in the same city in 1977.

126
LAWS, Leonard; (4th in Missouri)

Laws and his associate, George Gilmore, had killed an elderly couple during the course of a robbery in 1980. Laws was executed by lethal injection on 17 May; Gilmore would face death later in the year.

127
ANDERSON, Johnny Ray (35th in Texas)

Put to death by the same method and on the same date as Leonard Laws, Anderson had been convicted with Laura Anderson Goode and another man of killing his own brother-in-law, Ronald Gene Goode (Laura's husband), in an insurance fraud. Anderson's two partners in crime had been sentenced to life imprisonment, but were paroled in 1989, and he went to his death complaining that he was, as he put it, 'an excape goat'.

An interesting postscript to the two executions on 17 May was the publication in one of the British tabloid newspapers the following day of the menu requested by the two prisoners as their 'last supper'. For those fascinated by such minutae of execution craft, here is what they requested:

Anderson
Two hamburgers and a medium-rare cheeseburger;
Two pounds of french fries;
Green salad with blue-cheese dressing;
Iced lemon tea;
Two large chocolate chip ice creams with nuts.

Laws (apparently had appetite enough to eat two meals)
1. Fresh orange juice;
   Scrambled egg with hash browns;
   Wheat flakes;
   Six slices of brown toast with strawberry jam;
   Three mugs of coffee.
2. Kentucky fried chicken, coleslaw and mashed potato;
   Hot buttered rolls;
   Apple pie and cream;
   Two litres of iced Pepsi Cola.

But such nuggets are not the mere staple of overseas ghouls who, having lost their own, like to peep through the keyholes of other people's death cells. The same information is served up, so to speak, to an eager home market. Thus we learn from the *Atlanta Journal* that Dalton Prejean (see below) tucked into a seafood platter with french fries, salad, chocolate cake and two orange soft drinks.

The 'last supper' is usually served about three or four hours before the execution is scheduled to take place and can consist of anything 'within reason' that the prison kitchens can either prepare or have sent in. Looking through the list (yes, the last meal goes on official record!), the most striking feature is how remarkably prosaic the choice usually is: hamburgers, seafood platters, pizza, T-bone steaks, Kentucky fried chicken, all with french fries and the cola of choice. No *foie gras*, truffles or even a modest lobster Thermidor. No duck breast *en croûte* with savoury orange sauce, nor partridge poached in vine leaves. Just Kentucky fried chicken.

It was not always so. In London of the eighteenth century, the execution at Newgate Prison of a celebrated malefactor was the opportunity for revelry. Last supper? Last banquet was nearer the truth, last orgy. John Rann, the notorious highwayman known as 'Sixteen-string Jack' after his 'breeches worn with eight strings at each knee', was committed to Newgate in October 1774: 'When Rann was brought down to take his trial he was dressed in a new suit of pea-green clothes, his hat was bound round with silver strings, he wore a ruffled shirt . . . After conviction the behaviour of this malefactor was for some time very improper for one in his unhappy circumstances. On Sunday the 23rd of October he had seven girls to dine with him. The company were remarkably cheerful; nor was Rann less joyous than his companions.'

Another account describes the farewell party of Renwick Williams, known as 'The Monster of London': 'On the day preceding his journey to the gallows, Williams sent cards of invitation to about twenty couples, among whom were some of his alibi friends, his brothers, sisters and several of the more notorious prisoners. At four o'clock the party set to tea. This being over two violinists struck up accompanied by a flute, and the whole company proceeded to exercise their limbs. About eight o'clock the company partook of a farewell supper and a variety of wines such as would not discredit the most sumptuous gala'.

Quite the contrary was the case of violent sex-killer Stephen P. Morin, whose repentance for his crimes and apparently sincere conversion to Christianity led to his ordering, on 13 March 1985, the most sacramental of last meals – unleavened bread, the food of the Passover, Christ's own Last Supper.

128
PREJEAN, Dalton; (19th in Louisiana)

Convicted of the murder of a Louisiana state trooper for no more provocation than being pulled over for a broken tail light on his car, Prejean had been awaiting execution since 1977, when he was just seventeen years old. In fact Dalton Prejean was to make a little bit of legal history; he was the first 'juvenile' to be executed since the Supreme Court ruling of 26 June 1989 that the Constitution's ban on 'cruel and unusual punishment' did not prohibit the execution of mentally retarded murderers or young persons aged sixteen or seventeen at the time of their crime. The Prejean case had already aroused a torrent of anger among civil rights campaigners who made considerable political capital from the facts that the prisoner was not only a juvenile, not only mentally retarded through brain damage, but was typically a black youth convicted by an all-white jury. Despite the petitions and pleas (Prejean had already won ten delays of execution) on 17 May the Supreme Court refused to hear another appeal.

On 18 May 1990, at 10.30 pm – an hour and a half before Prejean, now thirty years old, was put to death – Governor Roemer spoke to him by telephone in the condemned cell at Angola Prison, Louisiana. He told Prejean that his execution was the only thing that would serve society and give the message to people who might think of killing a police officer. The prisoner countered, it was said, by suggesting to the governor that more crime might be deterred if he were kept alive and could tell his story so that people might learn a lesson from his example.

Giving his final statement from a microphone in front of the electric chair, his hands and feet shackled, Dalton Prejean addressed the witnesses, saying: 'Nothing is going to be accomplished. I have peace with myself. I'd like to thank all those who supported me all these years. I'd also like to thank my loved ones for being strong; my son [Dalton Junior, conceived during a conjugal visit at Lafayette parish jail] will be a better person for not letting something like this bring down his life . . . keep strong, keep pushing, keep praying.' Speaking of the victim's family, Prejean continued: 'They said it wasn't for the revenge, but it's hard for me to see, to understand. I hope they're happy. So I forfeit my life. I give my love to all. God bless.'

When he had been strapped into the chair, the condemned man was administered four jolts of electricity and at exactly 12.17 am he was certified dead.

129
BAAL, Thomas; (5th in Nevada)

When the Las Vegas bus driver gave Baal a miserable $20 during an armed robbery in 1988, he stabbed him to death and was, for his crime, convicted and himself sentenced to death. Although his parents had persisted in their campaign for clemency on the grounds of his mental retardation, Baal himself was anxious to face the supreme penalty for his misdeeds. Despite the lower court issuing a stay of execution, it was in no small part due to Joseph Baal ('I want to have this execution over so that I can pay my debt') that on 3 June the Supreme Court lifted the stay. Just hours later, Baal was put to death by lethal injection at Carson City, Nevada.

130
SWINDLER, John Edward; (1st in Arkansas)

Sentenced to die for shooting police officer Randy Basnett in 1976. Executed on 18 June in the electric chair at Varner, Arkansas, it was the first capital sentence to be carried out in the state since 1964.

131
SIMMONS, R. Gene; (2nd in Arkansas)

Only one week after the execution of John Swindler, Simmons

was put to death by lethal injection in the same prison on 25 June. Simmons had been charged and convicted of the muticide of sixteen people, many of them his relatives. He had pleaded for a swift execution to 'let the torture and suffering in me end'.

132
SMITH, James; (36th in Texas)

Killed and robbed a Houston, Texas, businessman in March 1983, Smith was executed by lethal injection on 26 June.

133
THOMAS, Wallace Norrell; (8th in Alabama)

Convicted of the abduction and fatal shooting of shop employee Quenette Shehane at Birmingham, Alabama, in 1976. Before he was strapped into the electric chair in Atmore on 13 July, Thomas read a statement to witnesses denouncing the death penalty as racist. During his time awaiting execution, Wallace Thomas had done considerable work towards founding Project Hope, an organization committed to the abolition of the death sentence and to the comfort of prisoners on death row and their families.

134
DERRICK, Mikel; (37th in Texas)

A male prostitute with a lengthy criminal record including car theft, robbery and soliciting. At his trial Derrick was accused of luring Edward Sonnier to his apartment in 1980, where he stabbed and robbed him. Derrick claimed he had been propositioned by the victim. Put to death by lethal injection at the Texas state prison at Huntsville on 18 July.

135
BOGGS, Richard T.; (9th in Virginia)

Convicted of stabbing and bludgeoning to death his neighbour, 87-year-old Treeby M. Shaw in her Portsmouth, Virginia, home in January 1984, 27-year-old Boggs had then stolen jewellery and silver in order to support his drug habit. Boggs's execution in the electric chair on 19 July was the first to take place in Governor Douglas Wilder's administration. Wilder was notable for completely upturning his former abolitionist stance to pressing for an *expansion* of capital crimes in the state of Virginia.

In an interesting piece of television reportage, viewers were recently taken behind the scenes at Mecklenburg Prison, Virginia, for a step-by-step visual description of the last day on earth of a condemned prisoner. It was not Richard T. Boggs, but only the name is different.

The prisoner is taken from the individual cell in which he has passed the previous two weeks and positioned in a wooden chair in the corridor. Here a warder will shave the man's head and then his right leg up to the knee; after this the prisoner takes a shower and is dressed in a special prison outfit: 'You may notice on this shirt the buttons have been removed and we put Velcro on. The purpose of this is the chair gets very hot – we use about 2400 volts to execute an inmate – and if we don't remove the buttons it'll burn the body.' This shaving and showering is taking place about three and three-quarter hours before execution is due. The prisoner, when he is dressed, is taken to Cell Number One, where a detachment of about half a dozen officers will watch his every move – most especially to guard against the inmate committing suicide. Against this strict security, the prisoner will often eat his last meal – with a plastic spoon.

At the time scheduled for execution the prisoner is taken to the death house and strapped into the electric chair: 'When the man is sat in and buckled secure into the chair, the first thing to be put on and connected will be the leg-piece [which has] a spring-action to fit it firmly to the inmate's leg; the [electric] cable is inserted and tightened with a wing-nut finger tight. Second step: A mask is inserted over the inmate's face which covers his forehead, nose and lips; the only thing exposed is his chin and the lower half of his neck. The back rest is adjusted so that you have a firm seat in the chair. Third step: The helmet is inserted on the inmate's head, [it] also has spring action, which gives you a tight fit. The chin strap is inserted round his chin and connected. At that point the connecting cables are inserted – also finger tight. The final thing that is done, all the straps are checked to make sure there is no slack and the belts are tight. Things to watch for: an inmate with a large body build, it will take more amperage to kill him; he will smoke extremely due to the size of his build. The smell is permeant; the thing is to put vaseline in your nostrils (you can use a Q-Tip to get it out). Also your clothes will have a smell in them, and it is suggested your clothes are soaked in water for two or three days before they are washed and you can re-use them again.' It is also apparently recommended that prisoners awaiting electrocution be encouraged to drink as much liquid as possible, not only to hasten death, but to reduce the smell of burning flesh.

[Another state's official guidlines for execution by electric chair are reproduced in Appendix 4]

136
BERTOLOTTI, Anthony; (23rd in Florida)

After the outrage that followed in the wake of Jesse Tafero's bungled execution in May, the US Court of Appeals had blocked the execution of five of Florida's death row inmates who had protested that the electric chair used to despatch Tafero was faulty and would as likely torture them to death. The Florida prisons' administration carried out lengthy tests and attributed the instrument's earlier temperament to the use of artificial instead of natural sponges to attach electrodes to the prisoner's head. The chair was now certified 'safe' and the execution of Bertolotti was the first since the Tafero incident. Anthony Bertolotti was convicted of robbing, raping, and stabbing to death a woman in 1983; he was put to death on 27 July 1990, at Starke.

137
GILMORE, George; (5th in Missouri)

Partnered Leonard Laws on his murderous spree and was executed by lethal injection at Potosi, Missouri, on 31 August. Laws had been put to death on 17 May.

138
COLEMAN, Charles Troy; (1st in Oklahoma)

The first time the death penalty had been carried out in the Sooner State since 1966. Coleman had been convicted of shooting dead a man who interrupted him during a burglary in 1979. Executed by lethal injection on 10 September at McAlester Prison at the age of 43.

139
WALKER, Charles; (1st in Illinois)

Executed for the 1983 murder of a young couple in Mascoutah, Illinois, whom he tied to a tree and robbed of the negligible sum of $40, 50-year-old Walker was executed by lethal injection at Joliet prison on 12 September.

140
HAMBLEN, James William; (24th in Florida)

Put to death in the electric chair at Starke on 21 September, Hamblen had been convicted of killing a lingerie store owner during an attempted robbery in 1984.

141
EVANS, Wilbert Lee; (10th in Virginia)

In 1981, while Evans was being held on suspicion of a murder in North Carolina, he attempted to escape from the Alexandria jail by shooting sheriff's deputy William Truesdale with his own gun. During the time he spent awaiting execution, Evans appeared to be the model prisoner – a reformed and rehabilitated man. Nowhere was this more apparent than in the riot on Death Row at Mecklenburg Correctional Centre, Richmond, in 1984, during which Evans intervened to save prison staff and female nurses from physical abuse. Despite the best efforts of civil rights campaigners, Evans's final appeal was turned down by the Supreme Court on 17 October, and he was electrocuted in Richmond jail on the same day. According to the *Washington Post*, eye-witnesses to the execution were appalled to see blood appear to flow from beneath the leather mask which covered Evans's face after the first burst of electricity had hit his body, and before the second and final jolt. Prison authorities claimed that the condition was due to a nose-bleed caused by the condemned man's high blood pressure.

142
CLARK, Raymond Robert; (25th in Florida)

Put to death in the electric chair at Starke on 19 November for the kidnapping and murder of a St Petersburg scrap-yard owner in 1977. Clarke's accomplice at the time, Ty Johnston, was only sixteen years of age when the killing occurred, and he was paroled in 1987 after serving nine years of a 25-year prison sentence. Johnston pleaded guilty and gave evidence against his partner.

THE GREAT HANGING DEBATE

On 17 December 1990, the right-wing of the British Conservative government made another of its periodic, desperate bids to reintroduce capital punishment to the country for certain categories of murder. It was the nineteenth such attempt since 'abolition' by the Murder (Abolition of Death Penalty) Act of 1965 – an average of once in every 22 months.

The previous vote, in June 1988, was based on a new clause in the Criminal Justice Bill which proposed: 'The maximum sentence available to the courts upon conviction for murder shall be death in a manner authorized by law.' The House of Commons rejected this new clause by 341 votes to 218 (with more than 80 abstentions). In the year before that, 1987, an attempt to reintroduce hanging for 'evil' murderers was rejected by a majority of 112.

Against any likelihood of success, hope for this latest attempt to turn back the clock rested on a more specific set of new clauses defining different categories of capital murder.

The first clause, *Punishment for murdering a police officer*, stated: 'A person aged eighteen years or above who is convicted of the murder of a police officer acting in the execution of his duty shall on conviction be sentenced to death.'

During the debate, John Greenaway, Conservative MP for Ryedale, himself a former police officer, pointed out that since the 1988 debate, 1500 people had been unlawfully killed, and went on to reflect on his own time spent as a constable in London in the 1960s and his battle against the 'riff-raff and deadbeats who infest Soho in the middle of the night'. The final result of the vote was 350 to 215, a majority of 135 against; (this same proposal had been rejected by a majority of only 81 in 1983).

A second clause put to the vote debated the emotive issue of *Terrorist murder*: 'A person aged eighteen years or above who is convicted of murder committed as, or in pursuit of, an act of terrorism shall on conviction be sentenced to death.'

It was left to a Conservative Party opponent of the rope, Sir John Wheeler, to sum up the fears of many if this clause were enacted: 'Terrorists are even less likely to be deterred by the death penalty than other murderers. They are fanatics who are perverted in their thinking and feelings, and see themselves fighting for a cause higher than themselves.' In short, the gallows would create martyrs and publicity on the one hand, and be likely to attract reprisals on the other. Some Members in the House may have recalled 1975, when after the execution of five terrorists in Spain, nine policemen were shot in revenge killings. As far as the situation in Northern Ireland was concerned, the problem of intimidation which has already made it impossible to try such a case by a jury would be exacerbated, and fear of reprisals would make informers less likely to co-operate with the police.

There was, though, the by now predictable contrary outburst by the outspoken Member for North Antrim, the Reverend Ian Paisley, who interrupted to point out to the House that 'the weapon of the IRA is capital punishment . . . I'm not making today any difference for anybody. I believe in capital punishment for all who commit murder.'

A third old chestnut to come under debate was the execution of killers using *Firearms, explosives or an offensive weapon* – rejected by 349 to 186 (a majority of 163).

Most controversial of the new issues presented to Parliament was that which proposed the restoration of the death sentence for *all* murderers over seventeen years of age, with each verdict being automatically referred to a special sitting of the Court of Appeal who could either uphold the penalty or commute the sentence to life imprisonment. The suggestion for such a blanket issue of death sentences was bound to be defeated, and it was by a large majority of 185 (367 to 182).

[Britain's most senior judge had already warned against imposing upon the judges of the Court of Appeal the responsibility of deciding whether a death sentence should stand, asking them in effect to rule on a case in which they had neither heard the evidence nor seen the witnesses.]

However, it was interesting for British observers to see how a new Cabinet under a new Prime Minister reacted to the debate. Prime Minister John Major is himself an outspoken opponent of capital punishment, and so is his new Home Secretary, Mr Kenneth Baker (predecessors in both offices – Mrs Margaret Thatcher and David Waddington respectively, were both pro-hanging). In his first major Commons speech as Home Secretary, Mr Baker warned that there were different categories of murder; different degrees between, for example, the callous multiple killer and the victim of insufferable violence in the home who kills out of desperation and fear.

Mr Baker continued: 'The possibility of a person being hanged by mistake cannot be dismissed with a shrug of the shoulders. There is no appeal from the grave.' This caution was taken up by the other side of the House when Labour MP for Walsall North, Mr David Winnick, reminded Members of the release of the 'Guildford Four' and the 'almost certain' release of the 'Birmingham Six',[1] all of whom would have been sentenced to death had the clause under discussion been active following their initial trials. He might also have added the case of David Blythe who, in 1987, confessed to the brutal double murder of elderly sisters Susan and Florence Egerton in Greater Manchester, was convicted and imprisoned for life. Blythe is now free, and the real killer of the Misses Egerton is serving life.

Looking back on the debate – indeed, the past 25 years of debate – it is puzzling how, in view of the rapidly dwindling support for the reintroduction of capital punishment, Parliament should continue these time-wasting exercises. For the arguments will arise again and again until the House finds the courage or the common sense to write the death penalty off the statute book totally. It could have been achieved in 1990, in a vote that narrowly rejected a complete repeal there was the opportunity to abolish capital punishment for those crimes for which it still, anachronistically, remains a mandatory punishment – dockyard arson, piracy and, under the unrepealed act of 1351, treason. The last time that a traitor was executed was in 1946, when William Joyce was sent to

[1] The 'Birmingham Six' *were* released in March 1991.

the gallows for broadcasting Nazi wartime propaganda under the name 'Lord Haw-Haw'. It may only have been Home Secretary Baker's promise to request the Law Commission to look into the whole question of treason that lost the vote for sanity by a majority of only 32 (289 to 257).

Meanwhile, it is rumoured, Britain's last working gallows remains ready for service at Wandsworth Prison in London.

APPENDIX 1
The McNaghten Rules

On 20 January in the year 1843, in Downing Street, a Glasgow wood-worker named Daniel McNaghten drew a pistol and shot and killed Edward Drummond, secretary to Prime Minister Sir Robert Peel (ironically founder of the Metropolitan police force). The ball had been intended for Sir Robert himself, but McNaghten seems to have been unfamiliar with the PM's appearance and to have shot the first likely candidate.

At McNaghten's subsequent trial before judge and jury at the Old Bailey, it transpired that he had entertained, with no apparent justification, an unreasoning suspicion that 'Tories' were persecuting him. The matter was a serious one – not only in that murder had been committed on the open street, but that Her Majesty's first Minister could so easily have been the victim. There was, then, a certain tinge of self-interest in the disquiet voiced by Parliament when the jury returned a verdict that McNaghten was insane and should therefore merely be confined to hospital. Great too was the public discomfort at this verdict, and it was contested in the House of Lords.

Their Lordships decided to require Her Majesty's judges to advise them on the matter – an ancient right of the House, though seldom exercised. The joint answer given by the fourteen judges formed what became the McNaghten Rules, and reads in essence as follows:

Jurors ought to be told in all cases that a man is presumed to be sane, and to possess a sufficient degree of reason to be responsible for his crimes, until the contrary be proved to their satisfaction; and that to establish a defence on the ground of insanity, it must be clearly proved that –

At the time of committing the act, the party accused was labouring unders such defect of reason, from disease of the mind as not to know:

a) The nature and quality of the act he was doing; or if he did know it

b) That he did not know he was doing what was wrong. The judges further allowed:

c) That if the accused labours under partial delusion only, and is not in other respects insane, we think he must be considered in the sane situation as to responsibility as if the facts with respect to which the delusion exists were real. (For example: if under the influence of his delusion he supposes another man to be in the act of attempting to take away his life, and he kills that man, as he supposes, in self-defence, he would be exempt from punishment. If his delusion was that the deceased had inflicted a serious injury to his character and fortune, and he killed in revenge for such supposed injury, he would be liable to punishment.)

APPENDIX 2
Life Sentence and Release on Licence

It is often a mystery to people not professionally involved with the law or law enforcement how some convicted criminals serve more years of a 'life' sentence than others. Despite the appearance of randomness, there is a very strict set of Home Office rules governing how long a person waits for release, or 'parole', and how that release date is decided.

Life Sentence

It is possible for an offender to be given a life sentence for many types of serious crime, though it is most commonly encountered in connection with homicide; in cases of murder, the life sentence is mandatory (as once was the death penalty). This is, in general, in accordance with sentencing procedure in many parts of the developed world.

Technically, in Britain there are several sentences that are covered by the term 'life':

1. Life imprisonment.
2. Custody for life under Section 8 of the Criminal Justice Act, 1982.
3. Detention during Her Majesty's pleasure, or life under Section 53 of the Children and Young Persons Act, 1933.

In both Britain and the United States, it is allowed for a judge in certain circumstances – where, for example, a crime has been particularly vicious, or directed at police or prison officers – to impose a minimum number of years of imprisonment. In the example of the Kray brothers (see page 187) that recommendation was thirty years. Otherwise, a 'life sentence' is, in effect, a sentence of indeterminate length.

Release on Licence

There is considerable flexibility within the justice system for rewarding good behaviour and rehabilitation during imprisonment by what is referred to as a 'life licence'. Here the Home Secretary may release a prisoner if that is the action recommended by a Parole Board, and after the Lord Chief Justice and, if practical, the original trial judge have had an opportunity to give their views on the matter. When a prisoner is considered for release on licence the two main determining factors are 1. Severity of the crime; and 2. Behaviour while in custody.

At the end of a defendant's trial, if he is convicted and sentenced, the trial judge will privately inform the Home Secretary through the Lord Chief Justice of his recommendation as to the appropriate term of imprisonment. As a result of this information the Home Secretary can determine when a case should be put before the Local Review Committee.

These committees are based on a prison and comprise the following members:

The Prison Governor or his Deputy (1).
A Member of the Board of Visitors (1).
A Senior Officer of the Probation Service (1).
Independent Members drawn from the local community (2).

Thus the LRC consists of five people whose responsibility is to the Home Secretary. The date for the committee review will usually be set some three years before the end of the judge's recommended sentence.

However, in the more serious cases of murder, account will be taken of aspects such as the degree of violence exhibited by the prisoner in the course of his crime, and properly to reflect the concern of the general public over the increasing incidence of violent crime.

In the 1988 Home Office advice booklet issued to life prisoners approaching licence, it is emphasized that for certain categories of murder it is customary for a period of twenty years to be spent in custody before review. These aggravating circumstances are:

Murder of police or prison officers.
Terrorist murders.
Sexual or sadistic murders of children.
Murder by firearm during the course of robbery.

When release on licence is being considered, the two criteria are whether a prisoner has served sufficient time to match the gravity of his crime, and whether it is safe to release the prisoner into society. This last consideration is of paramount importance, and a prisoner, no matter how many reviews are heard, will not be released until it is considered that the risk to the public is acceptable. Reviews are generally made at intervals not greater than three years.

Before a review is due to take place, a prisoner will have the opportunity (if he wishes) to be interviewed by one of the members of the LRC (except the Governor of the prison) and also to present the committee with any written representations that he may feel appropriate. The committee will also consider the regular written reports made on a prisoner during his time in custody.

The LRC report is then passed on to the Home Secretary's Office for consideration before being referred to a Parole Board. This board is made up of men and women 'whose personal and professional experience fits them to advise the Home Secretary on everything to do with parole and life sentences'.

It is finally the Home Secretary's responsibility to consider the recommendations of the Parole Board, plus those of the Lord Chief Justice and the trial judge before reaching a decision whether or not to release on licence. He may *not* consider release unless it is recommended by the Parole Board; on the other hand he is not obliged to release a prisoner simply because the Board recommends it.

A prisoner released on licence will, for an initial period at least, be subject to strict supervisory conditions which are monitored by his Probation Officer. This officer will generally be acting more as an advisor and counsellor than a 'warder', but a licensee must refer all matters such as where he is living, where he is working and any changes in these circumstances; and particular permission is needed to travel abroad. Although these conditions are gradually loosened and eventually cancelled, a released prisoner is on licence *until he dies*, and the licence can be revoked and the prisoner returned to custody in the event of serious failure to observe the conditions of release, or if he is convicted of another offence punishable by imprisonment.

As we can see, it is far easier to get into prison than to get out!

APPENDIX 3
The Sentence is Death

This book is not appropriate for a discussion on the rights and wrongs involved in the capital punishment debate, and any opinions expressed must necessarily be viewed as rhetorical. However, as I am asked so frequently, I will state here that the present author has been actively opposed to the imposition of the death penalty since 1955. Up to that point, like most children born in a pre-television age, my sense of right and wrong was the product of early Sunday school teaching and Sherlock Holmes. In short, everything was black and white, good or bad – a murder was committed, therefore the killer lost his life in turn; a clear case of good triumphing over evil, and being seen to do so.

Then on 13 July 1955, Ruth Ellis was hanged, and it was a remarkable and compassionate article penned by Sir William Conner ('Cassandra' of the *Daily Mirror*) under the headline 'The Woman Who Hangs This Morning' that shattered mine and many others' illusions, and brought close to home the fact that there were a lot more issues to be taken into account than a fanciful battle between the angels and the devils. I still have as a reminder of my humanity those yellowing articles so carefully clipped from my father's newspaper on that July morning.

The most frequently evoked argument in favour of capital punishment, and really the only one with a straight 'scientific' answer, is that it acts as a deterrent: that is to say, killing one offender dissuades others from committing the same crime.

Although this may seem plausible, it can only be relevant if the potential offender *at the time of his offence* makes a calculated decision. In most cases where a crime is committed for which the death penalty is applicable, the offender does not weigh up the possibilities before committing the act, or if he does, *per se* believes that there is a favourable chance that he will escape detection. This is particularly true of homicide where the majority of incidents are the result of angry exchanges and committed in 'hot blood'. Thus to remove capital punishment is not necessarily to invite bloodshed and anarchy. In its conclusion to the 1962 report on the state of capital punishment in the world, the United Nations committee studying abolition stated: 'All the information available appears to confirm that such a removal [of the death penalty] has, in fact, never been followed by a notable rise in the incidence of the crime no longer punishable with death.'

However, in one form or another, the death penalty is retained in 100 countries around the globe for what are termed 'ordinary' crimes.

The rest of the world is divided between three 'degrees' of abolition:

Abolitionist: Where a country's law does not provide at all for the death penalty (35 countries).

Abolitionist for Ordinary Crimes Only: The death penalty exists only for 'exceptional' crimes such as those committed under military law, or those committed in exceptional circumstances such as wartime (18 countries).

Abolitionist in Practice: Countries and territories which retain the death penalty on the statute, but have not exercised the option for ten or more years.

The Table below illustrates this distribution of Status, as well as other information on individual countries' use of the death penalty. The following notes explain the chart headings, and all information is based on the latest facts and figures derived from Amnesty International's report *When the State Kills*.

Number of Executions

Calculated between 1985 and the middle of 1988, these are the most recent reliable figures. However, as many retentionist states have proved reluctant either to issue their own figures or to co-operate with agencies collecting information, it can only serve as

a minimum calculation of the extent of the infliction of the death
penalty worldwide.

Date of Last Execution

Last date, if known, of those countries that are Abolitionist,
Abolitionist for Ordinary Crimes Only, and Abolitionist by
Practice. In some cases this date is of the last *known* execution
in countries where information is scant or unreliable.

Method of Execution

Varies from country to country, and in America from state to
state, ranging from the tokenly 'humane' lethal injection to the
decidedly barbaric stoning to death.

Beheading

Now that the guillotine has been renounced by France (abolitionist since 1981), the only survival of beheading is confined to
some Arab States and the Congo (which still uses the guillotine).
The prescribed method in Saudi Arabia, Qatar, Yemen and the
United Arab Emirates is decapitation with a sword. Manual
decapitation was a much-favoured method of execution among
the aristocracy of Europe in former times, though in Britain
the axe was generally preferred over the sword. At least one
King (Charles I) and a Queen (Anne Boleyn, who specified the
sword)[1] met their end in this fashion in London, along with some
four-score assorted lords who met their deaths on the block at
Tower Hill – from Sir Simon Burley in 1388 to the last, Simon
Fraser, Lord Lovat in 1747. The problem with the use of the
blade is that success is entirely dependent upon the skill of
the headsman, and a bungled execution could result in several
attempts being required to sever the spinal column.

In 'Another Exclusive' under the banner headline 'I Have
Chopped Off 600 Heads', one British tabloid in 1989 profiled
the life and times of Saudi Arabia's official executioner, Saeed
Al Sayaf. Describing the tools of his trade, the 60-year-old public
servant said: 'To chop off the heads of men I use a special sword,

---

[1]Anne's request generated some embarrassment as there was at the time
no headsman in England proficient with the use of the sword. In the end
an executioner was brought over from St Omer in northern France.

following the writings of the Prophet Mohammed, while I use a gun to execute women. The reason for using the gun is to avoid removing any part of the cover on the upper part of a woman's body.' All that are needed to cut off the hands of robbers are 'very sharp edged knives to ensure that the wrist is cut cleanly in one stroke'. Of job satisfaction there is apparently no shortage: 'When the job is done I get a sense of delight . . . and I thank God for giving me this power.'

Electrocution
See above 'Execution USA'.

Gassing
See above 'Execution USA'

Hanging
Although the United Kingdom became abolitionist for all but exceptional crimes in 1965, the gallows remains that most potent symbol of the British legal system.

Hanging, as an instrument of judicial execution, entered England by way of the Anglo-Saxons, who had inherited the method from their German ancestors. It became the established punishment for a great many crimes when Henry II organized trial-by-jury and the assize courts in the twelfth century. By the Middle Ages, the power to try, sentence and hang felons was vested in every town, abbey and manorial lord.

Executions until the present century were extremely crude affairs – carried out publicly and often preceded and succeeded by additional barbaric torture. Elaborations like hanging, drawing and quartering became popular spectator events; the prisoner was cut from the gallows while still alive, and his entrails torn out before his eyes; he was then beheaded and quartered – the head being exposed on a pole as a grim public warning. The first such punishment was meted out to one Maurice, a nobleman's son convicted of piracy in 1241.

But even at best, a simple hanging was little better than slow strangulation – sometimes lingering on for hours. Indeed, it was considered a great act of kindness on the part of the executioner to allow some relative or well-wisher to pull on the victim's legs, and so hasten death.

With the last public hanging in 1868, and the confinement of such practices to the execution shed of prisons, a more enlightened and humane procedure was developed to despatch the prisoner with the greatest speed and least pain. The act of hanging became a science based on the accurate relationship of weight to distance, and the hangman became its craftsman.

This is a description of the 'enlightened' method, still in use when the last person was hanged in England:

The executioner with his assistant arrives at the prison of execution on the day before the event. He is given details such as the weight and height of the condemned man, and is allowed to note his build and manner by peeping through the death cell's judas-hole.

Using a sack filled to the weight of the man to be hanged, the executioner adjusts the 'drop' of the rope – too short a drop, slow strangulation; too long a drop, decapitation. The trap on which the condemned stands consists of two hinged sections connected by long bolts. The executioner checks the smooth withdrawal of the bolts and the opening of the trap when the lever is pulled.

On the following morning, the executioner enters the condemned cell, straps the prisoner's arms behind his back and leads him to the gallows trap, where the assistant to the hangman straps the prisoner's legs together. The white hood over the head is followed by the noose, the knot of which is drawn tight to the left of the jaw and held in position by a sliding metal washer.

The executioner pulls the well-greased lever . . .

But hanging is far from extinct, and in the table of the retentionist favourites, the gallows rates second (78 countries) only to shooting (86 countries).

Lethal Injection
See above 'Execution USA'.

Shooting
There are two favoured methods of execution by shooting: with a firing squad or by a single executioner. Together they make up the most frequently used instrument of capital punishment.

Firing Squad: Rejected as a means of execution by the influential United Kingdom Royal Commission on Capital Punishment (1949–53) when it reviewed the various methods, on two main grounds. First that it required 'a multiplicity of executioners', and secondly that 'it does not possess the first requisite of an efficient method, the certainty of causing immediate death'.

Single Executioner: In practice, because the *coup de grâce* is delivered by a single point-blank pistol shot to the head, death is quicker and more certain than by firing squad, where the troop of executioners are farther away from the prisoner and generally aim at his trunk because it provides a larger target than the head.

Stoning

Confined mainly to the Arab nations, stoning is the most protracted and potentially painful 'official' means of administering the death sentence in use in the world today. Indeed, according to Article 119 of the Islamic Penal Code of Iran, that is exactly the way it should be: '. . . the stones should not be too large so that the person dies on being hit by one or two of them; nor should they be so small that they could not be defined as stones'.

The following graphic description is taken from the 1989 edition of Amnesty International's *When the State Kills* . . .:

The lorry deposited a large number of stones and pebbles beside the waste ground, and then two women were led to the spot wearing white and with sacks over their heads . . . [they] were enveloped in a shower of stones and transformed into two red sacks . . . The wounded women fell to the ground and Revolutionary Guards smashed their heads in with a shovel to make sure that they were dead.

Public Executions

Britain made its first move towards abolition when the Capital Punishment Within Prisons Bill received Royal Assent on 29 May 1868. Three days previously, Michael Barrett, the Irish Fenian condemned for conspiring to cause the Clerkenwell prison explosion, was the last person to be publicly hanged. The first to be executed behind prison walls was a youth named Thomas Wells, hanged at Maidstone county gaol on 13 August 1868 for the murder of a station master at the Dover Priory Railway Terminus.

In November 1849, Charles Dickens attended the hanging of Frederick and Maria Manning, an unlovely couple who had murdered their lodger for money and buried his body in quicklime beneath the kitchen floor of their home in south London. On the following morning the great novelist made his feelings on the subject of public executions known through the correspondence columns of *The Times*:

To the Editor of The Times

Sir – I was a witness of the execution at Horsemonger Lane this morning. I went there with the intention of observing the crowd gathered to behold it, and I had excellent opportunities of doing so, at intervals all through the night, and continuously from daybreak until after the spectacle was over.

I do not address you on the subject with any intention of discussing the abstract question of capital punishment, or any of the arguments of its opponents or advocates. I simply wish to turn this dreadful experience to some account for the general good by taking the readiest and most public means of [advertising] to an intimation given by Sir G. Grey in the last session of Parliament, that the Government might be induced to give its support to the measure making the infliction of capital punishment a private solemnity within the prison walls (with such guarantees for the last sentence of the law being inexorably and surely administered as should be satisfactory to the public at large), and of most earnestly beseeching Sir G. Grey as a solemn duty which he owes to society, and as a responsibility which he cannot for ever put away, to originate such a legislative change himself.

A sight so inconceivably awful as the wickedness and levity of the immense crowd collected at the execution this morning could be imagined by no man, and presented by no heathen kind under the sun. The horrors of the gibbet, and of the crime which brought the wretched murderers to it, faded in my mind before the atrocious bearing, looks, and language of the assembled spectators. When I came upon the scene at midnight, the shrillness of the cries and howls that were raised from time to time, denoting that they came from a concourse of boys and girls already assembled in the best places, made my blood run cold.

. . . When the day dawned, thieves, low prostitutes, ruffians, and vagabonds of every kind, flocked on to the ground, with every variety of offensive and foul behaviour. Fightings, faintings, whistlings, imitations of Punch, brutal jokes, tumultuous demonstrations of indecent delight, when swooning women

*were dragged out of the crowd by the police, with their dresses
disordered, gave a new zest to the general entertainment.*

*. . . I am solemnly convinced that nothing that ingenuity could
devise to be done in this city, in the same compass of time,
could work such ruin as some public execution, and I stand
astounded and appalled by the wickedness it exhibits. I do not
believe that any community can prosper where such a scene of
horror and demoralization as was enacted this morning outside
Horsemonger Lane Gaol is presented at the very doors of
good citizens, and is passed by unknown or forgotten. And
when, in our prayers and thanksgivings for the seasons, we
are humbly expressing before God our desire to remove the
moral evils of the land, I would ask your readers to consider
whether it is not time to think of this one, and to root it out.*

&c.

November 13th, 1847.   *Charles Dickens*

It would amaze, and almost certainly horrify Dickens to learn
that public executions, while no longer staining the reputation
of his native land, are regularly practised in many spots around
the globe, and, in China at least, never fail to attract as large and
appreciative a crowd as he will remember congregating outside
Newgate and Horsemonger Lane.

What Charles Dickens, along with most other people possessed
of the slightest humanity, would find incredulous, is that in the
country which welcomed and lauded him, the United States of
America, in San Francisco at least, there is a feeling in some
quarters that for the death penalty to work, it has to be seen.

KQED is a local television station that believes the United
States Constitution permits them not only to attend executions
like press journalists, but to broadcast them. So it came about that
at the beginning of 1991, KQED's current affairs chief brought
a lawsuit seeking a court ruling that its cameras may be set up
just outside the gas chamber. A spokesman insisted: 'We are
trying to cover a news story of major importance here. Executing
a condemned person is the ultimate act of government power
over an individual, and it's the ultimate act of justice in our
criminal justice system. Every other aspect of that system is open
to television coverage, so we believe we have a right to inform
people about what's going on.'

The prisoner under consideration for the starring role in this dubious landmark in modern legal history is Robert Harris – not because of any star quality, simply because he is first in line, having been on San Quentin's Death Row for twelve years.

It is an irony that both pro- and anti-capital punishment factions favour the public display of a condemned prisoner's last moments, the former because it would bring what they see as the potential deterrent live into the home, the latter because it feels that the public would be so antagonized by the sight they would demand an end to the death penalty. A position of great optimism in the face of polls showing 80% of Californians in favour of capital punishment.

The Execution of Children

The majority of the civilized world accepts, as a broad principle, that young people under the age of eighteen are not yet fully responsible for their actions, and so should not be expected to suffer the full sanction of the law. International figures show that 72 countries have specific laws setting the minimum age of eighteen as that below which the death penalty cannot be used and a further twelve countries because they are signatories to the International Covenant on Civil and Political Rights, which sets eighteen as the minimum age, can also be said to exercise this clemency. It is one of the great anachronisms of United States law that some states have condemned to death young people who were under the age of eighteen at the time their crime was committed, and a Supreme Court ruling of 26 June 1989 allowed the execution of people aged sixteen and seventeen at the time they committed their capital crime. This option was exercised by the state of Louisiana in 1990 when they sent Dalton Prejean, seventeen at the time of his crime in 1977, to the electric chair.

Crimes For Which the Death Penalty Applies

Although most retentionist countries or territories reserve the death penalty for homicide alone, it is possible to find capital crimes around the world ranging from adultery to causing the collapse of a government. What is most worrying, though, is the number of cases where the death sentence can be imposed for crimes that have not involved physical violence, let alone the taking of life.

Key to Table

* Not known/No information available.

1. *Key*: B = Beheading
   E = Electrocution
   F = Shooting, by Firing Squad (FS) or Single Executioner (SE)
   G = Lethal Gas
   H = Hanging
   L = Lethal Injection
   S = Stoning to Death

2. *Key*: A = Homicide (Murder and Manslaughter)
   B = Murder
   C = Terrorism
   D = Aggravated theft
   E = Aggravated robbery
   F = Rape
   G = Kidnap/Abduction
   H = Drug-trafficking
   I = Treason / Espionage
   J = Plotting the overthrow of government
   K = Economic sabotage
   L = Adultery
   M = Prostitution
   N = Embezzlement (usually of government funds)
   O = Crimes against the State
   P = Unlawful possession of firearms
   Q = Firearms trafficking
   R = Aggravated rape
   S = Piracy
   T = Sabotage
   U = Hijacking
   V = Sorcery and black magic (resulting in death)
   W = Mutiny
   Y = Genocide
   Z = Arson

3. In a state of emergency also Shooting.
4. Televised executions.
5. Last war crime punished by execution in 1949.
6. For adultery and homosexuality, though there are no recorded instances.

7. In certain cases, offenders may be executed with the weapon that was used in the crime.
8. Last war crime punished by execution in 1952.
9. Last war crime punished by execution in 1948.
10. According to Amnesty International report, two executions were carried out in October 1988, the first for over ten years.
11. Corpses may be crucified following execution.

COUNTRY	STATUS	EXECUTIONS	LAST EX.	METHOD[1]	PUBLIC	CHILDREN EX.	CRIMES PUNISHABLE[2]
Afghanistan	Retentionist	*		F(FS)			A, K, R, Mil.
Albania	Retentionist	*		F(FS), H			B
Algeria	Retentionist	12		F(FS)			
Andorra	Abolitionist in Practice		1943				A, O
Angola	Retentionist	15	1820s	F(FS)			
Anguilla	Abolitionist in Practice	1		H			B
Antigua & Barbuda	Retentionist			H			Mil.
Argentina	Abol. ex. Exceptional Crimes		1967	F(FS)			
Australia	Abolitionist		1950				
Austria	Abolitionist						
Bahamas	Retentionist	0		F(FS)			B, S
Bahrain	Abolitionist in Practice		1977	F(FS), H			B, K, T
Bangladesh	Retentionist	36+		F(FS), H		X	B, I, Mil.
Barbados	Retentionist	0		H		X	A, G, U, Mil.
Belgium	Abolitionist in Practice		1950	B (Guillotine), F(FS)			B, Mil.
Belize	Retentionist	1		H			B, I, V
Benin	Retentionist	8		F(FS)			B, I, S
Bermuda	Abolitionist in Practice		1977	H			B, I
Bhutan	Abolitionist in Practice		1964	*			
Bolivia	Abolitionist in Practice		1974	F(FS)			
Botswana	Retentionist	*		H			B, I, Mil.
Brazil	Abol. Ex. Exceptional Crimes		1855	F(FS)			B, S
British Virgin Islands	Abolitionist in Practice			H			B, H, P
Brunei Darussalam	Abolitionist in Practice		1957	H			
Bulgaria	Retentionist	32+		F(FS)			31 capital crimes on Statute, including 'preparing epidemi bacteria with the intention of causing infection in others'
Burkina Faso	Retentionist			F(FS)			B, I, Mil.

Country	Status	No./Year	Method		Codes / Crimes
Burma	Retentionist	*	H		B, I, H
Burundi	Retentionist	2	F(FS), H		A, B, I, Mil.
Cameroon	Retentionist		F(FS), H	X	B, D, Mil.
Canada	Abol. Ex. Exceptional Crimes	1962	F(FS)		Mil.
Cape Verde	Abolitionist	1835	H		
Cayman Islands	Abolitionist in Practice	1928	H		B, I
Central African Republic	Retentionist	0	F(FS)	X	A, I, W
Chad	Retentionist	0	F(FS)		B, I, Mil.
Chile	Retentionist	2	F(FS)		A, I, C, Mil.
China	Retentionist	500+	F(SE)	X	Murder, Rape, Robbery, Theft, Bribery, Embezzlement, Corruption, Smuggling, Swindling, Drug-trafficking, Assault and Battery, Kidnapping and trafficking in women & children, Leading a Criminal Gang, Enticing or forcing women into prostitution, Printing or showing pornographic material, Illegal making and trading of firearms, Organising reactionary secret societies, Use of poisons or explosives, Treason, Plotting overthrow of government, Hijacking, Illegal export of cultural relics.
Colombia	Abolitionist	1909			

Country	Status	No.	Year	Method	X	Codes
Comoros	Abolitionist in Practice	0		F(FS)		B, I
Congo	Retentionist		1878	B(Guillotine), F(FS)		B
Costa Rica	Abolitionist					B, I, Mil.
Côte D'Ivoire	Abolitionist in Practice	4		F(FS)		B, Mil.
Cuba	Retentionist		1962	F(FS)		I, S, Mil.
Cyprus	Abol. Ex. Exceptional Crimes			H		B, O, U, Y, Mil.
Czechoslovakia	Retentionist	5+		H,³		
Denmark	Abolitionist		1950			A, I, Mil.
Djibouti	Abolitionist in Practice	1		F(FS)		B, I
Dominica	Retentionist			H		
Dominican Republic	Abolitionist					
Ecuador	Abolitionist					
Egypt	Retentionist	12+	1973	F(FS), H		A, F, U, O, Mil.
El Salvador	Abol. Ex. Exceptional Crimes			F(FS)		Mil.
Equatorial Guinea	Retentionist	2+	1972	F(FS), H		B, O, Mil.
Ethiopia	Retentionist	*		F(FS), H	X	B, E, S, O, K, I, Mil.
Fiji	Abol. Ex. Exceptional Crimes		1964	H		I, Y
Finland	Abolitionist		1944			
France	Abolitionist		1977			
Gabon	Retentionist	1		F(FS)	X	B, I, J, Mil.
Gambia	Retentionist	0		H		B, I
Germany (United)	Abolitionist		1949			
Ghana	Retentionist	37+		F(FS)		B, E, K, N
Greece	Abolitionist in Practice		1972	F(FS)		B, E, O, Mil.
Grenada	Retentionist	0		H		B
Guatemala	Retentionist	0				B, R
Guinea	Retentionist	2+		F(FS)		B, N, J, O, Z
Guinea-Bissau	Retentionist	7+		F(FS)		B, O
Guyana	Retentionist	9				B, I, Mil.
Haiti	Abolitionist		1972	H		
Honduras	Abolitionist		1940			

Country	Status	Year	Number	Method			Crimes
Hong Kong	Abolitionist in Practice						B, I
Hungary	Retentionist	1966	2+	H			A, I, U, Y, Mil.
Iceland	Abolitionist	1830	*				
India	Retentionist			F(SE), H			A, E, J, Abetting suicide of a child or insane person, Fabricating evidence in capital case resulting in conviction. Military Crimes, Terrorism
Indonesia	Retentionist		19	F(FS)			B, Subversion, Rebellion
Iran	Retentionist		743+	F(FS), H, S	X	X	Murder, Drug offences, Political violence, other Political offences, Adultery, Prostitution, other 'Moral' offences, Being Corrupt on Earth, Being at Enmity with God.
Iraq	Retentionist		Hundreds per year *	F(FS), H	X	X	Murder, Treason, Sabotage using arms and explosives, Forgery of official documents, Economic corruption, Burglary and Theft in time of war, Desertion from army. Plus numerous categories of Crimes Against The State and Military Crimes.
Ireland	Abolitionist in Practice	1954		H			B, I

Country	Status	No.	Date	Method			Crimes
Israel (& occupied Territories)	Abol. Ex. Exceptional Crimes		1962	H			I, C, T, Y
Italy	Abol. Ex. Exceptional Crimes		1947	F(SE)			Mil.
Jamaica	Retentionist	30		H			B
Japan	Retentionist	9		H			B, E, R, O, U
Jordan	Retentionist	14+		F(FS), H			B, I, C, O, T, Z, Mil.
Kampuchea	Retentionist	*		F(FS)			B, I, R, Y
Kenya	Retentionist	32		H			B, I, E
Kiribati	Abolitionist						
Korea (Dem. People's Rep.)	Retentionist	*		F(FS)			B, F, L, N, T, Rebellion.
Korea (Republic of)	Retentionist	23		F(FS), H			B, R, E, J
Kuwait	Retentionist	6+		F(FS), H	X		B, O, R, False testimony leading to execution
Laos	[Retentionist]	*		*			
Lebanon	Retentionist	*		F(FS), H			B, I, Z, Mil.
Lesotho	Retentionist	0		H			B, I, F
Liberia	Retentionist	1+		F(FS), H	X		B, I, E, C, U, Mil.
Libya	Retentionist	9+		F(FS), H	X[4]	B, I, E,	B, I, E, O
Liechtenstein	Abolitionist		1785				
Luxembourg	Abolitionist		1948[5]				
Madagascar	Abolitionist in Practice		1958	F(FS)		B, I, E,	
Malawi	Retentionist	*		H			T, O, Z
Malaysia	Retentionist	52+		H			B, I, E, F
Maldives	Abolitionist in Practice		1952	*			B, E, H, P, G
Mali	Retentionist	0		F(FS)			B, I
Malta	Abol. Ex. Exceptional Crimes		1943	*			B, I, O, E
Marshall Islands	Abolitionist						I, Mil
Mauritania	Retentionist	3		F(FS), B, S,[6,7]	X		B, I, E, O, (Muslims may be sentenced to death for

unrepentant apostasy, rape, homosexuality, and adultery) Mil.

Country	Status	No.	Method	Year			Codes / Notes
Mauritius	Retentionist	1	H				B, I, W, H
Mexico	Abol. Ex. Exceptional Crimes		F(FS)	1937			
Micronesia (Fed. States of)	Abolitionist						
Monaco	Abolitionist	*		1847			
Mongolia	Retentionist	*	* [wars F(SE)]				B, D, E, I, C, T
Montserrat	Abolitionist in Practice		H	1961			B
Morocco & Western Sahara	Retentionist	0	F(FS)				A, E, O, Mil.
Mozambique	Retentionist	4+	F(FS)				O, Mil.
Namibia	Retentionist	9	H				B, E, F, I, O
Nauru	Abolitionist in Practice	0	*	1968			B
Nepal	Retentionist		F(SE), H				B, O, I
Netherlands	Abolitionist		H	1860[8]			
New Zealand	Abol. Ex. Exceptional Crimes			1957			I, Mil.
Nicaragua	Abolitionist			1930			
Niger	Abolitionist in Practice		F(FS)	1976			B, E, I,
Nigeria	Retentionist	439+	F(FS), H		X		B, E, I, O
Norway	Abolitionist		*	1876[9]			
Oman	Retentionist	*	*				*
Pakistan	Retentionist	115+	H, S		X	X	B, G, E, U, Defiling the name of the prophet Mohammad. Special Islamic courts may impose death penalty for various sexual offences.
Panama	Abolitionist			1903			
Papua New Guinea	Abol. Ex. Exceptional Crimes		H	1950			I, S

Paraguay	Abolitionist in Practice	1928		F(FS)		A, Y, O
Peru	Abol. Ex. Exceptional Crimes	1979		F(FS)		I (In time of war), O
Philippines	Abolitionist	1976				
Poland	Retentionist		11+	F(FS), H		B, I, K, Mil.
Portugal	Abolitionist	1846				
Qatar	Abolitionist in Practice		0^{10}	F(FS), H, B, (sword)		B, E, O
Romania	Retentionist		2+	F(FS)		B, I, Y, K, N, O
Rwanda	Retentionist		0	F(FS)		B, R, I, E
St Christopher & Nevis	Retentionist		1	H		B
St Lucia	Retentionist		1	H		B, I,
St Vincent & Grenadines	Retentionist		2	H		B, I,
San Marino (Rep. of)	Abolitionist	1468				
São Tomé & Príncipe	Abol. Ex. Exceptional Crimes			*		J, Mil.
Saudi Arabia	Retentionist		140	B(Sword), S	X	B, E, H, L, I, Y, Apostasy
Senegal	Abolitionist in Practice	1967		F(FS)		B, I, 'Acts of Barbarism'
Seychelles	Abol. Ex. Exceptional Crimes		*	*		I
Sierra Leone	Retentionist		*	F(FS), H		B, E, I, W
Singapore	Retentionist		2+	H		B, I, P, H
Solomon Islands	Abolitionist					
Somalia	Retentionist		150+	F(FS)	X	B, I, Y, O, N, Mil. Publishing or Distributing 'anti-state' propaganda, Several other political, religious and trade union activities – organising strikes, etc.
South Africa	Retentionist		537+	H		B, E, G, I, F, O, C
Spain	Abol. Ex. Exceptional Crimes	1975		F(FS)		Mil.
Sri Lanka of suicide	Abolitionist in Practice	1976		H	X	B, O, H, Abetment

Country	Status					
Sudan	Retentionist		9	F(FS), H, S		B, I, K, O, E. Plus 'offences against divine will' such as adultery and other several offences, and bearly false witness.
Suriname	Retentionist		0	F(FS)		A, O
Swaziland	Retentionist		0	H		B, I
Sweden	Abolitionist	1910				
Switzerland	Abol. Ex. Exceptional Crimes	1944				Mil.
Syria	Retentionist		31	F(FS), H		B, I, R, H, E, O, Mil.
Taiwan (Rep. of China)	Retentionist		17+	F(SE)	X	B, E, R, I, H, Q, S, Z
Tanzania	Retentionist		0	H		B, I
Thailand	Retentionist		34+	F(SE)		B, I, E, R, H
Togo	Abolitionist in Practice		0	F(FS)		B, I, O
Tonga	Retentionist		0	H		B, I
Trinidad & Tobago	Retentionist		0	H		B, I, Mil.
Tunisia	Retentionist		30	F(FS), H		B, E, R, O, I, Mil.
Turkey	Retentionist		0	H		B, O, Smuggling
Turks & Caicos Islands	Abolitionist in Practice			H		B
Tuvalu	Abolitionist					
Uganda	Retentionist		11+	F(FS), H		B, E, I, W, Armed Smuggling
Union of Soviet Socialist Reps.	Retentionist		63+	F(SE) H (War* Crimes only)		Large-scale theft of social property, Aggravated bribe-taking, Aggravated rape, Aggravated Murder, Aggravated hijacking, attempting to take the life of a police officer, war crimes, espionage.

United Arab Emirates	Retentionist	7		F(FS), B, S	X	B, E, I, F, L, Apostasy
United Kingdom	Abol. Ex. Exceptional Crimes		1964	H		I, S, Mil.
United States of America	Retentionist	66		F(FS), H, G, L	X	A, B, Mil
Uruguay	Abolitionist		late 19th cent.	H		
Vanuatu	Abolitionist					
Vatican City State	Abolitionist					
Venezuela	Abolitionist					
Viet Nam	Retentionist	3+		F(FS)		I, C, U, T, J
Western Samoa	Abolitionist in Practice			H		B, I
Yemen (Arab Republic)	Retentionist	34+		F(FS), B, S	X[11]	B, G, Mil, Plus 'offenses against divine will' such as adultery, sodomy, apostasy
Yemen (People's Dem. Rep. of)	Retentionist	5+		F(FS)		B, I, R, U, C, T, War Crimes
Yugoslavia	Retentionist	4		F(FS)		B, E, Abetting Suicide.
Zaire	Retentionist	4+		F(FS), H		B, G, R, E, I, O, Mil.
Zambia	Retentionist	11		H		B, I, E
Zimbabwe	Retentionist	24		H		B, I, F, E, P, Z, T, O

Note: Statistics derive from *When the State Kills*, Amnesty International, London 1989.

APPENDIX 4

Execution Guidelines

As issued by the Superintendent of Florida State Prison

Execution Day Minus Five

1. Execution squad selected.
2. Official and media witnesses selected.
3. Support personnel (entrance and checkpoints) selected.
4. Medical support staff for execution selected.
5. Electrical test of all execution equipment including telephone and emergency generator.
6. Briefing by Superintendent of all CO111 and above regarding execution activities.

Execution Day Minus Four

1. Security Co-ordinator notified.
2. Death Watch Supervisor assigned;
   Cell Front Monitor assigned.
3. Inmate reinventories property and seals for storage.
4. Chaplain notified to visit daily.
5. Visiting changed to 'non-contact'.
6. Check of outside telephone line by ASO.
7. Establish communications with DOC attorney for consultation as required.

8. Establish notification list and contact staff in the event of significant legal change.
9. Security-Coordinator schedules meeting for crowd control strategy, pursuant to FSP 10P No. 65.
10. Electrical test of all execution equipment, including emergency generator.
11. Inmate measured for clothing.
12. Inmate specifies funeral arrangments in writing.
13. Inmate specifies recipient of personal property in writing.
14. Execution squad drill.

Execution Day Minus Three

No Activities.

Execution Day Minus Two

1. Execution squad drill.
2. Assistant Superintendent Operations tests telephone.
3. Electrical test of all equipment.

Execution Day Minus One

1. Execution squad drill.
2. Assistant Superintendent Operations tests telephone.
3. Electrical test of all equipment including emergency generator.
4. Waiting area set up by Assistant Superintendent Operations.
5. Electrician makes up ammonium chloride solution and soaks sponges.
6. Inmate orders last meal.
7. Chief Medical Officer prepares certificate of death (ie. 'legal execution by electrocution').
8. Official witness list finalized (12 plus 4 alternatives)
9. Executioner contacted and liaison set up for execution day.
10. Funeral arrangements confirmed with family.
11. Information office arrives to handle media inquiries.
12. Security Meeting held.
13. External Death Watch Observer selected.
14. Information Office designates media pool observers.

Execution Day

4.30 am	Food Service Director personally prepares and serves last meal. Eating utensils allowed – plate and spoon.
5.00 am	Administrative Assistant or designate picks up executioner and proceeds to institution; enter through Sally Port, leaving executioner in Waiting Room of Death Chamber at 5.00 am. Security staff member posted in Chamber area.
6.00 am	

A. From 5.30, only staff authorized on Q-1-E are:
1. Observer designated by Secretary.
2. Superintendent.
3. Assistant Superintendent Operations.
4. Chief Correctional Officer IV.
5. Death Watch Supervisor.
6. Second Shift Lieutenant.
7. Chaplain.
8. Grille Gate Monitor.
9. Cell Front Monitor.

B. Assistant Superintendent Operations supervises the shaving of the condemned man's head and right leg.

C. Official witnesses report to Main Gate of prison no later than 5.30, received by Department of Corrections escort staff and transferred to staff dining room to await escort to witness room of execution chamber.

5.50 am	Media Witnesses collected at media onlooker area by Department of Corrections staff escort; transported to Main Entrance as a group, security cleared and escorted to Classification Department until escorted to witness room of execution chamber.
6.00 am	

A. Assistant Superintendent Operations supervises showering of condemned man. Immediately afterwards he will be returned to his cell and given a pair of shorts, a pair of trousers, a dress shirt, and socks. Correctional Officer Chief IV responsible for the delivery of clothes.

B. Switchboard operator instructed to wire calls through execution chamber from Governor's office via switchboard.

    C. Administrative Assistant (or designate), three electricians, Physician and Physician's assistant, report to execution chamber for preparation. Administrative Assistant checks telephones in chamber; electrician will ready the equipment; Physician and Assistant (Technician) will stand by.

6.30 am Administrative Assistant (or designate) establishes telephone communication with officials designated by Superintendent.

6.50 am A. Assistant Superintendent Operations supervises application of conducting gel to condemned man's right calf and crown of head.

    B. Superintendent reads Death Warrant to inmate.

    C. Official witnesses secured in witness room no later than 6.50 am.

    D. Authorized media witnesses secured in witness room no later than 6.50 am.

    E. Beginning at 6.55 am only persons permitted in execution chamber are: 12 official witnesses; 4 alternate witnesses; 1 physician; 1 medical technician; 12 authorized media representatives; 4 designated Department of Corrections staff escorts.

    Any exception must be approved by Superintendent.

6.56 am A. Beginning at 6.56 am only staff authorized in execution chamber are: Observer (designated by Secretary); Superintendent; Assistant Superintendent Operations; Correctional Officer Chief IV; Administrative Assistant (or designate); Chaplain (optional); 2 electricians; 1 executioner; 1 physician; 1 physician's assistant.

    Any exception must be approved by Superintendent.

    B. Superintendent, Assistant Superintendent Operations, and Correctional Officer Chief IV escort the condemned inmate to execution chamber. Administrative Assistant (or designate) records time inmate enters chamber.

    C. Assistant Superintendent Operations and Correctional Officer Chief IV place condemned inmate in chair.

    D. Superintendent and Assistant Superintendent

Operations secure back and arm straps and then forearm straps.

E. When inmate secured, Assistant Superintendent Operations and Correctional Officer Chief IV remove restraint apparatus, then secure lap, chest and ankle straps. Anklet laced and electrode attached.

7.00 am A. Superintendent permits condemned inmate to make last statement. Superintendent inquires over open telephone line of possible stays.

B. Electrician places sponges on inmate's head, secures head-set, attaches electrode.

C. Assistant Superintendent Operations engages circuit breaker.

D. Electrician in booth activates execution control panel.

E. Superintendent gives signal to executioner to turn switch and the automatic cycle begins. Administrative Assistant (or designate) records time switch is thrown.

F. Once cycle has run its course, electrician indicates current is off. Administrative Assistant (or designate) records time current is disengaged.

G. Assistant Superintendent Operations disengages manual circuit behind chair.

H. Superintendent invites doctor to conduct examination.

I. Inmate pronounced dead. Administrative Assistant (or designate) records time death pronounced.

J. Administrative Assistant (or designate) announces that sentence has been carried out and invites witnesses to exit: 'The sentence of [name] has been carried out. Please exit to the rear at this time.'

K. Witnesses escorted from witness room by staff escorts.

7.20 am A. O/S Lieutenant notified by Assistant
to   Superintendent Programs to bring ambulance
7.30 am attendants.

B. Inmate removed from chair by ambulance attendants supervised by Assistant Superintendent Programs.
C. Ambulance cleared through Sally Port by escorting officer.
D. Administrative Assistant (or designate) returns executioner and compensates him.

Post Execution

A. Physician signs death certificate.
B. Superintendent returns death warrant to governor indicating execution carried out.
C. Superintendent files copy with Circuit Court of Conviction.
D. Classification Supervisor advises Central Office Records by teletype.

APPENDIX 5
Aids as a Complicating Factor

Fear has always been a powerful generator of violence, and in combination with ignorance it can prove lethal. When a sense of helplessness envelops both, society faces tragedy.

Faced with the decimating spread of Aids, it is not surprising that the threefold enemy should clutch at people's emotions first, before robbing them of the power of rational thought. For despite considerable (if never enough) investment in research programmes into a cure, and despite well-meaning (if sometimes half-hearted or misguided) programmes of 'education', there remains a very real terror of what is seen as the twentieth-century plague. We should, as an intelligent and civilized species, have stopped pointing our blaming fingers at minority groups, for no matter who are the scapegoats, the homosexuals, blacks, drug-abusers, prostitutes, the problem remains. So it is no surprise to find some of the more vociferous, better organized of these groups leading a backlash: It is not, they say, a 'gay plague', it is *everybody's* plague!

June 1990 saw the world's biggest conference on Aids open in San Francisco. It provided, quite legitimately, a platform not only for the 15,000-odd delegates and visitors from all over the world, but also for groups like the militant gay ACT-UP (Aids Coalition To Unleash Power; slogan: 'Silence = Death') who used the occasion for active protest. In a city where more than 5000 people have died of Aids, and some 50,000 are HIV positive, feelings are bound to run high, and if militant gays gave the conference its backlash, then they too face a backlash from an America that is still broadly hostile to homosexuality.

In the weeks leading up to conference, extremist groups were said to be threatening to throw balloons filled with Aids-infected blood and contaminated needles at police officers attempting to curtail their protest. One policeman was widely reported in the press as replying to the question what he would do if confronted by a demonstrator waving a bag of blood, saying: 'I'm not saying I'd take a gun out and shoot him, but I'm not going to say I wouldn't.' It was a comment which was officially condemned, but that same authority nevertheless planned the issue of protective goggles and shields, and responded positively to the demand for a mobile decontamination centre where officers could be disinfected and given shots of the Aids-retarding drug AZT – just in case.

As a murder weapon, a virus – particularly one as little understood as Aids – poses a threat as deadly as any gun, and the mind of the murderer, fiendishly inventive as it is, has not been slow to adapt to modern times. Perhaps the officers of the San Francisco police department had reason for concern in the light of just two brief news stories from 1990. In July, a former police superintendent who had chased a bag snatcher through north London, was head-butted, kicked and bitten by a man who screamed at him, 'I've got Aids!' And in New York, a prisoner who knew he was infected with Aids and deliberately bit a prison officer was given a life sentence for attempted murder.

In what was described by police in Springfield, Missouri as 'a pretty bizarre situation', a man who had been jilted by his 36-year-old lover, attempted to exact a dreadful revenge when he paid an alleged $1000 to an accomplice to inject the woman with the Aids virus. It was certainly too bizarre for the hit-man, who confided in his intended victim and together they confided in the police.

Of course, such stories carry the very real danger that murder-by-Aids will join the 'Vanishing Hitch-Hiker' and the 'Kentucky Fried Rat' among the nation's best loved apocryphal tales. There was a saga that gained currency some years ago, which was picked up with apparent sincerity by one London tabloid (not noted for its seriousness) that told how the late, lovable Liberace, who had died in 1987 to the genuine sorrow of millions of his fans, was the 'Victim Of Aids Hit Man'. Undisclosed 'showbiz sources' were reported as saying that a blonde teenage choirboy, turned down by the star for a job in his show, had reacted with the threat: 'You'll be sorry you stupid old fool. Some day you will wish you never met me.' With that, according to the 'sources', the youth hired an airline steward (now seemingly deceased) to infect the pianist with Aids.

Another headline story from the Land of Extremes reinforced the almost ludicrous lengths to which the fear of Aids has pushed an ill-informed police and public. Linda Kean, a Los Angeles prostitute and heroin-user seeking her own 'Fifteen Minutes of Fame', gave an interview to the magazine *Newsweek* in June 1990, in the course of which she admitted she was suffering from Aids, probably picked up from a contaminated needle, but was still 'working'. Ms Kean pointed out, quite correctly, that 'telling customers or other hookers would be professional suicide'.

An observant officer with the Oakland police vice department who saw the article and recognized the photograph of Linda Kean as someone working his patch, did not think so much of suicide as homicide. Reasoning that she was knowingly risking the lives of her clients, Sergeant Miller arrested Ms Kean on suspicion of attempted murder: 'She had a deadly disease which she knew she could pass on to others, so we took her in.' There was never much chance that the charge would stick, because it required the prosecution to prove the defendant *intended* to kill, so Linda Kean was instead put inside for a couple of weeks for breaking probation. Clearly Ms Kean had tired of the attention, for when she next had access to the media, the reluctant celebrity announced that she did not, after all, have Aids.

But if it provides an extraordinary, and potentially lethal, weapon, then Aids has also proved to be a powerful *motive* for violence, and even murder. As a complication of the omnipresent trend to homophobia, gay-bashing has been aggravated by taunts of 'virus spreader', and groups monitoring attacks on the gay community have no doubt that HIV and Aids have exacerbated the problem – almost, it sometimes seems, to the point of the very existence of the disease being a *validation* of the violence.

To complicate matters for an already beleaguered police force, militant gays – in America at least – are mobilizing themselves into neighbourhood patrols, like the Pink Panthers (motto:

'Remember: lesbians and gays bash back'); though to their credit these groups are, so far, 'peace keeping forces'.

During February 1990, a jury at the Old Bailey in London sat in judgement of a young man who had been charged with the murder of his homosexual lover, 64-year-old John Radcliffe, manager of a gay club in London's Soho which was a meeting place for ageing homosexual men to pick up casual partners for sex. At the end of April 1989, he was found by the police and fire-brigade officers battered to death in his burned-out club. The young man, who had been Radcliffe's lover for some time, was taken into custody and found to be in possession of bloodstained clothing. He later admitted to investigating officers that he and Radcliffe had been drinking in the club after it closed. When the older man told him he was suffering from Aids he 'went berserk', and in a frenzied attack jumped up and down on his helpless victim, fracturing his ribs, crushing the wall of his chest and rupturing his heart. He then stole the dead man's gold watch and diamond ring and, soaking the body in alcohol from the bar, set light to the club and its owner.

Ironically, one of the most moving and compassionate cases to emerge from the horrors of 1990 also saw the tragedy of a relationship torn apart by Aids; with a far more dignified, if just as bloody, conclusion.

It was on 3 January in the Los Angeles 'Cedars-Sinai Medical Center' that the final dramatic scene in one of the city's increasing number of Aids-related tragedies was enacted before a horrifed audience of staff and patients.

Antique furniture dealer Philip Saylor was a familiar visitor at the Center, where he had been coming daily to comfort his long-term partner Steven Jenkins. At 5.30 in the evening a patient in the next-door room heard shots from Jenkins's suite, and entered to find both the patient and his companion dead: 'I went in and saw him lying there in bed on his side. The friend was on the floor lying right by the chair.' Some other patients were apparently unaware of the significance of the disturbance until Los Angeles Police Department officers began their investigation.

Steven Jenkins had come to die in suite 5906 of the Center's intensive care unit only three weeks previously, and in that brief time Saylor had watched the man with whom he had shared his life deteriorate to a state where he was continuously fed pain-killing morphine through intravenous tubes; his lungs had become choked with pneumonia, and a progressive disease of the eyes had rendered him all but sightless. A victim to frequent hallucinations, Steven Jenkins was powerless to stand, often even to move. In the final act of mercy, 40-old Philip Lee Saylor smuggled a .38 calibre revolver to his friend's bedside and shot both of them through the head.

Believed to be an Aids sufferer himself, Saylor gave no explanation for his action in a suicide note that only left practical instructions for the notification of family and friends. A close and private couple, Saylor and Jenkins lived almost reclusively at a fashionable West Hollywood apartment complex much favoured by members of the entertainment industry.

Commenting on what had clearly been a suicide pact, one hospital official observed: 'I'm somewhat surprised we don't see more of this; a lot of patients talk about it.'

FEB 2 9 1992